Philo for

By J. Clontz and T. E. Clontz

Cornerstone Publications

Printed in the United States of America.

Table of Contents

Preface

The Works of Philo are an important historical window into Roman and Jewish culture during the life of Jesus. Philo's works demonstrate that belief in the Son of God preceded the Christian New Testament. Philo's depiction of the Word parallels Christian concepts. Philo provides an account of Jewish leaders being crucified by Romans that confirms portions of the gospel account of Jesus' crucifixion. The Works of Philo display a variety of information about Roman and Jewish culture that precedes and parallels the Christian New Testament.

This book contains key passages from the Works of Philo translated by Yonge and lists the parallels in the New Testament based on the cross reference index in "The Comprehensive New Testament."

Allegorical Interpretation I (5-6)

(5) First, therefore, having desisted from the creation of mortal creatures on the seventh day, he began the formation of other and more divine beings. For God never ceases from making something or other; but, as it is the property of fire to burn, and of snow to chill, so also it is the property of God to be creating. And much more so, in proportion as he himself is to all other beings the author of their working. (6) Therefore the expression, "he caused to rest," is very appropriately employed here, not "he rested." For he makes things to rest which appear to be producing others, but which in reality do not affect anything; but he himself never ceases from creating. On which account Moses says, "He caused to rest the things which he had begun." For all the things that are made by our arts when completed stand still and remain; but all those which are accomplished by the knowledge of God are moved at subsequent times.

Parallels: Genesis 02:02-03; John 05:17

Comparison: John 05:17, "But [Jesus] answered them, "My Father is working still, and I am working.""

Allegorical Interpretation II (53-58)

(53) "And they were both naked, both Adam and his wife, and they were not ashamed; but the serpent was the most subtle of all the beasts that were upon the earth, which the Lord God had Made:"{Genesis 2:25; 3:1.}--the mind is naked, which is clothed neither with vice nor with virtue, but which is really stripped of both: just as the soul of an infant child, which has no share in either virtue or vice, is stripped of all coverings, and is completely naked: for these things are the coverings of the soul, by which it is enveloped and concealed, good being the garment of the virtuous soul, and evil the robe of the wicked soul. (54)

And the soul is made naked in these ways. Once, when it is in an unchangeable state, and is entirely free from all vices, and has discarded and laid aside the covering of all the passions. With reference to this Moses also pitches his tabernacle outside of the camp, a long way from the camp, and it was called the tabernacle of Testimony.{Exodus 33:7.} (55) And this has some such meaning as this: the soul which loves God, having put off the body and the affections which are dear to it, and having fled a long way from them, chooses a foundation and a sure ground for its abode, and a lasting settlement in the perfect doctrines of virtue; on which account testimony is borne to it by God, that it loves what is good, "for it was called the tabernacle of testimony," says Moses, and he has passed over in silence the giver of the name, in order that the soul, being excited, might consider who it is who thus bears witness to the dispositions which love virtue. (56) On this account the high priest "will not come into the holy of holies clad in a garment reaching to the feet; {Leviticus 16:1.} but having put off the robe of opinion and vain fancy of the soul, and having left that for those who love the things which are without, and who honor opinion in preference to truth, will come forward naked, without colors or any sounds, to make an offering of the blood of the soul, and to sacrifice the whole mind to God the Savior and Benefactor; (57) and certainly Nadab and Abihu, {Leviticus 10:1.} who came near to God, and left this mortal life and received a share of immortal life, are seen to be naked, that is, free from all new and mortal opinion; for they would not have carried it in their garments and borne it about, if they had not been naked, having broken to pieces every bond of passion and of corporeal necessity, in order that their nakedness and absence of corporeality might not be adulterated by the accession of atheistic reasoning; for it may not be permitted to all men to behold the secret mysteries of God, but only to those who are able to cover them up and guard them; (58) on which account Mishael and his partisans concealed them not in their own garments, but in those of Nadab and Abihu, who had been burnt with fire and taken upwards; for having stripped off all the garments that covered them, they brought their nakedness before God, and left their tunics about Mishael.

But clothes belong to the irrational part of the animal, which overshadow the rational part.

> Parallels: Genesis 02:25, 03:01; Exodus 33:07; Leviticus 10:01-05, 16:01; Matthew 27:35; John 19:23-24

Allegorical Interpretation II (86)

(86) Moreover, the soul falls in with a scorpion, that is to say, with dispersion in the wilderness; and the thirst, which is that of the passions, seizes on it until God sends forth upon it the stream of his own accurate wisdom, and causes the changed soul to drink of unchangeable health; for the abrupt rock is the wisdom of God, which being both sublime and the first of things he quarried out of his own powers, and of it he gives drink to the souls that love God; and they, when they have drunk, are also filled with the most universal manna; for manna is called something which is the primary genus of everything. But the most universal of all things is God; and in the second place the word of God. But other things have an existence only in word, but in deed they are at times equivalent to that which has no existence.

> Parallels: Numbers 20:08-21:18; Psalms 02:07; Matthew 07:24-25; Luke 01:35, 06:48; John 01:01-14, 06:32-35, 48-51; Acts 04:07, 08:10, 13:33; 1Corinthians 01:24, 10:03-04

> Comparison: 1Corinthians 10:03-04, "and all ate the same spiritual food, and all drank the same spiritual drink, for they drank from a spiritual rock which followed them, and the rock was Christ."

Allegorical Interpretation II (108)

(108) therefore do thou array against it the wisdom which contends with serpents; and struggle in this most glorious struggle, and labor to win the crown in the contest against pleasure, which subdues everyone else; winning a noble and glorious crown, such as no assembly of men can confer.

> Parallels: Leviticus 11:29-44; Numbers 21:06-09; Matthew 03:07, 10:16, 12:34, 23:33; Luke 03:07; 1Corinthians 09:24-27; 2Timothy 02:05, 04:07-08; James 01:12-15; 1Peter 05:01-04; Revelation 02:10
>
> Comparison: Matthew 10:16, "Behold, I send you out as sheep in the midst of wolves. Therefore be wise as serpents and innocent as doves." James 1:12-15 "Blessed is the man who perseveres under trial. For when he has stood the test, he will receive the crown of life that he has promised to those who love him. Let no one say when he is tempted, "I am being tempted by God"; for God cannot be tempted by evil, and he himself does not tempt anyone. But each one is tempted when he is carried away and enticed by his own desire. Then when desire has conceived, it gives birth to sin. And when sin is full-grown, it brings forth death."

Allegorical Interpretation III (82)

(82) But Melchizedek shall bring forward wine instead of water, and shall give your souls to drink, and shall cheer them with unmixed wine, in order that they may be wholly occupied with a divine intoxication, more sober than sobriety itself. For reason is a priest, having, as its inheritance the true God, and entertaining lofty and sublime and magnificent ideas about him, "for he is the priest of the most high God."{Genesis 14:18.} Not that there is

any other God who is not the most high; for God being one, is in the heaven above, and in the earth beneath, and there is no other besides Him." {Deuteronomy 4:39.} But he sets in motion the notion of the Most High, from his conceiving of God not in a low and groveling spirit, but in one of exceeding greatness, and exceeding sublimity, apart from any conceptions of matter.

> Parallels: Genesis 14:18-20; Deuteronomy 04:39; John 02:01-12; Hebrews 07:03

Allegorical Interpretation III (95-99)

(95) On which account God also calls Bezaleel by name, and says that "He will give him wisdom and knowledge, and that He will make him the builder and the architect of all the things which are in his Tabernacle;"{Exodus 31:2.} that is to say, of all the works of the soul, when he had up to this time done no work which any one could praise--we must say, therefore, that God impressed this figure also on the soul, after the fashion of an approved coin. And we shall know what the impression is if we previously examine the interpretation of the name. (96) Now, Bezaleel, being interpreted, means God in his shadow. But the shadow of God is his word, which he used like an instrument when he was making the world. And this shadow, and, as it were, model, is the archetype of other things. For, as God is himself the model of that image which he has now called a shadow, so also that image is the model of other things, as he showed when he commenced giving the law to the Israelites, and said, "And God made man according to the image of God."{Genesis 1:26.} As the image was modeled according to God, and as man was modeled according to the image, which thus received the power and character of the model. (97) Let us now, then, examine what the character which is impressed upon man is. The ancient philosophers used to inquire how we obtained our conceptions of the Deity? Men who, those who seemed to philosophize in the most excellent manner, said that from the world and form its several parts, and from the powers

which existed in those parts, we formed our notions of the Creator and cause of the world. (98) For as, if a man were to see a house carefully built and well provided with outer courts and porticoes, and men's chambers and women's chambers, and all other necessary apartments, he would form a notion of the architect; for he would never suppose that the house had been completed without skill and without a builder; (99) and, as he would argue in the same manner respecting any city, or any ship, or anything whatever that is made, whether it be great or small, so likewise anyone entering this world, as an exceedingly large house or large city, and seeing the heaven revolving round it in a circle and comprehending everything within it, and all the planets and fixed stars moving onwards in the same manner and on the same principles, all in regular order and in due harmony and in such a manner as is most advantageous for the whole created universe, and the earth stationed in the central situation, and the effusions of air and water affixed on the boundaries, and, moreover, all the animals, both mortal and immortal, and the different kinds of plants and fruits, he will surely consider that undoubtedly all these things were not made without skill, but that God both was and is the creator of this whole universe. They, then, who draw their conclusions in this manner perceive God in his shadow, arriving at a due comprehension of the artist through his works.

Parallels: Genesis 01:26; Exodus 31:02; Matthew 22:21; John 01:01-14, 02:19-21; Colossians 01:15-18; Hebrews 01:01-03

Comparison: John 01:03, "All things were made through him, and without him nothing was made…" Hebrews 01:02-03, "But in these last days he has spoken to us by his Son, whom he appointed heir of all things, and through whom also he made the world. He is the radiance of his glory and the exact representation of his being, and upholds all things by the word of his power. When he had made purification for sins, he sat down at the right hand of the Majesty on high."

Allegorical Interpretation III (104-106)

(104) Since therefore we find that there are two natures which have been created and fashioned and accurately and skillfully framed by God; the one being in its own intrinsic nature pernicious and open to reproach, and accursed, and the other beneficial and praiseworthy, the one too having a spurious stamp upon it, but the other having undergone a strict test; we will utter a beautiful and suitable prayer which Moses also addressed to God, praying that God may open his treasure house, and may lay before us his sublime word pregnant with divine lights, which he calls the heaven, and may bind fast the storehouses of evil. (105) For, just as there are storehouses of good things so are there also storehouses of evil things with God; as he says in his great song, "Behold are not these things collected with me, and sealed up in my treasure houses, against the day of vengeance when their foot shall be tripped Up?"{Deuteronomy 32:34.} You see then that there are several storehouses of evil things, and only one of good things. For since God is One, so also is his storehouse of good things one likewise. But there are many storehouses of evil things because the wicked are infinite in number. And in this observe the goodness of the true God, He opens the treasure house of his good things freely, but he binds fast that which contains the evil things. For it is an especial property of God to offer his good things freely and to be beforehand with men in bestowing gifts upon them, but to be slow in bringing evil on them, (106) and Moses dwelling at length upon the munificent and gracious nature of God, says that not only have his storehouses of evil things been sealed up in all other times, but also when the soul is tripped up in the path of right reason, when it is especially fair that it should be considered worthy of punishment; for he says that, "In the day of vengeance the storehouses of evil things have been sealed up," the sacred word of scripture showing that God does not visit with his vengeance even those who sin against him, immediately, but that he gives them time for repentance, and to remedy and correct their evil conduct.

Parallels: Deuteronomy 32:34; Luke 12:16-21

Allegorical Interpretation III (108-110)

(108) "Cursed indeed is he who causes the blind man to wander in the road." This also is done by that most impious thing pleasure, for the outward sense, inasmuch as it is destitute of reason, is a thing blinded by nature, since the eyes of its reason are put out. In reference to which we may say that it is by reason alone that we attain to a comprehension of things, and no longer by the outward sense; for they are bodies alone that we acquire a conception of by means of the outward senses. (109) Pleasure therefore has deceived the outward sense which is destitute of any proper comprehension of things, inasmuch as though it might have been turned to the mind, and have been guided by it, it has hindered it from being so, leading it to the external objects of outward sense, and making it desirous of everything which can call it into operation, in order that the outward sense being defective may follow a blind guide, namely the object of the outward sense, and then the mind being guided by the two things, which are themselves both blind, may plunge headlong to destruction and become utterly unable to restrain itself. (110) For if it were to follow its natural guide then it would be proper for defective things to follow reason which sees clearly, for in that way mischievous things would be less formidable in their attacks. But now, pleasure has put such great artifices in operation to injure the soul, that it has compelled it to use them as guides, cheating it, and persuading it to exchange virtue for evil habits, and to give good habits in exchange for vice.

Parallels: Deuteronomy 27:18; Matthew 15:14

Comparison: Matthew 15:14, "Let them alone. They are blind guides [of the blind]. And if a blind man leads a blind man, both will fall into a pit.""

Allegorical Interpretation III (172)

(172) There is a certain peculiarity which is attached to this word. For when it calls the soul to itself, it excites a congealing power in everything which is earthly, or corporeal, or under the influence of the external senses. On which account it is said to be "like the hoar-frost on the Earth."{Exodus 16:16.} For when the man who beholds God, meditates a flight from the passions, "the waves are frozen," that is to say, the impetuous rush, and the increase, and the haughty pride of the waves are arrested, in order that he who might behold the living God might then pass over the Passion.{Exodus 16:15.}

Parallels: Exodus 16:14-16; Matthew 14:23-33

Comparison: Matthew 14:28-29, "And Peter answered him, "Lord, if it is you, command me to come to you on the water." So he said, "Come." Then Peter got down out of the boat, walked on the water, and came toward Jesus."

Allegorical Interpretation III (173)

(173) Therefore the souls inquire of one another, those, that is, that have clearly felt the influence of the word, but which are not able to say what it is. For very often, when sensible of a sweet taste, we are nevertheless ignorant of the flavor which has caused it, and when we smell sweet scents, we still do not know what they are. And in the same manner also the soul very often, when it is delighted, is yet unable to explain what it is that has delighted it; but it is taught by the hierophant and prophet Moses, who tells it, "This is the bread, the food which God has given for the Soul,"{Exodus 16:15.} explaining that God has brought it, his own word and his own reason; for this bread which he has given us to eat is this word of his.

Parallels: Exodus 16:15; Matthew 04:04; John 01:01-14, 06:31-35, 48-51

Comparison: John 01:14, "And the Word became flesh and dwelt among us." John 06:31-35, "Our fathers ate the manna in the desert; as it is written, 'He gave them bread from heaven to eat.'" Jesus then said to them, "Truly, truly, I say to you, it was not Moses who has given you the bread from heaven; but my Father gives you the true bread from heaven. For the bread of God is he who comes down from heaven and gives life to the world." Then they said to him, "Lord, give us this bread always." Jesus said to them, "I am the bread of life. He who comes to me shall never hunger, and he who believes in me shall never thirst."

Allegorical Interpretation III (204-205)

(204) But some men have said that it is inconsistent with the character of God to swear at all; for that an oath is received for the sake of the confirmation which it supplies; but God is the only faithful being, and if anyone else who is dear to God; as Moses is said to have been faithful in all his House.{Numbers 12:7.} And besides, the mere words of God are the most sacred and holy of oaths, and laws, and institutions. And it is a proof of his exceeding power, that whatever he says is sure to take place; and this is the most especial characteristic of an oath. So that it would be quite natural to say that all the words of God are oaths confirmed by the accomplishment of the acts to which they relate. (205) They say, indeed, that an oath is a testimony borne by God concerning a matter which is the subject of doubt. But if God swears he is bearing testimony to himself, which is an absurdity. For the person who bears the testimony, and he on whose behalf it is borne, ought to be two different persons. What, then, are we to say? In the first place, that it is not a matter of blame for God to bear testimony to himself. For what other being could be competent to bear testimony to him? In the

second place, He himself is to himself everything that is most honorable--relative, kinsman, friend, virtue, prosperity, happiness, knowledge, understanding, beginning, end, entirety, universality, judge, opinion, intention, law, action, supremacy.

Parallels: Genesis 22:16-17; Numbers 12:07; Hebrews 06:13

Comparison: Hebrews 06:13, "For when God made a promise to Abraham, since he had no one greater by whom to swear, "he swore by himself."

Appendices A Treatise Concerning the World (1)

I. There is no existing thing equal in honor to God, but he is the one Ruler, and Governor, and King, to whom alone it is lawful to govern and regulate everything; for the verse - "A multitude of masters is not good, Let there one sovereign be, one king of All,"{hom. Il. 2.204.} is not more appropriate to be said with respect to cities and men than to the world and God, for it follows inevitably that there must be one Creator and Master of one world; and this position having been laid down and conceded as a preliminary, it is only consistent with sense to connect with it what follows from it of necessity. Let us now, therefore, consider what inferences these are. God being one being, has two supreme powers of the greatest importance. By means of these powers the incorporeal world, appreciable only by the intellect, was put together, which is the archetypal model of this world which is visible to us, being formed in such a manner as to be perceptible to our invisible conceptions just as the other is to our eyes. Therefore some persons, marveling at the nature of both these worlds, have not only worshipped them in their entirety as gods, but have also deified the most beautiful parts of them, I mean for instance the sun, and the moon, and the whole heaven, which, without any fear or reverence, they called gods. And Moses, perceiving the ideas which they entertained, says, "O Lord, King of all Gods,"{Deuteronomy 10:17.} in order to point out the great superiority of the Ruler to his subjects. And the original founder of the Jewish nation was a Chaldean by birth, being the son of a father who was much devoted to the study of astronomy, and being among people who were great studiers of mathematical science, who think the stars, and the whole heaven, and the whole world gods; and they say that both good and evil result from their speculations and belief, since they do not believe in anything as a cause which is apart from those things which are visible to the outward senses. But what can be worse than this, or more calculated to display the want of true nobility existing in the soul, than the notion of causes in general being secondary and created causes, combined with an ignorance of the one first cause, the uncreated God, the Creator of the universe, who for these and innumerable other reasons is most excellent, reasons which because of their magnitude human intellect is unable to apprehend? but this founder of the Jewish nation having conceived an idea of him in his mind, and looking upon him as the true God, forsook his native country and his family, and his father's house, knowing that if he remained, the deceits of the polytheistic doctrine also remaining in his soul would render his intellect incapable of discovering the nature of the one God, who is alone everlasting, and the father of everything else, whether appreciable only by the intellect or perceptible to the outward senses; but if he departed and emigrated, then he saw that deceit would also depart from his mind, which would then change its erroneous opinions into truth. And at the same time the oracular commands of God, which had been given to him, did further excite the desire which he felt to become acquainted with the living God. And he went forth like a man under the immediate guidance of others, with the most unhesitating promptness, to search after the knowledge of the one God; and he did not relax in his search till he had arrived at a more accurate and correct perception, not indeed of his essences (for that is impossible), but of his existence and of his providence; on which account he is the first man of whom it is said that he believed in God, since he was the first who had an accurate and positive notion of him, believing that there is one supreme cause of all things, which by his providence takes care of the world and of all things that are therein.

> Parallels: Genesis 01:01; Deuteronomy 10:17; Matthew 28:19; Luke 01:35; John 17:16, 18:36; Acts 04:07, 08:10; 1Corinthians 01:24
>
> Comparison: 1Corinthians 01:24, "but to those who are the called, both Jews and Greeks, Christ the power of God and the wisdom of God."

Concerning Noah's Work as a Planter (27)

(27) But he receives only the second honor of this summons, and the all-wise Moses shall have the first place assigned to him. For the former fashions shadows only, like painters do, in which it is not right to form any living thing. For the very name Bezeleel is interpreted to mean, "working in shadows." But Moses does not make shadows, but the task is assigned to him of forming the archetypal natures of things themselves. And in other places, also, the great Cause of all things is accustomed to reveal his secrets to some in a more conspicuous and visible manner, as if in the pure light of the sun, and to others more sparely, as though in the shade.

> Parallels: Exodus 31:02; Hebrews 08:05, 10:01
>
> Comparison: Hebrews 08:05, "They serve a copy and shadow of the heavenly sanctuary; for when Moses was about to erect the tabernacle, he was instructed by God, saying, "See that you make everything according to the pattern which was shown you on the mountain." Hebrews 10:01, "For since the law has only a shadow of the good things to come and not the true form of these realities, it can never perfect the worshippers by the same sacrifices which are continually offered year after year."

Concerning Noah's Work As A Planter (65-69)

(65) They tell an old story, that some man in ancient times, who had fallen madly in love with the beauty of wisdom, as if it had been the beauty of a most lovely woman, once, when he saw a most sumptuous preparation of unbounded and costly magnificence, looked towards some of his friends, and said, "Behold, O companions, how many things there are of which I have no need!" And yet he had nothing whatever of even necessary things beyond his mere clothes, so that he was not puffed up with the magnitude of his riches, which has been the case with numbers of people; so that, on this account, he spoke arrogantly against pomp and show. (66) The lawgiver teaches us that we should account those people wise who are not eager to be rich in created things, but who despise all created things in comparison of the friendship of the uncreated God, whom they look upon as the only true wealth, and the boundary of most perfect happiness. (67) Never, then, let those men boast, who have acquired power and sovereignty, as some do, because they have subdued one city, or country, or nation; and others, because they have acquired the dominion over all the countries of the earth, to its furthest borders, and over all Grecian and barbarous nations, and over all the rivers and seas, infinite both in number and magnitude. (68) For if, besides these things, they had made themselves masters (which it is impious even to mention) of that sublime nature which was the only thing that the Creator made free from the bond of slavery and servitude, they would still be looked upon but as private individuals in comparison with the great kings who have received God for their inheritance; for in proportion as that nature which has acquired a possession is better than the possession itself, and the Creator than the thing created, by so much also are they more royal. (69) Therefore, some people considered, that they who said that everything was the property of the one good Being, were speaking in an unreasonable manner, looking at the deficiencies and abundance which existed externally, and thinking no one rich who was in want of either money or

possessions. But Moses thinks wisdom a thing of such pre-eminent value, and deserving to be so eagerly sought after, that not only the whole world deserves to be his inheritance, but that he even looks upon the Governor of the universe in that light.

> Parallels: Numbers 18:20; Deuteronomy 10:09; Matthew 11:18-19; Acts 20:32; 1Corinthians 02:06-08

Concerning Noah's Work As A Planter (77-79)

(77) Therefore, some persons, departing from these numbers, as from signals, have said that God is the beginning and end of everything, which is a doctrine admirably calculated to engender piety. This doctrine, being implanted in the soul, produces a most beautiful and nutritious fruit, holiness; and the place most suitable for this fruit, (78) is the well which is called the oath, in which there is a report that no water could be found. For, says Moses, "the children of Israel, coming thither, reported to him concerning the well which they had dug: and they said, we found no water; and he called that place, "The Oath.' "{Genesis 26:32.} Let us now consider the meaning of this statement. (79) Those who investigate the nature of things as they actually exist, and who conduct their examinations of each individual matter in no negligent manner, behave very like those men who dig wells; for they also are seeking springs in an obscure place. And all men have one common desire, to find something to drink. But some men's nature is to be nourished by the food of the soul and that of others by the food of the body.

> Parallels: Genesis 26:32; Numbers 20:05-13; John 04:04-42, 06:31-58

> Comparison: John 04:32-34, "But he said to them, "I have food to eat of which you do not know." So the disciples said to one another, "Has any one brought him food?" Jesus said to them, "My food is to do the will of him who sent me, and to finish his work."

Concerning Noah's Work As A Planter (95-99)

(95) "When you go forth into the land which the Lord your God gives to you, and when you plant every tree which is good for food, you shall completely purify its uncleanness. For three years it shall be unclean as to its fruit, it shall not be eaten; but in the fourth year, all its fruit shall be holy, being praised by the Lord. And in the fifth year you shall eat the fruit thereof; and everything that it bears shall be useful to you: I am the Lord your God."{Leviticus 19:23.} Therefore it was impossible for the children of Israel, to plant those trees which are eatable, before they arrived in the country which had been given them by God; for he says, "When you go forth into the land... and when you plant every tree which is good for food." (96) So that while we are outside of the promised land, we should not be able to cultivate such trees; and this is very natural; (97) for as long as the mind has not entered upon the path of wisdom, but turns aside and wanders out of the road, it cares only for the trees which do not admit of being cultivated or used for food of men - trees which are barren and useless, and which, though they bear, bear no fruit which is eatable. (98) But when the mind, having entered upon the path of wisdom, marches along with its doctrines, and begins to keep pace with them all, it then cultivates the useful trees, which are capable of bearing eatable fruit, instead of caring for those useless kinds; it cultivates a mastery over, instead of the indulgence of the passions, and knowledge instead of ignorance, and good instead of evil. (99) Since therefore he who is led into the path of virtue is still at a long distance from the end, it is very naturally laid as an injunction upon the man who plants, to remove the uncleanness of that which is planted.

Parallels: Genesis 02:08-09; Leviticus 19:23-25; Matthew 07:16-21, 21:19; Mark 11:13-21; Luke 13:06-09

Concerning Noah's Work As A Planter (112-119)

(112) Therefore, to say that the tree is purified, contains a principle, the assertion of which is founded surely in truth, but to make the same statement with respect to the fruit is saying what is not equally clear or credible; for no cultivator of figs or grapes, or, in sort, of any fruit whatever, purifies them. (113) And again Moses says, "Its fruit shall be impure for three years, it shall not be eaten;"{Leviticus 19:23.} as if in fact it were customary for it to be purified forever. We must, therefore, say that this is one of those expressions which have a concealed meaning, since the words themselves are not quite consistent with it; for the expression is an ambiguous one; for it bears one sense of this kind, the fruit shall remain for three years; and then there is a distinct injunction, "it shall not be eaten before it is purified." But there is also another meaning, "the fruit of the tree shall for three years be unpurified, and while in that state it shall not be eaten." (114) According, then, to the former statement one may understand it in this manner: the three years being taken from time which is divided into three portions; for it is the nature of time to be divided into the past, the present, and the future; therefore the fruit of education will exist, and will endure, and will last unimpaired through all the divisions of time, a statement equivalent to - it will never receive any corruption, for the nature of good is imperishable. But the fruit which is not purified shall not be eaten; inasmuch as virtuous reasons, duly purified and rendered sound, nourish the soul, and give vigor to the mind; but the opposite kinds are not nutritious, but bring disease and destruction on the soul. (115) According to the other meaning, as in the disputes of dialecticians, the word "undemonstrated" is used in a double sense, either of a proposition which it is hard to demonstrate by reason of its difficulty, or of one which is intrinsically so plain as to require no demonstration, and the truth of which is established not by the testimony of anyone else, but by its own internal evidence. So also fruit may be understood as not being purified, either when it is so impure as to be difficulty to purify,

or when it requires no purification, but is bright, and clear, and pure of itself. (116) Such now is the fruit of education; being for three years, that is to say for all time, divided as it is into three portions, most completely pure and brilliant, being overshadowed by no injurious thing, and having no need whatever of any washings or purifications, or anything else whatever which tends to cleansing. (117) "But in the fourth year," says the scripture, "all the fruit of the tree shall be sacred, being praised by the Lord."{Leviticus 19:25.} The prophetic books appear often to dignify the number four in many places of the exposition of the law, and most especially in the account of the creation of the universe; (118) for the light which is perceptible by the outward senses, and held in honor, being that which throws the most brilliant light both upon itself and upon other things, and upon its own parents the sun and the moon, and upon the most sacred company of the stars, which by their rising and setting fix the boundaries of night and day, and moreover, of months and years, and which have shown the nature of number, to which, also, the greatest good of the soul is attributed, Moses says was created on the fourth day. (119) And now he honors this day in a remarkable degree, assigning the fruit of the trees to God, in accordance with no other time than with the fourth year after they are planted.

> Parallels: Genesis 02:08-09; Leviticus 19:23-25; Matthew 07:16-21, 21:19; Mark 11:13-21; Luke 13:06-09
>
> Comparison: Luke 13:06-09, “He told this parable: “A man had a fig tree planted in his vineyard, and he came seeking fruit on it and found none. And he said to the keeper of his vineyard, ‘Look, for three years I have come seeking fruit on this fig tree and find none. [So] cut it down; why should it use up the ground?’ And he answered him, ‘Sir, let it alone this year also, until I dig around it and fertilize it. And if it bears fruit next year, fine; but if not, you can cut it down.’”

Concerning Noah's Work As A Planter (177)

(177) Someone then will say in opposition that, according to the argument that has been advanced, the wise man must never have a bilious attack, and never go to sleep, and above all must never die. But he to whom some of these things happen is either an inanimate being or a divine one; but beyond all question he is not a man at all. Imitating this perversion of the arguments, one may apply it equally to a bilious man, or to a sleeping man, or to a dying man; for no one in his senses would tell a secret to a man in any of these conditions, but it would be reasonable for him to tell it to a wise man, for the wise man is never bilious, never goes to sleep, and never dies.

Parallels: Acts 02:31, 03:18-26

Every Good Man Is Free (3)

(3) and all men who have studied philosophy in a genuine spirit, showing themselves obedient to this injunction, have looked upon it as a sentence, or rather as a law of equal weight with a divine oracle; and, departing from the common opinions of men, they have cut out for themselves a new and hitherto untraveled path, inaccessible to such as have no experience of wise maxims and doctrines, building up systems of ideas, which no one who is not pure either may or can handle.

Parallels: Matthew 07:13-14

Comparison: Matthew 07:13-14, "Enter by the narrow gate. For the gate is wide, and the way is easy that leads to destruction, and many are those who enter by it. How narrow is the gate and hard the way, that leads to life, and few those who find it!"

Every Good Man Is Free (20)

(20) For, in real truth, that man alone is free who has God for his leader; indeed, in my opinion, that man is even the ruler of all others, and has all the affairs of the earth committed to him, being, as it were, the viceroy of a great king, the mortal lieutenant of an immortal sovereign. However, this assertion of the actual authority of the wise man may be postponed to a more suitable opportunity. We must at present examine minutely the question of his perfect freedom.

Parallels: Exodus 04:16, 07:01; Acts 03:18-26; Romans 06:06-07
Comparison: Romans 06:06-07, "We know that our old self was crucified with him so that the body of sin might be done away with, that we should no longer be slaves to sin. For he who has died has been freed from sin."

Every Good Man Is Free (25)

(25) On which account he will neither obey everyone who imposes a command upon him, not even if he threatens him with insults, and tortures, and even still more formidable evils; but he will bear a gallant spirit, and will cry out in reply to such menaces -- "Yes, burn and scorch my flesh, and glut your hate, drinking my life-warm blood; for heaven's stars shall quit their place, and darken 'neath the earth, and earth rise up and take the place of heaven, before you wring from me a word of flattery." {this is a fragment of Euripides from the Syleus. Fr. 2.}

Parallels: Matthew 27:33-56; Luke 23:33-45; John 06:53-56; Fragment of Euripides From the Syleus. Fr. 2

Comparison: John 06:53-56, "So Jesus said to them, "Truly, truly, I say to you, unless you eat the flesh of the Son of Man and drink his blood, you have no life in you. Whoever eats my flesh and drinks my blood has eternal life, and I will raise him up at the last day. For my flesh is true food, and my blood is true drink. He who eats my flesh and drinks my blood abides in me, and I in him." Matthew 27:45, 50-51, "Now from the sixth hour until the ninth hour there was darkness over all the land… And Jesus cried out again with a loud voice, and yielded up his spirit. And behold, the veil of the temple was torn in two, from top to bottom. And the earth shook. And the rocks were split."

Every Good Man Is Free (42-43)

(42) Besides all this, would not any one affirm that the friends of God are free? unless indeed one can think it consistent to attribute to the companions of kings, not only freedom but even at times a great degree of authority, when they commit magistracies to them, and when they, in consequence, fulfill the offices of subordinate rulers; and yet, at the same time, to speak of slavery in connection with the gods of heaven, when those men, on account of the love which they have shown to God, have also at once become beloved by God, being requited by him with good will equal to their own, truth being the judge, so that they as the poets say, are universal princes and kings of kings. (43) But the lawgiver of the Jews ventures upon a more bold assertion even than this, inasmuch as he was, as it is reported, a student and practitioner of plain philosophy; and so he teaches that the man who is wholly possessed with the love of God and who serves the living God alone, is no longer man, but actually God, being indeed the God of men, but not of the parts of nature, in order to leave to the Father of the universe the attributes of being both and God.

Parallels: Exodus 04:16, 07:01; Matthew 17:25-26; Acts 03:18-26, 20:32; 1Timothy 06:15

Comparison: Matthew 17:25b-26, "…And when he came into the house, Jesus spoke to him first, saying, "What do you think, Simon? From whom do the kings of the earth take customs or taxes, from their sons or from others?" And when he said, "From others," Jesus said to him, "Then the sons are free.""

Every Good Man Is Free (68)

(68) And yet, what need is there, either of long journeys over the land, or of long voyages, for the sake of investigating the seeking out virtue, the roots of which the Creator has laid not at any great distance, but so near, as the wise lawgiver of the Jews says, {Deuteronomy 30:14.} "They are in thy mouth, and in thy heart, and in thy hands:" intimating by these figurative expressions the words, and actions, and designs of men; all of which stand in need of careful cultivation.

Parallels: Deuteronomy 30:14; Matthew 22:37; Mark 12:28-34; Luke 10:27-28, 17:20-21

Comparison: Mark 12:32-34, "And the scribe said to him, "You are right, Teacher. You have well said that 'He is one, and there is no other but he'; and to 'love him with all the heart, and with all the understanding, and with all the strength', and to 'love one's neighbor as oneself', is much more than all whole burnt offerings and sacrifices." And when Jesus saw [him,] that he answered wisely, he said to him, "You are not far from the kingdom of God." And after that no one dared to ask him any question."

Every Good Man Is Free (72)

(72) It is owing to this that the whole earth and sea are full of men who are rich and of high reputation, and who indulge in all kinds of pleasure; but that the number of those who are prudent, and just, and virtuous, is very small; but that of which the numbers are small, though it may be rare, is nevertheless not non-existent.

Parallels: Deuteronomy 30:14-19; Matthew 07:13-14

Comparison: Matthew 07:13-14, "Enter by the narrow gate. For the gate is wide, and the way is easy that leads to destruction, and many are those who enter by it. How narrow is the gate and hard the way, that leads to life, and few those who find it!"

Every Good Man Is Free (74)

(74) And in the land of the barbarians, in which the same men are authorities both as to words and actions, there are very numerous companies of virtuous and honorable men celebrated. Among the Persians there is the body of the Magi, who, investigating the works of nature for the purpose of becoming acquainted with the truth, do at their leisure become initiated themselves and initiate others in the divine virtues by very clear explanations. And among the Indians there is the class of the gymnosophists, who, in addition to natural philosophy, take great pains in the study of moral science likewise, and thus make their whole existence a sort of lesson in virtue.

Parallels: Matthew 02:01

Comparison: Matthew 02:01, "Now after Jesus was born in Bethlehem of Judea in the days of Herod the king, behold, wise men from the East came to Jerusalem…" Note: wise men or astrologers Greek magi.

Every Good Man Is Free (75-91)

(75) Moreover Palestine and Syria too are not barren of exemplary wisdom and virtue, which countries no slight portion of that most populous nation of the Jews inhabits. There is a portion of those people called Essenes, in number something more than four thousand in my opinion, who derive their name

from their piety, though not according to any accurate form of the Grecian dialect, because they are above all men devoted to the service of God, not sacrificing living animals, but studying rather to preserve their own minds in a state of holiness and purity. (76) These men, in the first place, live in villages, avoiding all cities on account of the habitual lawlessness of those who inhabit them, well knowing that such a moral disease is contracted from associations with wicked men, just as a real disease might be from an impure atmosphere, and that this would stamp an incurable evil on their souls. Of these men, some cultivating the earth, and others devoting themselves to those arts which are the result of peace, benefit both themselves and all those who come in contact with them, not storing up treasures of silver and of gold, nor acquiring vast sections of the earth out of a desire for ample revenues, but providing all things which are requisite for the natural purposes of life; (77) for they alone of almost all men having been originally poor and destitute, and that too rather from their own habits and ways of life than from any real deficiency of good fortune, are nevertheless accounted very rich, judging contentment and frugality to be great abundance, as in truth they are. (78) Among those men you will find no makers of arrows, or javelins, or swords, or helmets, or breastplates, or shields; no makers of arms or of military engines; no one, in short, attending to any employment whatever connected with war, or even to any of those occupations even in peace which are easily perverted to wicked purposes; for they are utterly ignorant of all traffic, and of all commercial dealings, and of all navigation, but they repudiate and keep aloof from everything which can possibly afford any inducement to covetousness; (79) and there is not a single slave among them, but they are all free, aiding one another with a reciprocal interchange of good offices; and they condemn masters, not only as unjust, inasmuch as they corrupt the very principle of equality, but likewise as impious, because they destroy the ordinances of nature, which generated them all equally, and brought them up like a mother, as if they were all legitimate brethren, not in name only, but in reality and truth. But in their view this natural relationship of all men to one another has been thrown into disorder by designing covetousness, continually wishing to surpass others in good fortune, and which has therefore engendered alienation instead of affection, and hatred instead of friendship; (80) and leaving the logical part of philosophy, as in no respect necessary for the acquisition of virtue, to the word-catchers, and the natural part, as being too sublime for human nature to master, to those who love to converse about high objects (except indeed so far as such a study takes in the contemplation of the existence of God and of the creation of the universe), they devote all their attention to the moral part of philosophy, using as instructors the laws of their country which it would have been impossible for the human mind to devise without divine inspiration. (81) Now these laws they are taught at other times, indeed, but most especially on the seventh day, for the seventh day is accounted sacred, on which they abstain from all other employments, and frequent the sacred places which are called synagogues, and there they sit according to their age in classes, the younger sitting under the elder, and listening with eager attention in becoming order. (82) Then one, indeed, takes up the holy volume and reads it, and another of the men of the greatest experience comes forward and explains what is not very intelligible, for a great many precepts are delivered in enigmatical modes of expression, and allegorically, as the old fashion was; (83) and thus the people are taught piety, and holiness, and justice, and economy, and the science of regulating the state, and the knowledge of such things as are naturally good, or bad, or indifferent, and to choose what is right and to avoid what is wrong, using a threefold variety of definitions, and rules, and criteria, namely, the love of God, and the love of virtue, and the love of mankind. (84) Accordingly, the sacred volumes present an infinite number of instances of the disposition devoted to the love of God, and of a continued and uninterrupted purity throughout the whole of life, of a careful avoidance of oaths and of falsehood, and of a strict adherence to the principle of looking on the Deity as the cause of everything which is good and of nothing which is evil. They also furnish us with many proofs of a love of virtue, such as abstinence from all covetousness of money, from ambition, from indulgence in pleasures, temperance, endurance, and also moderation, simplicity, good temper, the absence of pride, obedience to the laws, steadiness, and everything of that kind; and, lastly, they bring forward as proofs of the love of mankind, goodwill, equality beyond all power of description, and fellowship, about which it is not unreasonable to say a few words. (85) In the first place, then, there is no one who has a house so absolutely his own private property, that it does not in some sense also belong to every one: for besides that they all dwell together in companies, the house is open to all those of the same notions, who come to them from other quarters; (86) then there is one magazine among them all; their expenses are all in common; their garments belong to them all in common; their food is common, since they all eat in messes; for there is no other people among which you can find a common use of the same house, a common adoption of one mode of living, and a common use of the same table more thoroughly established in fact than among this tribe: and is not this very natural? For whatever they, after having been working during the day, receive for their wages, that they do not retain as their own, but bring it into the common stock, and give any advantage that is to be derived from it to all who desire to avail themselves of it; (87) and those who are sick are not neglected because they are unable to contribute to the common stock, inasmuch as the tribe have in their public stock a means of supplying their necessities and aiding their weakness, so that from their ample means they support them liberally and abundantly; and they cherish respect for their elders, and honor them and care for them, just as parents are honored and cared for by their lawful children: being supported by them in all abundance both by their personal exertions, and by innumerable contrivances. (88) Such diligent practitioners of virtue does philosophy, unconnected with any superfluous care of examining into Greek names render men, proposing to them as necessary exercises to train them towards its attainment, all praiseworthy actions by which a freedom, which can never be enslaved, is firmly established. (89) And a proof of this is that, though at different times a great number of chiefs of every variety of disposition and character, have occupied their country, some of whom have endeavored to surpass even ferocious wild beasts in cruelty, leaving no sort of inhumanity unpracticed, and have never ceased to murder their subjects in whole troops, and have even torn them to pieces while living, like cooks cutting them limb from limb, till they themselves, being overtaken by the vengeance of divine justice, have at last experienced the same miseries in their turn: (90) others again having converted their barbarous frenzy into another kind of wickedness, practicing an ineffable degree of savageness, talking with the people quietly, but through the hypocrisy of a more gentle voice, betraying the ferocity of their real disposition, fawning upon their victims like treacherous dogs, and becoming the causes of irremediable miseries to them, have left in all their cities monuments of their impiety, and hatred of all mankind, in the never to be forgotten miseries endured by those whom they oppressed: (91) and yet no one, not even of those immoderately cruel tyrants, nor of the more treacherous and hypocritical oppressors was ever able to bring any real accusation against the multitude of those called Essenes or Holy.{the Greek is essaioμn eμ hosioμn, as if essaioμn was only a variety of the word hosioμn, "holy."} But everyone being subdued by the virtue of these men, looked up to them as free by nature, and not subject to the frown of any human being, and have celebrated their manner of messing together, and their fellowship with one another beyond all description in respect of its mutual good faith, which is an ample proof of a perfect and very happy life.

Parallels: Acts 02:42-47

Comparison: Acts 02:42-47, "They devoted themselves to the apostles' teaching and to the fellowship, to the breaking of bread and to prayer. Everyone was filled with awe. And many wonders and signs were done through the apostles. And all who believed were together and had all things in common. And they sold their possessions and goods and distributed them to all, as anyone had need. And day by day, attending the temple together and breaking bread in their homes, they ate together with glad and sincere hearts, praising God and having favor with all the people. And the Lord added to them day by day those who were being saved."

Every Good Man Is Free (131-136)

(131) And moreover anyone who considers the matter may find even among the brute beasts examples of the freedom which exists among men, as he may of all other human blessings. At all events, cocks are accustomed to contend with one another, and to display such an actual affection for danger, that in order to save themselves from yielding or submitting, even if they are inferior in power to their adversary they will not bear to be inferior in courage, for they endure even to death. (132) And Miltiades, the famous general of the Athenians, seeing this, when the king of the Persians having roused up all the might of Asia, was invading Europe with many myriads of soldiers, as if he were going to destroy all Greece with the mere shout of his army, having collected all the allies at the festival called the panathenaea, showed them a battle between these birds, thinking that the encouragement which they would derive from such a sight would be more powerful than any argument. (133) And he was not deceived, for when they had seen the patient enduring and honorable feeling of these irrational animals, which could not be subdued by any means short of death itself, they snatched up their arms and rushed eagerly to war, as resolving to fight against their enemies with their bodies, and being utterly indifferent to wounds and death, being willing to die for their freedom, so that at all events they might be buried in the still free soil of their native country; for there is nothing which acts so forcibly in the way of exhortation so as to improve the character, as an unhoped for success in the case of those whom men look upon as inferior to themselves. (134) Moreover the tragic writer, Ion, mentions the contentious spirit of those birds in the following lines: "Nor though wounded in each limb,

nor though his eyes with blows are dim, will he forget his might; but still, though much fatigued, will crow, preferring death to undergo than slavery, or slight." (135) And why, then, should we think that wise men will not cheerfully encounter death in preference to slavery? And is it not absurd to imagine that the souls of young and nobly born men will turn out inferior to those of game-cocks in the contest of virtue, and will be barely fit to stand in the second place? (136) And yet who is there who has even the least tincture of education who does not know this fact, that freedom is a noble thing and slavery a disgraceful one, and that what is honorable belongs to virtuous men, and what is disgraceful to worthless ones? From which it is seen most undeniably, that no virtuous man can ever be a slave, not if ten thousand persons, with all imaginable deeds to prove themselves masters, threaten them; and that no foolish or worthless man can ever be free, not even if he were Croesus, or Midas, or the great king of Persia himself.

Parallels: Matthew 26:33-35, 75; Mark 13:35, 14:30, 72; Luke 22:34, 61; John 13:38; Greek Playwright Ion

Comparison: Matthew 26:33-35, "But Peter declared to him, "If all fall away because of you, I will never fall away." Jesus said to him, "Truly I say to you, this very night, before the rooster crows, you will deny me three times." Peter said to him, "Even if I have to die with you, I will never deny you." And so said all the disciples."

Every Good Man Is Free (159)

(159) For if it is driven to and fro by appetite, or if it is attracted by pleasure, or turned out of the way by fear, or contracted by grief, or tortured by want, it then makes itself a slave, and makes him who possesses such a soul the slave of ten thousand masters. But if it has resisted and subdued ignorance by prudence, and intemperance by temperance, and cowardice by

bravery, and covetousness by justice; it then adds to its indomitable free spirit, power and authority.

Parallels: Matthew 07:28-29, 28:18; Mark 05:01-20; Ephesians 01:20-22

Comparison: Matthew 28:18, "And Jesus came and said to them, "All authority in heaven and on [the] earth has been given to me." Ephesians 01:20-22, "...which he worked in Christ when he raised him from the dead and seated him at his right hand in the heavenly places, far above all rule and authority and power and dominion, and above every name that is named, not only in this age but also in the one to come. And he put all things under his feet and appointed him to be the head over all things for the church..."

Every Good Man Is Free (160)

(160) And all the souls which are not as yet partakers of either of these two classes, neither of that which is enslaved, nor of that by which prudence is confirmed, but which are still naked like those of completely infant children; those we must nurse and cherish carefully, prescribing for them at first tender food instead of milk, namely, instruction in the encyclical sciences, and after that stronger food, such as is prepared by philosophy, by which they will be strengthened so as to become manly, and in good condition, and conducted on to a favorable end, not more that are recommended by you than enjoined by the oracle, "To live in conformity to nature."

Parallels: Hebrews 05:11-13

Comparison: Hebrews 05:11-13, "About this we have much to say which is hard to explain, since you have become dull of hearing. For though by this time you ought to be teachers, you need someone to teach you again the first elements of God's word. You need milk, [and] not solid food; for every one who lives on milk is unskilled in the word of righteousness, for he is a babe."

Flaccus (36-38)

(36) There was a certain madman named Carabbas, afflicted not with a wild, savage, and dangerous madness (for that comes on in fits without being expected either by the patient or by bystanders), but with an intermittent and more gentle kind; this man spent all his days and nights naked in the roads, minding neither cold nor heat, the sport of idle children and wanton youths; (37) and they, driving the poor wretch as far as the public gymnasium, and setting him up there on high that he might be seen by everybody, flattened out a leaf of papyrus and put it on his head instead of a diadem, and clothed the rest of his body with a common door mat instead of a cloak and instead of a scepter they put in his hand a small stick of the native papyrus which they found lying by the way side and gave to him; (38) and when, like actors in theatrical spectacles, he had received all the insignia of royal authority, and had been dressed and adorned like a king, the young men bearing sticks on their shoulders stood on each side of him instead of spear-bearers, in imitation of the bodyguards of the king, and then others came up, some as if to salute him, and others making as though they wished to plead their causes before him, and others pretending to wish to consult with him about the affairs of the state.

Parallels: Matthew 27:19-31

Comparison: Matthew 27:19-31, "While he was sitting on the judgment seat, his wife sent word to him, "Have nothing to do with that righteous man, for I have suffered greatly today in a dream because of him." But the chief priests and the elders persuaded the crowds to ask for Barabbas and destroy Jesus. The governor answered them, "Which of the two do you want me to release to you?" They said, "Barabbas!" Pilate said to them, "Then what shall I do with Jesus who is called Christ?" They all said, "Let him be crucified!" And he said, "Why, what evil has he done?" But they shouted all the more, "Let him be crucified!" When Pilate saw that he was gaining nothing, but rather that a riot was starting, he took water and washed his hands before the crowd, saying, "I am innocent of this man's blood. See to it yourselves." And all the people answered, "His blood be on us and on our children!" Then he released Barabbas to them. And when he had scourged Jesus, he delivered him to be crucified. Then the soldiers of the governor took Jesus into the Praetorium and gathered the whole garrison around him. And they stripped him and put a scarlet robe on him. And when they had twisted a crown of thorns, they put it on his head, and a reed in his right hand. And they bowed the knee before him and mocked him, saying, "Hail, King of the Jews!" And they spat on him, and took the reed and struck him on the head. And when they had mocked him, they took the robe off him, and put his own clothes on him, and led him away to crucify him."

Flaccus (74-77)

(74) for he arrested thirty-eight members of our council of elders, which our Savior and benefactor, Augustus, elected to manage the affairs of the Jewish nation after the death of the king of our own nation, having sent written commands to that effect to Manius Maximus when he was about to take upon himself for the second time the government of Egypt and of the country, he arrested them, I say, in their own houses, and commanded them to be thrown into prison, and arranged a splendid procession to send through the middle of the market-place a body of old men prisoners, with their hands bound, some with thongs and others with iron chains, whom he led in this plight into the theatre, a most miserable spectacle, and one wholly unsuited to the times.

(75) And then he commanded them all to stand in front of their enemies, who were sitting down, to make their disgrace the more conspicuous, and ordered them all to be stripped of their clothes and scourged with stripes, in a way that only the most wicked of malefactors are usually treated, and they were flogged with such severity that some of them the moment they were carried out died of their wounds, while others were rendered so ill for a long time that their recovery was despaired of. (76) And the enormity of this cruelty is proved by many other circumstances, and it will be further proved most evidently and undeniably by the circumstance which I am about to mention. Three of the members of this council of elders, Euodius, and Trypho, and Audro, had been stripped of all their property, being plundered of everything that was in their houses at one onset, and he was well aware that they had been exposed to this treatment, for it had been related to him when he had in the first instance sent for our rulers, under pretence of wishing to promote a reconciliation between them and the rest of the city; (77) but nevertheless, though he well knew that they had been deprived of all their property, he scourged them in the very sight of those who had plundered them, that thus they might endure the twofold misery of poverty and personal ill treatment, and that their persecutors might reap the double pleasure of enjoying riches which did in no respect belong to them, and also of feasting their eyes to satiety on the disgrace of those whom they had plundered.

Parallels: Matthew 27:26-35; Luke 23:26-37

Comparison: Matthew 27:26-35, "Then he released Barabbas to them. And when he had scourged Jesus, he delivered him to be crucified. Then the soldiers of the governor took Jesus into the Praetorium and gathered the whole garrison around him. And they stripped him and put a scarlet robe on him. And when they had twisted a crown of thorns, they put it on his head, and a reed in his right hand. And they bowed the knee before him and mocked him, saying, "Hail, King of the Jews!" And they spat on him, and took the reed and struck him on the head. And when they had mocked him, they took the robe off him, and put his own clothes on him, and led him away to crucify him. Now as they came out, they found a man of Cyrene, Simon by name, and they compelled him to carry his cross. And when they came to a place called Golgotha (which means the place of a skull), they offered him wine to drink, mingled with gall. But when he tasted it, he would not drink it. And when they had crucified him, they divided his garments among them by casting lots."

Flaccus (83-85)

(83) I have known instances before now of men who had been crucified when this festival and holiday was at hand, being taken down and given up to their relations, in order to receive the honors of sepulture, and to enjoy such observances as are due to the dead; for it used to be considered, that even the dead ought to derive some enjoyment from the natal festival of a good emperor, and also that the sacred character of the festival ought to be regarded. (84) But this man did not order men who had already perished on crosses to be taken down, but he commanded living men to be crucified, men to whom the very time itself gave, if not entire forgiveness, still, at all events, a brief and temporary respite from punishment; and he did this after they had been beaten by scourging in the middle of the theatre; and after he had tortured them with fire and sword; (85) and the spectacle of their sufferings was divided; for the first part of the exhibition lasted from the morning to the third or fourth hour, in which the Jews were scourged, were hung up, were tortured on the wheel, were condemned, and were dragged to execution through the middle of the orchestra; and after this beautiful exhibition came the dancers, and the buffoons, and the flute-players, and all the other diversions of the theatrical contests.

Parallels: Mark 15:15-33; Luke 23:33-45

Comparison: Mark 15:15-33, "So Pilate, wanting to satisfy the crowd, released Barabbas to them. And he delivered Jesus, after he had scourged him, to be crucified. The soldiers led him away into the palace (that is, the Praetorium) and they called together the whole battalion. And they dressed him in a purple cloak, and they twisted a crown of thorns and put it on him. And they began to salute him, "Hail, King of the Jews!" Then they struck him on the head with a reed and spat on him. And falling on their knees, they paid homage to him. And when they had mocked him, they took the purple robe off him, and put his clothes on him. Then they led him out to crucify him. Then they compelled a certain man, Simon of Cyrene, the father of Alexander and Rufus, as he was coming out of the country and passing by, to carry his cross. And they brought him to the place called Golgotha (which means the place of a skull). Then they offered him wine mingled with myrrh, but he did not take it. And they crucified him, and 'divided his garments, casting lots for them' to determine what each man should take. And it was the third hour, when they crucified him. And the inscription of the charge written against him read: THE KING OF THE JEWS. And with him they crucified two robbers, one on his right and one on his left. And those who passed by hurled insults at him, wagging their heads, and saying, "Aha! You who would destroy the temple and build it in three days, save yourself by coming down from the cross!" So also the chief priests mocked him among themselves with the scribes, and said, "He saved others? He cannot save himself! Let the Christ, the King of Israel, come down now from the cross, that we may see and believe." Those who were crucified with him also reviled him. And when the sixth hour had come, there was darkness over the whole land until the ninth hour."

Flaccus (112)

(112) And when he heard that he was supping at some persons' house in company with Flaccus, he did not relax in his speed, but hastened onward to the dwelling of his entertainer; for the man with whom they were feasting was Stephanion, one of the freedmen of Tiberius Caesar; and withdrawing to a short distance, he sends forward one of his own followers to reconnoiter, disguising him like a servant in order that no one might notice him or perceive what was going forward. So he, entering in to the banqueting-room, as if he were the servant of one of the guests, examined everything accurately, and then returned and gave information to Bassus.

Parallels: Matthew 26:57-27:56; John 18:15-27

Comparison: John 18:15-27, "Simon Peter followed Jesus, and so did another disciple. As this disciple was known to the high priest, he went with Jesus into the courtyard of the high priest. But Peter stood at the door outside. Then the other disciple, the one known by the high priest, went out and spoke to the girl who kept the door, and brought Peter in. Then the girl who kept the door said to Peter, "You are not also one of this man's disciples, are you?" He said, "I am not." Now the servants and officers had made a charcoal fire, because it was cold, and they were standing and warming themselves. And Peter also was with them, standing and warming himself. The high priest then questioned Jesus about his disciples and his teaching. Jesus answered him, "I have spoken openly to the world. I always taught in synagogues and in the temple, where all the Jews come together, and I have said nothing in secret. Why do you ask me? Ask those who have heard me what I said to them. They know what I said." And when he had said this, one of the officers standing by struck Jesus with his hand, saying, "Is that the way you answer the high priest?" Jesus answered him, "If I have spoken wrongly, bear witness to the wrong. But if I have spoken rightly, why do you strike me?" So Annas sent him bound to Caiaphas the high priest. Now Simon Peter stood warming himself. Therefore they said to him, "You are not also one of his disciples, are you?" He denied it and said, "I am not." One of the servants of the high priest, a relative of him whose ear Peter had cut off, said, "Did I not see you in the garden with him?" Peter again denied it; and at once a rooster crowed.

Flaccus (159)

(159) What a change is this! In the middle of the day, as if an eclipse had come upon me, night has overshadowed my life. What shall I say of this little islet? Shall I call it my place of banishment, or my new country, or harbor and refuge of misery? A tomb would be the most proper name for it; for I, miserable that I am, am now in a manner conducted to my grave, attending my own funeral, for either I shall destroy my miserable life through my sorrow, or if I am able to cling to life among my miseries, I shall in that case find a distant death, which will be felt all the time of my life."

Parallels: Luke 23:44-55

Comparison: Luke 23:44-55, "And it was now about the sixth hour, and there was darkness over the whole land until the ninth hour – the sun failed; and the veil of the temple was torn in two. (Note: the sun failed or the sun eclipsed active) And Jesus, crying out with a loud voice, said, "Father, into your hands I commit my spirit." And having said this, he breathed his last. Now when the centurion saw what had happened, he began to praise God, saying, "Certainly this was a righteous man!" When all the multitudes who had gathered to witness this sight saw what had taken place, they beat their breasts, and returned home. But all his acquaintances, and the women who had followed him from Galilee, stood at a distance, watching these things. Now there was a man named Joseph, a member of the Council, [and] a good and righteous man, who had not consented to their decision and deed. He came from Arimathea, a city of the Jews, and he was waiting for the kingdom of God. This man went to Pilate and asked for the body of Jesus. Then he took it down and wrapped it in linen cloth, and laid it in a tomb that was hewn out of the rock, where no one had ever yet been laid."

On Abraham (56)

(56) We must, however, not remain in ignorance that the sacred historian has represented the first man, him who was formed out of the earth as the father of all those who existed before the deluge; and him who, with his whole family, was the only person left out of so universal a destruction, because of his justice and his other excellencies and virtues, as the founder of the new race of men which was to flourish hereafter. And that venerable, and estimable, and glorious triad is comprehended by the sacred scriptures under one class, and called, "A royal priesthood, and a holy Nation."{Exodus 19:6.}

Parallels: Exodus 19:06; Matthew 28:19; 1Peter 02:09

Comparison: 1Peter 02:09, "But you are a chosen race, a royal priesthood, a holy nation, a people for God's own possession, that you may declare the praises of him who called you out of darkness into his marvelous light."

On Abraham (59)

(59) for the roads which lead upwards to him are laborious and slow, but the descent down the declivity, being rather like a rapid dragging down than a gradual descent, is swift and easy.

And there are many things urged downwards, in which there is no use whatever, when God having made the soul to depend on his own powers, drags it up towards himself with a more vigorous attraction.

> Parallels: Deuteronomy 30:19; Psalms 01:01-06; Jeremiah 21:08; Matthew 07:13-14; Luke 01:35; Acts 04:07, 08:10; 1Corinthians 01:24
>
> Comparison: Matthew 07:13-14, "Enter by the narrow gate. For the gate is wide, and the way is easy that leads to destruction, and many are those who enter by it. How narrow is the gate and hard the way, that leads to life, and few those who find it!

On Abraham (62-63)

(62) He being impressed by an oracle by which he was commanded to leave his country, and his kindred, and his father's house, and to emigrate like a man returning from a foreign land to his own country, and not like one who was about to set out from his own land to settle in a foreign district, hastened eagerly on, thinking to do with promptness what he was commanded to do was equivalent to perfecting the matter. (63) And yet who else was it likely would be so undeviating and unchangeable as not to be won over by and as not to yield to the charms of one's relations and one's country? The love for which has in a manner -- "Grown with the growth and strengthened with the strength," of every individual, and even more, or at all events not less than the limbs united to the body have done.

> Parallels: Genesis 12:01-04; Hebrews 11:10-16

On Abraham (107-109)

(107) It has been said then that the disposition of the Egyptians is inhospitable and intemperate; and the humanity of him who has been exposed to their conduct deserves admiration, for He {Genesis 18:1, etc.} in the middle of the day beholding as it were three men travelling (and he did not perceive that they were in reality of a more divine nature), ran up and entreated them with great perseverance not to pass by his tent, but as was becoming to go in and receive the rites of hospitality: and they knowing the truth of the man not so much by what he said, as by his mind which they could look into, assented to his request without hesitation; (108) and being filled as to his soul with joy, he took every possible pains to make their extemporaneous reception worthy of them; and he said to his wife, "Hasten now, and make ready quickly three measures of fine meal," and he himself went forth among the herds of oxen, and brought forth a tender and well-fed heifer, and gave it to his servant; (109) and he having slain it, dressed it with all speed. For no one in the house of a wise man is ever slow to perform the duties of hospitality, but both women and men, and slaves and freemen, are most eager in the performance of all those duties towards strangers.

> Parallels: Genesis 18:01-08; Luke 13:20-21; John 08:56-58
>
> Comparison: Luke 13:20-21, "And again he said, "To what shall I compare the kingdom of God? It is like leaven, which a woman took and hid in three measures of flour till it was all leavened."

On Abraham (132)

(132) For when the wise man entreats those persons who are in the guise of three travelers to come and lodge in his house, he speaks to them not as three persons, but as one, and says, "My lord, if I have found favor with thee, do not thou pass by thy

Servant."{Genesis 18:3.} For the expressions, "my lord," and "with thee," and "do not pass by," and others of the same kind, are all such as are naturally addressed to a single individual, but not to many. And when those persons, having been entertained in his house, address their entertainer in an affectionate manner, it is again one of them who promises that he by himself will be present, and will bestow on him the seed of a child of his own, speaking in the following words: "I will return again and visit thee again, according to the time of life, and Sarah thy wife shall have a Son."{Genesis 18:10.}

> Parallels: Genesis 18:03, 10; Matthew 01:01, 28:19; John 08:56-58
>
> Comparison: John 08:56-58, "Your father Abraham rejoiced to see my day; he saw it and was glad." The Jews then said to him, "You are not yet fifty years old, and have you seen Abraham?" Jesus said to them, "Truly, truly, I say to you, before Abraham was, I am.""

On Abraham (161)

(161) But the eyes in a single moment can reach from earth to heaven, and taking in the extremist boundaries of the universe, reaching at the same moment to the east and to the west, and to the north and to the south, so as to survey them all at once, drag the mind towards what is visible.

> Parallels: Genesis 18:02; Matthew 18:09; Mark 09:47

On Abraham (220-222)

(220) Each then of these dispositions has, as it were, flocks and herds. The one which desires external things has for its flocks, gold and silver, and all those things which are materials and furniture of wealth; and, moreover, arms, engines, triremes, armies of infantry and cavalry, and fleets of ships, and all kinds

of provisions to procure domination, by which firm authority is secured. But the lover of excellence has for his flock the doctrines of each individual virtue, and its speculations respecting wisdom. (221) Moreover, there are overseers and superintendents of each of these flocks, just as there are shepherds to flocks of sheep. Of the flock of external things, the superintendents are those who are fond of money, those who are fond of glory, those who are eager for war, and all those who love authority over multitudes. And the managers of the flocks of things concerning the soul are all those who are lovers of virtue and of what is honorable, and who do not prefer spurious good things to genuine ones, but genuine to spurious good. (222) There is therefore a certain natural contest between them, inasmuch as they have no opinions in common with one another, but are always at variance and difference respecting the matter which has of all others the greatest influence in the maintenance of life as it should be, that is to say, the judgment of what things are truly good.

Parallels: Genesis 13:05-17; Matthew 06:24

Comparison: Matthew 06:24, "No one can serve two masters. For either he will hate the one and love the other, or he will be devoted to the one and despise the other. You cannot serve God and mammon."

On Abraham (225)

(225) Therefore the virtuous man was not only peaceful and a lover of justice, but also a man of courage and of a warlike disposition; not for the sake of making war, for he was not of a contentious and quarrelsome character, but for the sake of a lasting peace for the future, which hitherto his adversaries had destroyed.

Parallels: Genesis 14:13-20; Matthew 26:47-56

On Abraham (235)

(235) And when the great high priest of the most high God beheld him returning and coming back loaded with trophies, in safety himself, with all his own force uninjured, for he had not lost one single man of all those who went out with him; marveling at the greatness of the exploit, and, as was very natural, considering that he had never met with this success but through the favor of the divine wisdom and alliance, he raised his hands to heaven, and honored him with prayers in his behalf, and offered up sacrifices of thanksgiving for his victory, and splendidly feasted all those who had had a share in the expedition; rejoicing and sympathizing with him as if the success had been his own, and in reality it did greatly concern him. For as the proverb says: -- "All that befalls from friends we common call." And much more are all instances of good fortune common to those whose main object it is to please God.

Parallels: Genesis 14:13-20; John 18:09

Comparison: John 18:09, "This happened so that the words which he had spoken would be fulfilled, that "Of those whom you gave me I have lost none.""

On Dreams That they Are God-Sent (1.50-1.51)

(1.50) Blessed therefore are they to whom it has happened to enjoy the delights of wisdom, and to feast upon its speculations and doctrines, and even of the being cheered by them still to thirst for more, feeling an insatiable and increasing desire for knowledge. (1.51) And those will obtain the second place who are not allured indeed to enjoy the sacred table, but who nevertheless refresh their souls with its odors; for they will be excited by the fragrances of virtue like those languid invalids who, because they are not as yet able to take solid food, nevertheless feed on the smell of such viands as the sons of the physicians prepare as a sort of remedy for their impotency.

Parallels: Matthew 05:06

On Dreams That they Are God-Sent (1.85-86)

(1.85) But according to the third signification, when he speaks of the sun, he means the divine word, the model of that sun which moves about through the heaven, as has been said before, and with respect to which it is said, "The sun went forth upon the earth, and Lot entered into Segor, and the Lord rained upon Sodom and Gomorrah brimstone and fire." (1.86) For the word of God, when it reaches to our earthly constitution, assists and protects those who are akin to virtue, or whose inclinations lead them to virtue; so that it provides them with a complete refuge and salvation, but upon their enemies it sends irremediable overthrow and destruction.

Parallels: Genesis 19:24; Psalms 02:07, 33:06, 119:01-176; Luke 09:54; John 01:01-14; Acts 13:33

Comparison: Luke 9:54, "And when the disciples James and John saw this, they said, "Lord, do you want us to command fire to come down from heaven and consume them?""

On Dreams That they Are God-Sent (1.114)

(1.114) Moreover, while God pours upon you the light of his beams, do you hasten in the light of day to restore his pledge to the Lord; for when the sun has set, then you, like the whole land of Egypt, {Exodus 10:21.} will have an everlasting darkness which may be felt, and being stricken with blindness and ignorance, you will be deprived of all those things of which you thought that you had certain possession, by that sharp-sighted

Israel, whose pledges you hold, having made one who was by nature exempt from slavery a slave to necessity.

Parallels: Exodus 10:21; Jude 01:06

Comparison: Jude 01:06, "And the angels who did not keep their own domain, but abandoned their proper abode, he has kept in eternal chains under darkness for the judgment of the great day."

On Dreams That they Are God-Sent (1.124-1.126)

(1.124) Now no such person as this is a pupil of the sacred word, but those only are the disciples of that who are real genuine men, lovers of temperance, and orderliness, and modesty, men who have laid down continence, and frugality, and fortitude, as a kind of base and foundation for the whole of life; and safe stations for the soul, in which it may anchor without danger and without changeableness: for being superior to money, and pleasure, and glory, they look down upon meats and drinks, and everything of that sort, beyond what is necessary to ward off hunger: being thoroughly ready to undergo hunger, and thirst, and heat, and cold, and all other things, however hard they may be to be borne, for the sake of the acquisition of virtue. And being admirers of whatever is most easily provided, so as to not be ashamed of ever such cheap or shabby clothes, think rather, on the other hand, that sumptuous apparel is a reproach and great scandal to life. (1.125) To these men, the soft earth is their most costly couch; their bed is bushes, and grass, and herbage, and a thick layer of leaves; and the pillows for their head are a few stones, or any little mounds which happen to rise a little above the surface of the plain. Such a life as this, is, by luxurious men, denominated a life of hardship, but by those who live for virtue, it is called most delightful; for it is well adapted, not for those who are called men, for those who really are such. (1.126) Do you not see, that even now, also, the sacred historian represents the practitioner of honorable pursuits, who abounds in all royal materials and appointments, as sleeping on the ground, and using a stone for his pillow; and a little further on, he speaks of himself as asking in his prayers for bread and a cloak, the necessary wealth of nature? like one who has at all times held in contempt, the man who dwells among vain opinions, and who is inclined to revile all those who are disposed to admire him; this man is the archetypal pattern of the soul which is devoted to the practice of virtue, and an enemy of every effeminate person.

> Parallels: Genesis 28:11, 20-21; Matthew 03:01-17, 06:28, 08:20; Luke 07:22-28
>
> Comparison: Matthew 03:04, "Now John wore a garment of camel's hair, and a leather belt around his waist; and his food was locusts and wild honey." Matthew 8:20, "And Jesus said to him, "Foxes have holes and birds of the air have nests, but the Son of Man has nowhere to lay his head.""

On Dreams That they Are God-Sent (1.137-1.139)

(1.137) Is it not then absurd that that element, by means of which the other elements have been filled with vitality, should itself be destitute of living things? Therefore let no one deprive the most excellent nature of living creatures of the most excellent of those elements which surrounds the earth; that is to say, of the air. For not only is it not alone deserted by all things besides, but rather, like a populous city, it is full of imperishable and immortal citizens, souls equal in number to the stars. (1.138) Now of these souls some descend upon the earth with a view to be bound up in mortal bodies, those namely which are most nearly connected with the earth, and which are lovers of the body. But some soar upwards, being again distinguished according to the definitions and times which have been appointed by nature. (1.139) Of these, those which are influenced by a desire for mortal life, and which have been familiarized to it, again return to it. But others, condemning the body of great folly and trifling, have pronounced it a prison and a grave, and, flying from it as from a house of correction or a tomb, have raised themselves aloft on light wings towards the aether, and have devoted their whole lives to sublime speculations.

Parallels: Genesis 22:17, 26:04, 28:12; John 01:51; Acts 01:04-11; 1Thessalonians 04:16-17

On Dreams That they Are God-Sent (1.148)

(1.148) Now the God and governor of the universe does by himself and alone walk about invisibly and noiselessly in the minds of those who are purified in the highest degree. For there is extant a prophecy which was delivered to the wise man, in which it is said: "I will walk among you, and I will be your God."{Leviticus 26:12.} But the angels--the words of God--move about in the minds of those persons who are still in a process of being washed, but who have not yet completely washed off the life which defiles them, and which is polluted by the contact of their heavy bodies, making them look pure and brilliant to the eyes of virtue.

Parallels: Leviticus 26:11-12; Matthew 17:01-02; John 13:05-14, 17:01-26

On Dreams That they Are God-Sent (1.149)

(1.149) But it is plain enough what vast numbers of evils are driven out, and what a multitude of wicked inhabitants is expelled in order that one good man may be introduced to dwell there. Do thou, therefore, O my soul, hasten to become the abode of God, his holy temple, to become strong from having been most weak, powerful from having been powerless, wise from having been foolish, and very reasonable from having been doting and childless.

Parallels: Leviticus 26:11-12; Mark 05:01-20; John 02:19-21; 1Peter 02:05

On Dreams That they Are God-Sent (1.151-1.152)

(1.151) And perhaps this is no incorrect statement; for the wise have obtained the heavenly and celestial country as their habitation; having learnt to be continually mounting upwards, but the wicked have received as their share the dark recesses of hell, having from the beginning to the end of their existence practiced dying, and having been from their infancy to their old age familiarized with destruction. (1.152) But the practitioners of virtue, for they are on the boundary between two extremities, are frequently going upwards and downwards as if on a ladder, being either drawn upwards by a more powerful fate, or else being dragged down by that which is worse; until the umpire of this contention and conflict, namely God, adjudges the victory to the more excellent class and utterly destroys the other.

> Parallels: Genesis 28:12; Exodus 14:30; Matthew 07:13-14, 25:29-30, 46; John 01:51; Acts 01:04-11; 1Thessalonians 04:16-17; Hebrews 11:01-16; Revelation 20:10-15

On Dreams That they Are God-Sent (1.164-1.165)

(1.164) Now is it not fitting that even blind men should become sharp sighted in their minds to these and similar things, being endowed with the power of sight by the most sacred oracles, so as to be able to contemplate the glories of nature, and not to be limited to the mere understanding of the words? But even if we voluntarily close the eye of our soul and take no care to understand such mysteries, or if we are unable to look up to them, the hierophant himself stands by and prompts us. And do not thou ever cease through weariness to anoint thy eyes until you have introduced those who are duly initiated to the secret light of the sacred scriptures, and have displayed to them the hidden things therein contained, and their reality, which is invisible to those who are uninitiated. (1.165) It is becoming then for you to act thus; but as for ye, O souls, who have once tasted of divine love, as if you had even awakened from deep sleep, dissipate the mist that is before you; and hasten forward to that beautiful spectacle, putting aside slow and hesitating fear, in order to comprehend all the beautiful sounds and sights which the president of the games has prepared for your advantage.

> Parallels: Deuteronomy 29:04; Isaiah 06:09-10; Matthew 11:25, 13:03-53; Luke 10:21, 18:31-34, 24:25-27, 44-47; 1Corinthians 02:6-16; 2Corinthians 03:12-18, 04:03; Ephesians 03:09; Colossians 01:26, 02:02-03
>
> Comparison: 1Corinthians 02:06-14, "Yet we do speak a wisdom among the mature; a wisdom, however, not of this age nor of the rulers of this age, who are passing away. But we speak of God's secret wisdom, a wisdom that has been hidden and which God destined for our glory before the ages. None of the rulers of this age understood it; for if they had, they would not have crucified the Lord of glory. But, as it is written, "No eye has seen, nor ear heard, nor the heart of man conceived, what God has prepared for those who love him," But God has revealed them to us through the Spirit. For the Spirit searches all things, even the depths of God. For who among men knows the thoughts of a man except the man's spirit which is in him? Even so no one knows the thoughts of God except the Spirit of God. Now we have received not the spirit of the world, but the Spirit who is from God, that we may understand the things freely given to us by God. This is what we speak, not in words taught us by human wisdom but in words taught by the Spirit, expressing spiritual truths in spiritual words. But the natural man does not accept the things of the Spirit of God, for they are foolishness to him; and he cannot understand them, because they are spiritually discerned."

On Dreams That they Are God-Sent (1.175-1.176)

(1.175) But the race of wisdom is likened to the sand of the sea, by reason of its boundless numbers, and because also the sand, like a fringe, checks the incursions of the sea; as the reasonings of instruction beat back the violence of wickedness and iniquity. And these reasonings, in accordance with the divine promises, are extended to the very extremities of the universe. And they show that he who is possessed of them is the inheritor of all the parts of the world, penetrating everywhere, to the east, and to the west, to the south, and to the north. For it is said in the scripture: "He shall be extended towards the sea, and towards the south, and towards the north, and towards the East."{Genesis 28:14.} (1.176) But the wise and virtuous man is not only a blessing to himself, but he is also a common good to all men, diffusing advantages over all from his own ready store. For as the sun is the light of all those beings who have eyes, so also is the wise man light to all those who partake of a rational nature.

Parallels: Genesis 28:14; Isaiah 06:09-10; Matthew 05:14, 11:25; Luke 10:21, 18:31-34; John 19:17-18; Acts 03:18-26; 1Corinthians 02:06-16; 2Corinthians 04:03; Ephesians 03:09; Colossians 01:26, 02:02-03

Comparison: Matthew 05:14, "You are the light of the world. A city set on a hill cannot be hidden."

On Dreams That they Are God-Sent (1.215)

(1.215) For there are, as it seems, two temples belonging to God; one being this world, in which the high priest is the divine word, his own firstborn son. The other is the rational soul, the priest of which is the real true man, the copy of whom, perceptible to the senses, is he who performs his paternal vows and sacrifices, to whom it is enjoined to put on the aforesaid tunic, the representation of the universal heaven, in order that the world may join with the man in offering sacrifice, and that the man may likewise co-operate with the universe.

Parallels: Genesis 01:01, 19:24; Exodus 04:11, 28:03-42; Psalms 02:07, 33:06, 119:01-176; John 01:01-14, 02:19-21; Acts 13:33; Hebrews 07:26-28

Comparison: Hebrews 07:26-28, "For it was indeed fitting that we should have such a high priest, holy, blameless, unstained, separated from sinners, exalted above the heavens. He does not need, like those high priests, to offer up daily sacrifices, first for his own sins and then for the sins of the people, because he did this once for all when he offered up himself. For the Law appoints men as high priests who are weak. But the word of the oath, which came after the Law, appoints a Son who has been made perfect forever."

On Dreams That they Are God-Sent (1.218)

(1.218) And these injunctions contain this figurative meaning, that of those who in a pure and a guileless spirit serve the living God, there is no one who does not at first depend upon the firmness and obstinacy of his mind, despising all human affairs, which allure men with their specious bait, and injure them, and produce weakness in them. In the next place, he aims at immortality, laughing at the blind inventions with which mortals delude themselves. And last of all, he shines with the unclouded and most brilliant light of truth, no longer desiring any of the things which belong to false opinion, which prefer darkness rather than light.

Parallels: Matthew 15:14, 17:01-21; John 03:19, 12:25; Acts 01:04-11, 02:31

Comparison: Matthew 17:02, "And he was transfigured before them. His face shone like the sun, and his clothes became as white as light."

On Dreams That they Are God-Sent (1.237-1.239)

(1.237) For we must be content if such men can be brought to a proper state, by the fear which is suspended over them by such descriptions; and one may almost say that these are the only two paths taken, in the whole history of the law; one leading to plain truth, owing to which we have such assertions as, "God is not as a Man;"{Numbers 23:19.} the other, that which has regard to the opinions of foolish men, in reference to whom it is said, "The Lord God shall instruct you, like as if a man instructs his Son."{Deuteronomy 1:31.} (1.238) Why then do we any longer wonder, if God at times assumes the likeness of the angels, as he sometimes assumes even that of men, for the sake of assisting those who address their entreaties to him? so that when he says, "I am the God who was seen by thee in the place of God;"{Genesis 31:13.} we must understand this, that he on that occasion took the place of an angel, as far as appearance went, without changing his own real nature, for the advantage of him who was not, as yet, able to bear the sight of the true God; (1.239) for as those who are not able to look upon the sun itself, look upon the reflected rays of the sun as the sun itself, and upon the halo around the moon as if it were the moon itself; so also do those who are unable to bear the sight of God, look upon his image, his angel word, as himself.

Parallels: Genesis 19:24, 31:13, 32:24-32; Numbers 23:19; Deuteronomy 01:31; Psalms 02:07, 33:06, 119:01-176; John 01:01-14; Acts 13:33; 1Timothy 03:16; Hebrews 01:02-03

Comparison: Hebrews 01:02-03, "But in these last days he has spoken to us by his Son, whom he appointed heir of all things, and through whom also he made the world. He is the radiance of his glory and the exact representation of his being, and upholds all things by the word of his power. When he had made purification for sins, he sat down at the right hand of the Majesty on high."

On Dreams That they Are God-Sent (1.255-1.256)

(1.255) Why then, O my soul, do you any longer waste yourself in vain speculations and labors? And why do you not go as a pupil to the practitioner of virtue, taking up arms against the passions, and against vain opinion, to learn from him the way to wrestle with them? For as soon as you have learnt this art, you will become the leader of a flock, not of one which is destitute of marks, and of reason, and of docility, but of one which is well approved, and rational, and beautiful, (1.256) of which, if you become the leader, you will pity the miserable race of mankind, and will not cease to reverence the Deity; and you will never be weary of blessing God, and moreover you will engrave hymns suited to your sacred subject upon pillars, that you may not only speak fluently, but may also sing musically the virtues of the living God; for by these means you will be able to return to your father's house, being delivered from a long and profitless wandering in a foreign land.

Parallels: Genesis 31:18, 32:07-32; John 10:11-14, 14:02; Acts 03:18-26; Galatians 05:24; Hebrews 11:10-16, 13:12-15

Comparison: Hebrews 13:12-15, "And so Jesus also suffered outside the gate to sanctify the people through his own blood. Let us, then, go to him outside the camp, bearing the disgrace he bore. For here we do not have an enduring city, but we are looking for the city which is to come. Through him [then] let us continually offer up a sacrifice of praise to God, that is, the fruit of lips that acknowledge his name. "

On Dreams That they Are God-Sent (2.8)

(2.8) Let these things be laid down first by way of foundation; and on this foundation let us raise up the rest of the building, following the rules of that wise architect, allegory, and accurately investigating each particular of the dreams; but first we must mention what it is requisite should be attended to before the dreams. Some persons have extended the nature of good over many things, and others have attributed it to the most excellent Being alone; some again have mixed it with other things, while others have spoken of it as unalloyed.

> Parallels: Genesis 37:05-11; Matthew 19:17; Luke 06:48-49
>
> Comparison: Luke 06:48-49, "he is like a man building a house, who dug deep and laid the foundation on the rock. And when a flood arose, the stream broke against that house and could not shake it, because it was well built. But he who hears and does not do them is like a man who built a house on the ground without a foundation; against which the stream broke, and immediately it collapsed. And the ruin of that house was great."" Matthew 19:17a, "And he said to him, "Why do you ask me about what is good? There is only one who is good."

On Dreams That they Are God-Sent (2.11)

(2.11) for he does not indeed neglect the virtues of the soul, but he likewise shows anxiety about the stability and permanence of the body, and also desires an abundance of worldly treasures; and it is in strict accordance with natural truth, that he is represented as drawn in different directions, since he proposes to himself many different objects in life; and being attracted by each of them, he is kept in a state of commotion and agitation, without being able to stand firm.

Parallels: Genesis 37:05-11; Matthew 14:28-31, 19:16-30; Mark 10:21-30

On Dreams That they Are God-Sent (2.25)

(2.25) Now the reaping a harvest is like cutting a second time what has been cut already; which when some persons fond of novelty applied themselves to they found a circumcision of circumcision, and a purification of purification; {Numbers 6:2.} that is to say, they found that the purification of the soul was itself purified, attributing the power of making bright to God, and never fancying that they themselves were competent, without the assistance of the divine wisdom, to wash and cleanse a life which is full of stains.

Parallels: Numbers 06:01-27; Matthew 03:05-16; John 03:03-07

Comparison: John 03:03-07, "Jesus answered him, "Truly, truly, I say to you, unless one is born again, he cannot see the kingdom of God." Nicodemus said to him, "How can a man be born when he is old? Can he enter a second time into his mother's womb and be born?" Jesus answered, "Truly, truly, I say to you, unless one is born of water and the Spirit, he cannot enter the kingdom of God. That which is born of the flesh is flesh, and that which is born of the Spirit is spirit. Do not marvel that I said to you, 'You must be born again.'

On Dreams That they Are God-Sent (2.140)

(2.140) And are the offspring of us too to come likewise? And are we all to stand in a row, laying aside all our former dignity, and holding up our hands and praying to thee? And are we then to prostrate ourselves on the ground, and endeavor to propitiate and adore thee? But may the sun never shine upon such transactions, since deep darkness is suited to evil deeds, and brilliant light to good deeds. And what could be a greater evil than for pride, that deceiver and beguiler, to be praised and admired, instead of sincere and honest simplicity?

Parallels: Matthew 06:01-06; Acts 26:18

Comparison: Matthew 06:05-06, "And when you pray, you shall not be like the hypocrites. For they love to pray standing in the synagogues and on the street corners, that they may be seen by men. Truly, I say to you, they have received their reward. But when you pray, go into your room, shut the door and pray to your Father, who is in secret. And your Father, who sees in secret, will reward you."

On Dreams That they Are God-Sent (2.170-2.176)

(2.170) When any one leading us along the road, deserted by the passions and by acts of wickedness, the rod, that is, of philosophy, has led right reason to a height, and placed it like a scout upon a watch-tower, {Numbers 13:18.} and has commanded it to look around, and to survey the whole country of virtue, and to see whether it be blessed with a deep soil, and rich, and productive of herbage and of fruit, since deep soil is good to cause the learning which has been sown in it to increase, and to make the doctrines which have been planted in it, and which have grown to trees, to form solid trunks, or whether it be of a contrary character; and also to examine into actions, as one might into cities, and see whether they are strongly fortified, or whether they are defenseless and deprived of all the security which might be afforded by walls around them. Also to inquire into the condition of the inhabitants, whether they are considerable in numbers and in valor, or whether their courage is weak and their numbers scanty, the two causes acting reciprocally on one another. (2.171) Then because we were not able to bear the weight of the whole trunk of wisdom, we cut off one branch and one bunch of grapes, and carried it with us as a most undeniable proof of our joy, and a burden very easy to be borne, wishing to display at the same time the branch and the fruit of excellence to those who are gifted with acuteness of mental sight, to show them, that is, the strongly-shooting and grape bearing vine. (2.172) They then very fairly compare this vine of which we were only able to take a part, to happiness. And one of the ancient prophets bears his testimony in favor of my view of the matter, who speaking under divine inspiration has said, "The vineyard of the Lord Almighty is the house of Israel."{Isaiah 5:7.} (2.173) Now Israel is the mind inclined to the contemplation of God and of the world; for the name Israel is interpreted, "seeing God," and the abode of the mind is the whole soul; and this is the most sacred vineyard, bearing as its fruit the divine shoot, virtue: (2.174) thus thinking well (to eu phronein) is the derivation of the word joy (euphrosyneμ), being a great and brilliant thing so that, says Moses, even God himself does not disdain to exhibit it; and most especially at that time when the human race is departing from its sins, and inclining and bending its steps towards justice, following of its own accord the laws and institutions of nature. (2.175) "For," says Moses, "the Lord thy God will return, that he may rejoice in thee for thy good as he rejoiced in thy fathers, if thou wilt hear his voice to keep all his commandments and his ordinances and his judgments which are written in the book of this Law."{Deuteronomy 30:9.} (2.176) Who could implant in man a desire for virtue and excellence, more strongly than is here done? Dost thou wish, says the scripture, O mind, that God should rejoice? Do thou rejoice in virtue thyself, and bring no costly offering, (for what need has God of anything of thine?) But, on the other hand, receive with joy all the good things which he bestows upon thee.

Parallels: Numbers 13:17-21; Deuteronomy 30:09; Isaiah 05:07; Matthew 24:42-51; John 15:01-06

Comparison: John 15:01-06, ""I am the true vine, and my Father is the vinedresser. Every branch in me that bears no fruit he takes away; and every branch that does bear fruit he prunes, so that it may bear more fruit. You are already pruned because of the word which I have spoken to you. Abide in me, and I in you. As the branch cannot bear fruit by itself, unless it abides in the vine, neither can you, unless you abide in me. I am the vine, you are the branches. He who abides in me, and I in him, he bears much fruit; for apart from me you can do nothing. If anyone does not abide in me, he is like a branch that is cast away and withers; and they gather them and throw them into the fire, and it is burned."

On Dreams That they Are God-Sent (2.212-2.214)

(2.212) Therefore the birds, that is to say, the chances which never could have been anticipated by conjecture, coming from outward quarters and hovering around him, will attack and kindle everything like fire, and will destroy everything with their all-devouring power, so that there is not a single fragment left to the bearer of the baskets for his enjoyment though he had hoped to proceed with his inventions and contrivances, forever and ever carrying them on in a safe place, so that they could never be taken from him. (2.213) And thanks be to God who give the victory and who renders the labors of the man who is a slave to his passions, though ever so carefully carried out, still unproductive and useless, sending down winged natures in an invisible manner for their destruction and overthrow. Therefore, the mind, being deprived of those things which it had made for itself, having, as it were, its neck cut through, will be found headless and lifeless, and like those who are fixed to a cross, nailed as it were to the tree of hopeless and helpless ignorance. (2.214) For as long as none of these things come upon one which arrive suddenly and unexpectedly, then those acts which are directed to the enjoyment of pleasure appear to be successful; but when such evils descend upon them unexpectedly, they are overthrown, and their maker is destroyed with them.

Parallels: Genesis 40:18-22; Matthew 03:11-12, 27:05; Luke 23:33-45; Revelation 15:07-17:01, 19:17-21

On Dreams That they Are God-Sent (2.229-2.231)

(2.229) at all events, it says, "And I stood in the midst between the Lord and You," {Deuteronomy 10:10.} not meaning by these words that he was standing on his own feet, but wishing to indicate that the mind of the wise man, being delivered from all storms and wars, and enjoying unruffled calm and profound peace, is superior indeed to man, but inferior to God. (2.230) For the ordinary human mind is influenced by opinion, and is thrown into confusion by any passing circumstances; but the other is blessed and happy, and free from all participation in evil. And the good man is on the borders, so that one may appropriately say that he is neither God nor man, but that he touches the extremities of both, being connected with the mortal race by his manhood, and with the immortal race by his virtue. (2.231) And there is something which closely resembles this in the passage of scripture concerning the high priest; "For when," says the scripture, "he goes into the holy of holies, he will not be a man till he has gone out again."{Leviticus 16:17.} But if at that time he is not a man, it is clear that he is not God either, but a minister of God, belonging as to his mortal nature to creation, but as to his immortal nature to the uncreated God.

Parallels: Leviticus 16:17; Deuteronomy 10:10; 1Timothy 02:05; Hebrews 07:26-28

Comparison: 1Timothy 02:05, “For there is one God, and one mediator also between God and men, the man Christ Jesus.”

On Dreams That they Are God-Sent (2.246-2.249)

(2.246) There is also another expression in the Psalms, such as this, "The course of the river makes glad the city of God."{Psalm 45:5.} What city? For the holy city, which exists at present, in which also the holy temple is established, at a great distance from any sea or river, so that it is clear, that the writer here means, figuratively, to speak of some other city than the visible city of God. (2.247) For, in good truth, the continual stream of the divine word, being borne on incessantly with rapidity and regularity, is diffused universally over everything, giving joy to all. (2.248) And in one sense he calls the world the city of God, as having received the whole cup of the divine draught, ... and being gladdened thereby, so as to have derived from it an imperishable joy, of which it cannot be deprived forever. But in another sense he applies this title to the soul of the wise man, in which God is said also to walk, as if in a city, "For," says God, "I will walk in you, and I will be your God in You."{Leviticus 26:12.} (2.249) And who can pour over the happy soul which proffers its own reason as the most sacred cup, the holy goblets of true joy, except the cup-bearer of God, the master of the feast, the word? Not differing from the draught itself, but being itself in an unmixed state, the pure delight and sweetness, and pouring forth, and joy, and ambrosial medicine of pleasure and happiness; if we too may, for a moment, employ the language of the poets.

Parallels: Genesis 19:24, 32:24-32; Leviticus 26:12; Psalms 02:07, 33:06, 45:05, 119:01-176; Matthew 26:26-29; John 01:01-14, 02:07-11, 06:53-56, 14:17-23, 17:20-23; Acts 13:33; 1Corinthians 10:16-18; Hebrews 11:08-16

Comparison: Comparison: Hebrews 11:08-16, "By faith Abraham obeyed when he was called to go out to a place which he was to receive as an inheritance. And he went out, not knowing where he was going. By faith he lived in a land of promise, as in a foreign land, dwelling in tents with Isaac and Jacob, heirs with him of the same promise. For he was looking forward to the city which has foundations, whose architect and builder is God. By faith Sarah herself, when she was barren, received power to conceive, even when she was past the age, because she considered him faithful who had promised. Therefore from one man, and him as good as dead, were born descendants as many as the stars of heaven and as the innumerable grains of sand by the seashore. These all died in faith, not having taken hold of the promises, but having seen them and greeted them from a distance, and having acknowledged that they were strangers and exiles on the earth. For people who say such things make it clear that they are seeking a country of their own. And if they had been thinking of that country from which they had gone out, they would have had opportunity to return. But as it is, they desire a better country, that is, a heavenly one. Therefore God is not ashamed to be called their God, for he has prepared for them a city." John 14:17-23, "the Spirit of truth, whom the world cannot receive, because it neither sees nor knows him. You know him, for he dwells with you and will be in you. I will not leave you orphans. I will come to you. A little while longer, and the world will see me no more, but you will see me. Because I live, you will live also. In that day you will know that I am in my Father, and you in me, and I in you. He who has my commandments and keeps them, it is he who loves me. And he who loves me will be loved by my Father, and I will love him and reveal myself to him." Judas (not Iscariot) said to him, "Lord, [then] how is it that you will reveal yourself to us, and not to the world?" Jesus answered him, "If anyone loves me, he will keep my word, and my Father will love him, and we will come to him and make our home with him."

On Dreams That they Are God-Sent (2.272-2.273)

(2.272) What, then, shall we say? When we bring home the legitimate fruit of the mind, does not the sacred scripture enjoin us to display in our reason, as in a sacred basket, the first fruits of our fertility; a specimen of the glorious flowers, and shoots, and fruits which the soul has brought forth, bidding us speak out distinctly, and to utter panegyrics on the God who brings things to perfection, and to say, "I have cleared away the things which were holy out of my house, and I have arranged them in the house of God:"{Deuteronomy 26:13.} appointing as stewards and guardians of them, men selected for their superior merit, and giving them the charge of these sacred things; (2.273) and these persons are Levites, proselytes, and orphans, and widows. But some are suppliants, some are emigrants and fugitives, some are persons widowed and destitute of all created things, but enrolled as belonging to God, the genuine husband and father of the soul which is inclined to worship.

Parallels: Deuteronomy 26:13; Matthew 10:01, 19:27

On Dreams That they Are God-Sent (2.282)

(2.282) For no glorious thing can be invisible, but should be brought to the light and brilliancy of the sun. For so also the contrary, namely evil, should be thrust into deep darkness, and should be accounted deserving of night. And it may indeed by chance happen to some one to behold this: but what is really good should be always beheld by more piercing eyes. And what is so good as that what is good should live, and what is evil should die?

Parallels: Genesis 28:12; Exodus 14:30; Matthew 07:13-14; Acts 26:18

On Dreams That they Are God-Sent (2.302)

(2.302) For our present discussion is not about the history of rivers but about ways of life, which are compared to the streams of rivers, running in opposite directions to one another. For the life of the good man consists in actions; but that of the wicked man is seen to consist only in words. And speech [...] in the tongue, and mouth, and lips, and [...]

Parallels: Deuteronomy 30:14; James 02:01-26

Comparison: James 02:14-17, "What good is it, my brothers, if a man says he has faith but has no works? Can such faith save him? If a brother or sister is without clothing and in need of daily food, and one of you says to them, "Go in peace, be warmed and filled," and yet you do not give them what is necessary for their body, what use is that? So faith by itself, if it has no works, is dead."

On Drunkenness (72-76)

(72) This is he "who says to his father and to his mother," his mortal parents, "I have not seen you," ever since I have beheld the things of God, who "does not recognize his sons," ever since he has become an acquaintance of wisdom, who "disowns his Brethren,"{Deuteronomy 33:9.} ever since he has ceased to be disowned by God, and has been thought worthy of perfect salvation. (73) This is he who "took as coadjutor," that is to say, who searched for and sought out the things of corruptible creation, of which the chief happiness is laid up in eating and drinking, and who went, Moses says, "to the chimney," which was burning and flaming with the excesses of wickedness, and which could never be extinguished, namely, the life of man, and who, after that, was able even to pierce the woman through her belly, {Numbers 25:8.} because she appeared to be the cause of bringing forth, being, in real truth, rather the patient than the

agent, and even every "man," and every reasoning which follows the opinion which attributes passions to the essence of God, who is the cause of all things. (74) Will not this person be justly looked upon as a murderer, by many who are influenced by the customs which have so much weight among women? But with God, the ruler and father of the universe, he will be thought worthy of infinite praises and panegyrics, and of rewards which can never be taken away; and the rewards are great, and akin to one another, being peace and the priesthood: (75) for it was an illustrious achievement, after having put to flight the almost invincible troops of men who live according to the common fashion, and having put down the civil war of the appetites in the soul, to establish a peace firmly; and for this great exploit to receive nothing else, not riches, not glory, not honor, not authority, not beauty, not strength, not any of the advantages of the body, nor, on the other hand, earth or heaven, or all the world, but that most important and valuable of all things, the rank of the priesthood, the office of serving and paying honor to Him who is in truth the only being worthy of honor and service; this is an admirable thing, an object worthy of contention. (76) And I was not wrong when I called those rewards, brothers to one another, but I said so, knowing that he cannot be made a true priest who is still serving in human and mortal warfare, in which vain opinions are the officers of the companies; and that he cannot be a peaceful man, who does not in sincerity cultivate and serve, with all simplicity, the only Being who has no share in warfare, and everlasting peace.

Parallels: Numbers 25:08; Deuteronomy 33:09; Matthew 19:29; Luke 14:26

Comparison: Matthew 19:29, "And whoever has left houses or brothers or sisters or father or mother or children or lands, for my name's sake, will receive a hundredfold, and inherit eternal life."

On Flight And Finding (13)

(13) For the animal when first created is imperfect as to quantity; and a proof of this is the gradual growth which takes place at each successive age. But it is perfect as to quality. For the same quality remains in it, as having been stamped upon it by the divine word which abides permanently and never changes.

Parallels: Psalms 119:160; John 01:01-14; Hebrews 13:08

Comparison: Hebrews 13:08, "Jesus Christ is the same yesterday and today and forever."

On Flight And Finding (55-58)

(55) for how else does anyone die, who dies at all, except dying the death? Therefore, betaking myself for instruction to a wise woman, whose name is Consideration, I was released from my difficulty, for she taught me that some persons who are living are dead, and that some who are dead are still alive: she pronounced that the wicked, even if they arrive at the latest period of old age, are only dead, inasmuch as they are deprived of life according to virtue; but that the good, even if they are separated from all union with the body, live forever, inasmuch as they have received an immortal portion. (56) Moreover, she confirmed this opinion of hers by the sacred scriptures, one of which ran in this form: "You who cleave unto the Lord your God are all alive to this Day:"{Deuteronomy 4:4.} for she saw that those who sought refuge with God and became his suppliants, were the only living persons, and that all others were dead. And Moses, it seems, testifies to the immortality of those persons, when he adds, "You are all alive to this day;" (57) and this day is interminable eternity, from which there is no departure; for the period of months, and years, and, in short, all the divisions of time, are only the inventions of men doing honor to number. But the unerring proper name of eternity is "today;" for the sun is

always the same, without ever changing, going at one time beneath the earth, and at another time above the earth, and by him it is that day and night, the measures of time, are distinguished. (58) She also confirmed her statement by another passage in scripture of the following purport: "Behold, I have set before thy face life and death, and good and Evil."{Deuteronomy 30:15.} Therefore, O all-wise man, good and virtue mean life, and evil and wickedness mean death. And in another passage we read, "This is thy life, and thy length of days, to love the Lord thy God."{Deuteronomy 30:20.} This is the most admirable definition of immortal life, to be occupied by a love and affection for God unembarrassed by any connection with the flesh or with the body.

> Parallels: Deuteronomy 04:04, 30:15, 20; Matthew 08:22; Mark 12:27; Luke 09:60; Acts 02:31; 1Corinthians 15:36-57; Ephesians 02:01
>
> Comparison: Matthew 08:22, "But Jesus said to him, "Follow me, and let the dead bury their own dead."" Luke 20:38, "Now he is not the God of the dead but of the living, for all live to him."

On Flight and Finding (68-71)

(68) On this account, I imagine it is, that when Moses was speaking philosophically of the creation of the world, while he described everything else as having been created by God alone, he mentions man alone as having been made by him in conjunction with other assistants; for, says Moses, "God said, Let us make man in our Image."{Genesis 1:26.} The expression, "let us make," indicating a plurality of makers. (69) Here, therefore, the Father is conversing with his own powers, to whom he has assigned the task of making the mortal part of our soul, acting in imitation of his own skill while he was fashioning the rational part within us, thinking it right that the dominant part within the soul should be the work of the Ruler of all things, but that

the part which is to be kept in subjection should be made by those who are subject to him. (70) And he made us of the powers which were subordinate to him, not only for the reason which has been mentioned, but also because the soul of man alone was destined to receive notions of good and evil, and to choose one of the two, since it could not adopt both. Therefore, he thought it necessary to assign the origin of evil to other workmen than himself, --but to retain the generation of good for himself alone. (71) On which account, after Moses had already put in God's mouth this expression, "Let us make man," as if speaking to several persons, as if he were speaking only of one, "God made man." For, in fact, the one God alone is the sole Creator of the real man, who is the purest mind; but a plurality of workmen are the makers of that which is called man, the being compounded of external senses;

> Parallels: Genesis 01:26; Matthew 28:19; Luke 01:35; John 08:58; Acts 04:07, 08:10; 1Corinthians 01:24; Irenaeus Against Heresies Book IV.20.1
>
> Comparison: 1Corinthians 01:24, "but to those who are the called, both Jews and Greeks, Christ the power of God and the wisdom of God." Irenaeus Against Heresies Book IV.20.1, "We also then were made, along with those things which are contained by Him. And this is He of whom the Scripture says, "And God formed man, taking clay of the earth, and breathed into his face the breath of life." It was not angels, therefore, who made us, nor who formed us, neither had angels power to make an image of God, nor any one else, except the Word of the Lord, nor any Power remotely distant from the Father of all things. For God did not stand in need of these [beings], in order to the accomplishing of what He had Himself determined with Himself beforehand should be done, as if He did not possess His own hands. For with Him were always present the Word and Wisdom, the Son and the Spirit, by whom and in whom, freely and spontaneously, He made all things, to whom also He speaks, saying, "Let Us make

man after Our image and likeness;" He taking from Himself the substance of the creatures [formed], and the pattern of things made, and the type of all the adornments in the world."

On Flight And Finding (73-74)

(73) In accordance with this he has also not attributed the blessing of the virtuous and the cursing of the wicked to the same ministers, though both these offices receive praise. But since the blessing of the good has the precedence in panegyrics, and the affixing curses on the wicked is in the second rank of those who are appointed for these duties (and they are the chiefs, and leaders of the race, twelve in number, whom it is customary to call the patriarchs), he has assigned the better six, who are the best for the task of blessing, namely, Simeon, Levi, Judah, Issachar, Joseph, and Benjamin; and the others he has appointed for the curses, namely, the first and last sons of Leah, Reuben, and Zebulon, and the four bastard sons by the handmaidens; (74) for the chiefs of the royal tribe, and of the tribe consecrated to the priesthood, Judah and Levi, are reckoned in the former class. Very naturally, therefore, does God give up those who have done deeds worthy of death to the hands of others for punishment, wishing to teach us that the nature of evil is banished to a distance from the divine choir, since even punishment, which, though a good, has in it some imitation of evil, is confirmed by others.

Parallels: Deuteronomy 27:11-28:68; Matthew 05:01-12, 07:13-14; Luke 06:13-26

On Flight And Finding (75-76)

(75) And the expression, "I will give thee a place to which he who has slain a man unintentionally shall flee," appears to me to be spoken with exceeding propriety; for what he calls a place is not a region filled by the body, but is rather, in a figure, God

himself, because he, surrounding all things, is not surrounded himself, and because he is that to which all things flee for refuge. (76) It is proper, therefore, for him who appears to have been involuntarily changed to say that this change has come upon him by the divine will, just as it is not proper for him to say so who has done evil of his own accord; and he says that he will give this place, not to him who has slain the man, but to him with whom he is conversing, so that the inhabitant of it shall be one person, but he who flees to it for refuge another; for God has given his own word a country to inhabit, namely, his own knowledge, as if it were a native of it. But to the man who is under the pollution of involuntary error he has given a foreign home as to a stranger, not a country as to a citizen.

Parallels: Genesis 31:08-13; Exodus 25:22; Numbers 35:01-34; Deuteronomy 06:10-11, 33:27; John 01:01-14; Hebrews 11:10-16

On Flight And Finding (79-80)

(79) There is nothing therefore of the wicked actions which are done secretly, and treacherously, and of malice aforethought, which we can properly say are done through the will of God, but they are done only through our own will. For, as I have said before, the storehouses of wickedness are in us ourselves, and those of good alone are with God. (80) Whosoever therefore flees for refuge, that is to say, whosoever accuses not himself, but God as the cause of his offence, let him be punished, being deprived of that refuge to the altar which tends to salvation and security, and which is meant for suppliants alone. And is not this proper? For the altar is full of victims, in which there is no spot, I mean of innocent and thoroughly purified souls. But to pronounce the Deity the cause of evil is a spot which it is hard to cure, or rather which is altogether incurable.

Parallels: Leviticus 35:16-21; Luke 06:45, 12:16-21

Comparison: Luke 12:16-21, "And he told them a parable, saying: "The ground of a certain rich man yielded plentifully. And he thought to himself, 'What shall I do, since I have no place to store my crops?' And he said, 'I will do this: I will pull down my barns and build larger ones; and there I will store all the wheat and my goods. And I will say to my soul, "Soul, you have many goods laid up for many years; take your ease; eat, drink, and be merry."' But God said to him, 'Fool! This night your soul will be required of you; then whose will those things be which you have prepared?' So is he who lays up treasure for himself, and is not rich toward God.""

On Flight And Finding (88-92)

(88) We must, therefore, say what is suitable on each of these heads, beginning with the first order. It is with exceeding propriety that the command is given to flee only to those cities which have been assigned to the tribe of Levi; for the Levites themselves are in a manner fugitives, inasmuch as they, for the sake of pleasing God, have left parents, and children, and brethren, and all their mortal relations. (89) Therefore the original leader of the company is represented as saying to his father and mother, "I have not seen you, and my brethren I do not know, and my sons I Disown,"{Deuteronomy 33:9.} in order to be able to serve the living God without allowing any opposite attraction to draw him away. But real flight is a deprivation of all that is nearest and dearest to man. And it introduces one fugitive to another, so as to make them forget what they have done by reason of the similarity of their actions. (90) Either, therefore, it is for this reason alone, or perhaps for this other also, that the Levitical tribe of the persons set apart for the service of the temple ran up, and at one onset slew those who had made a god of the golden calf, the pride of Egypt, killing all who had arrived at the age of puberty, being inflamed with righteous anger, combined with enthusiasm, and a certain heaven-sent

inspiration: "And every one slew his brother, and his neighbor, and him that was nearest to Him."{Exodus 32:26.} The body being the brother of the soul, and the irrational part the neighbor of the rational, and the uttered speech that which is nearest to the mind. (91) For by the following means alone can that which is most excellent within us become adapted for and inclined to the service of him who is the most excellent of all existing beings. In the first place, if a man be resolved into soul, the body, which is akin to it as a brother, being separated and cut off from it, and also all its insatiable desires; and in the second place when the soul has, as I have already said, cast off the irrational part, which is the neighbor of the rational part; for this, like a torrent, being divided into five channels, excites the impetuosity of the passions through all the external senses, as so many aqueducts. (92) Then, in regular order, the reason removes to a distance and separates the uttered speech which appeared to be the nearest to it of all things, in order that speech, according to the intention, might alone be left, free from the body, free from the entanglements of the outward senses, and free from all uttered speech; for when it is left in this manner existing in a solitary manner, it will embrace that which alone is to be embraced with purity, and in such a way that it cannot be drawn away.

> Parallels: Exodus 32:26; Numbers 35:01-34; Deuteronomy 33:09; Matthew 19:29; Luke 14:26
>
> Comparison: Matthew 19:29, "And whoever has left houses or brothers or sisters or father or mother or children or lands, for my name's sake, will receive a hundredfold, and inherit eternal life."

On Flight And Finding (95-112)

(95) But the other five, being as it were colonies of that one, are the powers of Him who utters the word, the chief of which is his creative power, according to which the Creator made the world with a word; the second is his kingly power, according to which

he who has created rules over what is created; the third is his merciful power, in respect of which the Creator pities and shows mercy towards his own work; the fourth is his legislative power, by which he forbids what may not be done. [...](96) And these are the very beautiful and most excellently fenced cities, the best possible refuge for souls which are worthy to be saved for ever; and the establishment of them is merciful and humane, calculated to excite men, to aid and to encourage them in good hopes. Who else could more greatly display the exceeding abundance of his mercy, all of the powers which are able to benefit us, towards such an exceeding variety of persons who err by unintentional misdeeds, and who have neither the same strength nor the same weakness? (97) Therefore he exhorts him who is able to run swiftly to strain onwards, without stopping to take breath, to the highest word of God, which is the fountain of wisdom, in order that by drinking of that stream he may find everlasting life instead of death. But he urges him who is not so swift of foot to flee for refuge to the creative power which Moses calls God, since it is by that power that all things were made and arranged; for to him who comprehends that everything has been created, that comprehension alone, and the knowledge of the Creator, is a great acquisition of good, which immediately persuades the creature to love him who created it. (98) Him, again, who is still less ready he bids flee to his kingly power; for that which is in subjection is corrected by the fear of him who rules it, and by necessity which keeps it in order, even if the child is not kept in the right way by love for his father. Again, in the case of him who is not able to reach the boundaries which have been already mentioned, in respect of their being a long way off, there are other goals appointed for them at a shorter distance, the cities namely of the necessary powers, the city of the power of mercy, the city of the power which enjoins what is right, the city of the power which forbids what is not right: (99) for he who is already persuaded that the deity is not implacable, but is merciful by reason of the gentleness of his nature, then, even if he has previously sinned, subsequently repents from a hope of pardon. And he who has adopted the notion that God is a lawgiver obeys all the injunctions which as such he imposes, and so will be happy; and he who is last of all will find the last refuge, namely, the escape from evil, even though he may not be able to arrive at a participation in the more desirable good things. (100) These, then, are the six cities which Moses calls cities of refuge, five of which have had their figures set forth in the sacred scriptures, and their images are there likewise. The images of the cities of command and prohibition are the laws in the ark; that of the merciful power of God is the covering of the ark, and he calls it the mercy-seat. The images of the creative power and of the kingly power are the winged cherubim which are placed upon it. (101) But the divine word which is above these does not come into any visible appearance, inasmuch as it is not like to any of the things that come under the external senses, but is itself an image of God, the most ancient of all the objects of intellect in the whole world, and that which is placed in the closest proximity to the only truly existing God, without any partition or distance being interposed between them: for it is said, "I will speak unto thee from above the mercy seat, in the midst, between the two Cherubim."{Exodus 25:22.} So that the word is, as it were, the charioteer of the powers, and he who utters it is the rider, who directs the charioteer how to proceed with a view to the proper guidance of the universe. (102) Therefore, he who is so far removed from committing any intentional misdeeds, that he is even free from all unintentional offence, will have God himself for his inheritance, and will dwell in him alone. But those who fall into errors which proceed not from willful purpose, but which are done without premeditation, will have the aforesaid places of refuge in all abundance and fullness. (103) Now of the cities of refuge there are three on the other side of Jordan , which are at a great distance from our race. What cities are they? The word of the Governor of the universe, and his creative power, and his kingly power: for to these belong the heaven and the whole world. (104) But those which, as it were, participate in us, and which are near to us, and which almost touch the unfortunate race of mankind which is alone capable of sinning, are the three on this side of the river; the merciful power, the power which enjoins what is to be done, the power which prohibits what ought not to be done: for these powers touch us. (105) For what need can there be of prohibition to persons who are not likely to do wrong? And what need of injunction to people who are not by nature inclined to stumble? And what need of mercy can those persons have who will absolutely never do wrong at all? But our race of mankind has need of all these things because it is by nature inclined and liable to offences both voluntary and involuntary. (106) The fourth and last of the points which we proposed to discuss, is the appointing as a period for the return of the fugitives the death of the high priest, which, if taken in the literal sense, causes me great perplexity; for a very unequal punishment is imposed by this enactment on those who have done the very same things, since some will be in banishment for a longer time, and others for a shorter time; for some of the high priests live to a very old age, and others die very early, (107) and some are appointed while young men, and others not until they are old. And again of those who are convicted of unintentional homicide, some have been banished at the beginning of the high priest's entrance into office, and some when the high priest has been at the very point of death. So that some are deprived of their country for a very long time, and others suffer the same infliction only for a day, if it chance to be so; after which they lift up their heads, and exult, and so return among those whose nearest relations have been slain by them. (108) This difficult and scarcely explicable perplexity we may escape if we adopt the inner and allegorical explanation in accordance with natural philosophy. For we say that the high priest is not a man, but is the word of God, who has not only no participation in intentional errors, but none even in those which are involuntary. (109) For Moses says that he cannot be defiled neither in respect of his father, that is, the mind, nor his mother, that is, the external sense; {Leviticus 21:11.} because, I imagine, he has received imperishable and wholly pure parents, God being his father, who is also the father of all things, and wisdom being his mother, by means of whom the universe arrived at creation; (110) and also because he is anointed with oil, by which I mean that the principal part of him is illuminated with a light like the beams of the sun, so as to be thought worthy to be clothed with garments. And the most ancient word of the living God is clothed with the word as with a garment, for it has put on earth, and water, and air, and fire, and the things which proceed from those elements. But the particular soul is clothed with the body, and the mind of the wise man is clothed with the virtues. (111) And it is said that he will never take the miter off from his head, he will never lay aside the kingly diadem, the symbol of an authority which is not indeed absolute, but only that of a viceroy, but which is nevertheless an object of admiration. Nor will he "rend his clothes;" (112) for the word of the living God being the bond of everything, as has been said before, holds all things together, and binds all the parts, and prevents them from being loosened or separated. And the particular soul, as far as it has received power, does not permit any of the parts of the body to be separated or cut off contrary to their nature; but as far as depends upon itself, it preserves everything entire, and conducts the different parts to a harmony and indissoluble union with one another. But the mind of the wise man being thoroughly purified, preserves the virtues in an unbroken and unimpaired condition, having adapted their natural kindred and communion with a still more solid good will. (113) This high priest, as Moses says, "shall not enter into any soul that is dead." But the death of the soul is a life according to wickedness; so that he must never touch any pollution such as folly is fond of dealing with. (114) And to him also "a virgin of the sacred race is joined;" that is to say, an opinion for ever pure, and undefiled, and imperishable; for he "may never become the husband of a widow, or of one who has been divorced, or of one who is a profane person, or of one who is a harlot," since he is always proclaiming an endless and irreconcilable war against them. For it is a hateful thing to him to be widowed with respect to virtue, and to be divorced and driven away by her; and in like manner all persuasion of this kind is profane and unholy. But that promiscuous evil abandoned to many husbands, and to the worship of many gods, that is, a harlot, he does not think fit even to look upon, being content with her who has chosen for herself one husband and father only, the all-governing God.

Parallels: Genesis 31:08-13; Exodus 25:22, 28:32; Leviticus 10:06, 36, 21:10-14; Numbers 23:19, 35:01-34; Deuteronomy 01:31; Psalms 119:160; Jeremiah 02:13; Matthew 08:22, 11:19, 17:01-21; Mark 12:27; Luke 01:26-27, 35, 07:35, 09:60; John 01:01-14, 18, 04:04-42, 06:47, 19:23-24; Acts 03:18-26, 04:07, 08:10; 1Corinthians 01:24; Ephesians 02:01; Hebrews 07:26-28; 1Peter 02:09

Comparison: Hebrews 07:26-28, "For it was indeed fitting that we should have such a high priest, holy, blameless, unstained, separated from sinners, exalted above the heavens. He does not need, like those high priests, to offer up daily sacrifices, first for his own sins and then for the sins of the people, because he did this once for all when he offered up himself. For the Law appoints men as high priests who are weak. But the word of the oath, which came after the Law, appoints a Son who has been made perfect forever.

On Flight And Finding (117-118)

(117) As long, therefore, as this most sacred word lives and survives in the soul, it is impossible for any involuntary error to enter into it; for it is by nature so framed as to have no participation in, and to be incapable of admitting any kind of error. But if it dies (not meaning by this that it is itself destroyed, but that it is separated from our soul), then a return is at once granted to intentional offences. (118) For if while the word remained and was healthy in us, error was driven to a distance, by all means, when the word departs, error will be introduced. For the undefiled high priest, conscience, has derived from nature this most especial honor, that no error of the mind can find any place within him; on which account it is worth our while to pray that the high priest may live in the soul, being at the same time both a judge and a convictor, who having received jurisdiction over the whole of our minds, is not altered in his

appearance or purpose by any of those things which are brought under his judgment.

> Parallels: Genesis 31:08-13; Exodus 25:22, 28:32; Leviticus 10:06, 36, 21:11, 35:25; Numbers 23:19, 35:01-34; Deuteronomy 01:31; Psalms 119:160; John 01:01-14; Hebrews 07:24-28; Revelation 20:11-15

> Comparison: Hebrews 07:24-28, "But he holds his priesthood forever, because he continues forever. Therefore he is able also to save forever those who draw near to God through him, since he always lives to make intercession for them. For it was indeed fitting that we should have such a high priest, holy, blameless, unstained, separated from sinners, exalted above the heavens. He does not need, like those high priests, to offer up daily sacrifices, first for his own sins and then for the sins of the people, because he did this once for all when he offered up himself. For the Law appoints men as high priests who are weak. But the word of the oath, which came after the Law, appoints a Son who has been made perfect forever.

On Flight And Finding (122-123)

(122) For whoever despises his teacher, and under the influence of an innate and habitual indolence forsakes what is in front of him, by means of which it may be in his power to see, and to hear, and to exert his other powers, so as to form a judgment in things of nature, and turns his head round so as to keep his eyes on what is behind him, that man has an admiration for blindness in the affairs of life, as well as in the parts of the body, and becomes a pillar, like a lifeless and senseless stone. (123) For, as Moses says, "such men have not hearts to understand, nor eyes to see, nor ears to Hear,"{Deuteronomy 29:4.} but make the whole of their life blind, and deaf, and senseless and mutilated

in every respect, so as not to be worth living, caring for none of those matters which deserve their attention.

> Parallels: Deuteronomy 29:04; Matthew 11:15
>
> Comparison: Matthew 11:15, "He who has ears, let him hear."

On Flight And Finding (175)

(175) And the lawgiver appears to me to be recommending most manifestly that kind of discovery which is not preceded by any search, in the following words, "When the Lord thy God shall lead thee into the land which he swore to thy fathers that he would give thee, large and beautiful cities which thou build not, houses full of all good things which thou filled not, cisterns hewn out of the quarries which thou hewed not, vineyards and olive gardens which thou planted not." {Deuteronomy 6:10.}

> Parallels: Numbers 35:06, 09-32; Deuteronomy 06:10-11, 33:27; Matthew 21:33-41; Hebrews 11:08-16
>
> Comparison: Hebrews 11:08-16, "By faith Abraham obeyed when he was called to go out to a place which he was to receive as an inheritance. And he went out, not knowing where he was going. By faith he lived in a land of promise, as in a foreign land, dwelling in tents with Isaac and Jacob, heirs with him of the same promise. For he was looking forward to the city which has foundations, whose architect and builder is God. By faith Sarah herself, when she was barren, received power to conceive, even when she was past the age, because she considered him faithful who had promised. Therefore from one man, and him as good as dead, were born descendants as many as the stars of heaven and as the innumerable grains of sand by the seashore. These all died in faith, not having taken hold of the promises, but

> having seen them and greeted them from a distance, and having acknowledged that they were strangers and exiles on the earth. For people who say such things make it clear that they are seeking a country of their own. And if they had been thinking of that country from which they had gone out, they would have had opportunity to return. But as it is, they desire a better country, that is, a heavenly one. Therefore God is not ashamed to be called their God, for he has prepared for them a city."

On Flight And Finding (197-210)

(197) We must now speak also concerning that highest and most excellent of fountains which the Father of the universe spoke of by the mouths of the prophets; for he has said somewhere, "They have left me, the fountain of life, and they have dug for themselves cisterns already worn out, which will not be able to hold Water;"{Jeremiah 2:13.} (198) therefore, God is the most ancient of all fountains. And is not this very natural? For he it is who has irrigated the whole of this world; and I am amazed when I hear that this is the fountain of life, for God alone is the cause of animation and of that life which is in union with prudence; for the matter is dead. But God is something more than life; he is, as he himself has said, the everlasting fountain of living. (199) But the wicked having fled away, and having passed their time without ever tasting the draught of immortality, have dug, insane persons that they are, for themselves, and not first for God, having preferred their own actions to the heavenly and celestial things, and the things which proceed from care to those which are spontaneous and ready. (200) Then they dig, not as the wise men Abraham and Isaac did, making wells, but cisterns, which have no good nutritious stream belonging to and proceeding from themselves, but requiring an influx from without, which must proceed from instruction. While the teachers are always pouring into the ears of their disciples all kinds of doctrines and speculations of science altogether, admonishing them to retain them in their

minds, and to preserve them when faithfully committed to memory. (201) But now they are but worn-out cisterns, that is to say, all the channels of the ill-educated soul are broken and leaky, not being able to hold and to preserve the influx of those streams which are able to profit. (202) We have now then said as much as the time will permit us to say on the subject of the fountains, and it is with great accuracy and propriety that the sacred scriptures represent Hagar as found at the fountain, and not as drawing water from it: for the soul has not as yet made such an advance as to be fit to use the unmixed draught of wisdom; but it is not forbidden from making its abode in its neighborhood. (203) And all the road which is made by instruction is easy to travel, and most safe, and most solid, and strong, on which account the scripture tells us that she was found in the road leading to Shur; and the name Shur being interpreted means a wall or a direction. Therefore its convicter, speaking to the soul, says, "Whence comes thou, and whither goes thou?" And it says, not because it doubts, and not so much by the way of asking a question, as in a downcast and reproachful spirit, for an angel cannot be ignorant of anything that concerns us, and a proof of this is, (204) that he is well acquainted even with the things that are in the womb, and which are invisible to the creature, inasmuch as he says, "Behold thou art with child, and thou shall bring forth a son, and shall call his name Ishmael;" for to know that that which is conceived is a male child does not belong to human power, any more than it does to foretell the destruction of life which the child who is not yet born will adopt, namely, that it will be rude life, and not that of a citizen or of a polished man. (205) The expression, "Whence comes thou?" is said by way of reproving the soul, which is fleeing from the better and dominant opinion, of which she is the handmaiden, not in name more than in fact, and by remaining in subjection to which she would gain great glory. And the expression, "And whither goes thou?" means, you are running after uncertain things, having discarded and thrown away confessed good. (206) It is well, therefore, to praise her for rejoicing at this admonition. And she shows a proof of her delighting in it, by not bringing any accusation against her mistress, and by attributing the cause of her running away to her own self, and by her making no reply to the second question, "Whither goes thou?" for it is a matter of uncertainty; and it is both safe and necessary to restrain one's self from speaking of what is uncertain. (207) Therefore the convicter of the soul approving of her in respect of her obedience says, Return unto thy mistress; for the government of the teacher is profitable to the disciple, and servitude in subjection to wisdom is advantageous to her who is imperfect; and when thou return, "be thou humbled under her hands:"--a very beautiful humiliation, comprehending the destruction of irrational pride. (208) For thus, after a gentle travail, thou wilt bring forth a male child, by name Ishmael, corrected by divine admonitions; for Ishmael, being interpreted, means "the hearing of God;" and hearing is considered as entitled to only the second prize after seeing; but seeing is the inheritance of the legitimate and first-born son, Israel; for the name Israel, being interpreted, means "seeing God." For it is possible for a man to hear false statements as though they were true, because hearing is a deceitful thing; but seeing is a sense which cannot be deceived, by which a man perceives existing things as they really are. (209) But the angel describes the characteristics of the disposition which is born of Hagar, by saying that he will be a rude man; as if he had said that he would be a man wise about rude matters, and not as yet thought worthy of that which is the truly divine and political portion of life: and this is virtue, by means of which it is the nature of the moral character to be humanized. And by his saying, "His hand shall be against every man, and every man's hand against him," he means to describe the design and plan of life of a sophist, who professes an overcurious skepticism, and who rejoices in disputatious arguments. (210) Such a man shoots at all the followers of learning, and in his own person opposes all men, both publicly and privately, and is shot at by all who very naturally repel him as if they were acting in defense of their own offspring, that is to say, of the doctrines which their soul has brought forth.

Parallels: Jeremiah 02:13; John 04:04-42

Comparison: John 04:04-42, "Now he had to go through Samaria. So he came to a city of Samaria which is called Sychar, near the plot of ground that Jacob gave to his son Joseph. Jacob's well was there, and Jesus, wearied as he was from his journey, sat down by the well. It was about the sixth hour. There came a woman of Samaria to draw water. Jesus said to her, "Give me a drink." For his disciples had gone away into the city to buy food. Then the woman of Samaria said to him, "How is it that you, being a Jew, ask a drink from me, a Samaritan woman?" For Jews have no dealings with Samaritans. Jesus answered her, "If you knew the gift of God, and who it is that is saying to you, 'Give me a drink,' you would have asked him, and he would have given you living water." [The woman] said to him, "Sir, you have nothing to draw with, and the well is deep. So where do you get that living water? Are you greater than our father Jacob, who gave us the well, and drank from it himself, as well as his sons and his cattle?" Jesus answered her, "Everyone who drinks of this water will thirst again, but whoever drinks of the water that I shall give him will never thirst. The water that I shall give him will become in him a spring of water welling up to eternal life." The woman said to him, "Sir, give me this water, that I may not thirst, nor should come all the way here to draw." He said to her, "Go, call your husband, and come here." The woman answered and said to him, "I have no husband." Jesus said to her, "You are right in saying, 'I have no husband.' For you have had five husbands, and the one whom you now have is not your husband. This you have said truly." The woman said to him, "Sir, I perceive that you are a prophet. Our fathers worshipped on this mountain, and you Jews say that in Jerusalem is the place where men ought to worship." Jesus said to her, "Woman, believe me, the hour is coming when neither on this mountain nor in Jerusalem will you worship the Father. You worship what you do not know; we worship what we know, for salvation is from the Jews. But the hour is coming, and now is, when the true worshippers will worship the Father in spirit and truth, for such the Father seeks to worship him. God is spirit, and those who worship him must worship in spirit and truth." The woman said to him, "I know that Messiah is coming" (who is called Christ). "When he comes, he will tell us all things." "I am he," Jesus said to her, "the one speaking to you." Just then his disciples came. And they were amazed that he was talking with a woman. But no one said, "What do you wish?" or, "Why are you talking with her?" Then the woman left her water jar, and went away into the city, and said to the people, "Come, see a man who told me all that I ever did. Could this be the Christ?" They went out of the city and came to him. Meanwhile the disciples urged him, saying, "Rabbi, eat." But he said to them, "I have food to eat of which you do not know." So the disciples said to one another, "Has any one brought him food?" Jesus said to them, "My food is to do the will of him who sent me, and to finish his work. Do you not say, 'There are yet four months and then comes the harvest'? Behold, I tell you, lift up your eyes, and look at the fields! They are white for harvest. Already the reaper is receiving wages, and gathering fruit for eternal life, so that sower and reaper may rejoice together. For here the saying is true, 'One sows and another reaps.' I sent you to reap that for which you have not labored. Others have labored, and you have entered into their labor." Many of the Samaritans from that city believed in him because of the woman's testimony, "He told me all that I did." So when the Samaritans came to him, they urged him to stay with them; and he stayed there two days. And many more believed because of his word. They said to the woman, "We no longer believe just because of what you said; now we have heard for ourselves, and we know that this man is indeed the Savior of the world."

On Husbandry (9-11)

(9) What can man be but the kind that is in every one of us, which is accustomed to reap the advantage from all that is sown or planted? But since milk is the food of infants, but cakes made of wheat are the food of full grown men, so also the soul must have a milk-like nourishment in its age of childhood, namely, the elementary instruction of encyclical science. But the perfect food which is fit for men consists of explanations dictated by prudence, and temperance, and every virtue. For these things being sown and implanted in the mind will bring forth most advantageous fruit, namely, good and praiseworthy actions. (10) By means of this husbandry, all the trees of the passions and vices, which shoot forth and grow up to a height, bringing forth pernicious fruits, are rooted up, and cut down, and cleared away, so that not even the smallest fragment of them is left, from which any new shoots of evil actions can subsequently spring up. (11) And if, besides, there are any trees which produce no fruit at all, neither good nor bad, the husbandman will cut them down too, but still he will not suffer them to be completely destroyed, but he will apply them to some appropriate use, making them into stakes and fixing them as pales all round his homestead, or using them as a fence for a city to serve instead of a wall.

Parallels: Deuteronomy 20:20; Matthew 07:16-21; Hebrews 05:12-14

Comparison: Matthew 07:16-21, "You will know them by their fruits. Do men gather grapes from thorn bushes, or figs from thistles? Even so, every good tree bears good fruit, but a bad tree bears bad fruit. A good tree cannot bear bad fruit, nor can a bad tree bear good fruit. Every tree that does not bear good fruit is cut down and thrown into the fire. Thus you will know them by their fruits. "Not every one who says to me, 'Lord, Lord,' shall enter the kingdom of heaven, but he who does the will of my

Father who is in heaven." Hebrews 05:12-14, "For though by this time you ought to be teachers, you need someone to teach you again the first elements of God's word. You need milk, [and] not solid food; for every one who lives on milk is unskilled in the word of righteousness, for he is a babe. But solid food is for the mature – those who have their sense trained by practice to distinguish good from evil."

On Husbandry (12-20)

(12) For Moses says, "Every tree which brings not forth fruit good to eat thou shall cut down; and thou shall make it into stakes against the city which shall make war upon them."{Deuteronomy 20:20.} And these trees are likened to those powers developed in words alone, which have nothing in them but mere speculation, (13) among which we must class medical science, when unconnected with practice, by which it is natural that such persons may be cured, and also the oratorical and hireling species of rhetoric, which is conversant not about the discovery of the truth, but solely about the means of deceiving the hearers by plausible persuasion; and in the same class we must place all those parts of dialectics and geometry which have no connection with a proper regulation of the character or morals, but which only sharpen the mind, not suffering it to exercise a dull apprehension towards each question which is raised and submitted to it, but always to dissect the question and divide it, so as to distinguish the peculiar character of each thing from the common qualities of the whole genus. (14) At all events, men say, that the ancients compared the principles of philosophy, as being threefold, to a field; likening natural philosophy to trees and plants, and moral philosophy to fruits, for the sake of which the plants are planted; and logical philosophy to the hedge or fence: (15) for as the wall, which is erected around, is the guardian of the plants and of the fruit which are in the field, keeping off all those who wish to do them injury and to destroy them, in the same manner, the logical part

of philosophy is the strongest possible sort of protection to the other two parts, the moral and the natural philosophy; (16) for when it simplifies twofold and ambiguous expressions, and when it solves specious plausibilities entangled in sophisms, and utterly destroys seductive deceits, the greatest allurement and ruin to the soul, by means of its own expressive and clear language, and its unambiguous demonstrations, it makes the whole mind smooth like wax, and ready to receive all the innocent and very praiseworthy impressions of sound natural and moral philosophy. (17) These then are the professions and promises made by the husbandry of the soul, "I will cut down all the trees of folly, and intemperance, and injustice, and cowardice; and I will eradicate all the plants of pleasure, and appetite, and anger, and passion, and of all similar affections, even if they have raised their heads as high as heaven. And I will burn out their roots, darting down the attack of flame to the very foundations of the earth, so that no portion, nay, no trace, or shadow whatever, of such things shall be left; (18) and I will destroy these things, and I will implant in those souls which are of a childlike age, young shoots, whose fruit shall nourish them. And those shoots are as follows: the practice of writing and reading with facility; an accurate study and investigation of the works of wise poets; geometry, and a careful study of rhetorical speeches, and the whole course of encyclical education. And in those souls which have arrived at the age of puberty or of manhood, I will implant things which are even better and more perfect, namely, the tree of prudence, the tree of courage, the tree of temperance, the tree of justice, the tree of every respective virtue. (19) And if there be any tree belonging to what is called the wild class, which does not bear eatable fruit, but which is able to be a fence to and a protector of that which is eatable, that also I will manage, not for its own sake, but because it is calculated by nature to be of use to what is necessary and very useful. (20) Therefore, the all wise Moses attributes to the just man a knowledge of the husbandry of the soul, as an act consistent with his character, and thoroughly suited to him, saying, "Noah began to be a husbandman." But to the unjust man he attributes the task of tilling the ground, which is an employment bearing the heaviest burdens without any knowledge.

> Parallels: Genesis 09:20; Deuteronomy 20:20; Matthew 07:16-21.
>
> Comparison: Matthew 07:16-21, "You will know them by their fruits. Do men gather grapes from thorn bushes, or figs from thistles? Even so, every good tree bears good fruit, but a bad tree bears bad fruit. A good tree cannot bear bad fruit, nor can a bad tree bear good fruit. Every tree that does not bear good fruit is cut down and thrown into the fire. Thus you will know them by their fruits. "Not every one who says to me, 'Lord, Lord,' shall enter the kingdom of heaven, but he who does the will of my Father who is in heaven."

On Husbandry (23-25)

(23) Moreover, the general crowd of men, travelling over the different climates of the earth and penetrating to its furthest boundaries, and traversing the seas, and investigating the things that lie hid in the recesses of the ocean, and leaving no single part of the whole universe unexplored, is continually providing from every quarter the means by which it can increase pleasure. (24) For as fishermen let down their nets at times to the most extraordinary depths, comprehending a vast surface of the sea in their circle, in order to catch the greatest possible number of fish enclosed within their nets, like people shut up within the walls of a besieged city; so in the same manner the greatest part of men having extended their universal nets to take everything, as the poets somewhere say, not only over the parts of the sea, but also over the whole nature of earth, and air, and water, seek to catch everything from every quarter for the enjoyment and attainment of pleasure. (25) For they dig mines in the earth, and they sail across the seas, and they achieve every other work both of peace and war, providing unbounded materials for pleasure,

as for their queen, being utterly uninitiated in that husbandry of the soul which sows and plants the virtues and reaps their fruit, which is a happy life. But they laboring to procure, and reducing to a system those things which are pleasant to the flesh, cultivate with all imaginable care that composite mass, that carefully fashioned statue, the narrow house of the soul, which, from its birth to its death it can never lay aside, but which it is compelled to bear till the day of its death, burdensome as it is.

Parallels: Genesis 09:20; Luke 05:03-09; John 21:06

Comparison: Luke 05:03-09, "Then he got into one of the boats, which was Simon's, and asked him to put out a little from the land. And he sat down and taught the people out of the boat. When he had finished speaking, he said to Simon, "Put out into the deep, and let down your nets for a catch." And answering, Simon said, "Master, we toiled all night and caught nothing! But at your word I will let down the nets." And when they had done this, they caught a great number of fish, and their nets were breaking. So they signaled to their partners in the other boat to come and help them. And they came and filled both the boats, so that they began to sink. When Simon Peter saw it, he fell down at Jesus' knees, saying, "Depart from me, for I am a sinful man, O Lord!" For he and all who were with him were astonished at the catch of fish which they had taken."

On Husbandry (41-42)

(41) These, then, are the occupations of shepherds who prefer those things which are useful, though mixed with unpleasantness, to those which are pleasant but pernicious. Thus, at all events, the occupation of a shepherd has come to be considered a respectable and profitable employment, so that the race of poets has been accustomed to call kings the shepherds of the people; but the law giver gives this title to the wise, who are

the only real kings, for he represents them as rulers of all men of irrational passions, as of a flock of sheep. (42) On this account he has attributed to Jacob, the man who was made perfect by practice, a skill in the science of a shepherd, saying: "For he is the shepherd of Laban's Sheep."{Genesis 30:36.} That is, of the sheep of the foolish soul, which thinks only those things good which are the objects of the outward senses and apparent to them, being deceived and enslaved by colors and shadows; for the name, Laban, being interpreted, means "whitening."

> Parallels: Genesis 30:36, 46:31-47:06; John 10:11-14; 1Peter 05:01-04
>
> Comparison: John 10:11-14, “I am the good shepherd. The good shepherd lays down his life for the sheep. He who is a hireling and not the shepherd, who does not own the sheep, sees the wolf coming and leaves the sheep and flees; and the wolf snatches and scatters them. This is because he is a hireling and cares nothing for the sheep. I am the good shepherd; I know my sheep, and my own know me.” 1Peter 05:01-04, “So I exhort elders among you, as a fellow elder and a witness of the sufferings of Christ and a partaker in the glory that is to be revealed, shepherd the flock of God that is under your care, [serving as overseers] – not under compulsion, but voluntarily, according to the will of God; and not for sordid gain, but with eagerness; not as lording it over those in your charge, but being examples to the flock. And when the Chief Shepherd appears, you will receive the unfading crown of glory.”

On Husbandry (51-53)

(51) … For God, like a shepherd and a king, governs (as if they were a flock of sheep) the earth, and the water, and the air, and the fire, and all the plants, and living creatures that are in them, whether mortal or divine; and he regulates the nature of the

heaven, and the periodical revolutions of the sun and moon, and the variations and harmonious movements of the other stars, ruling them according to law and justice; appointing, as their immediate superintendent, his own right reason, his first-born son, who is to receive the charge of this sacred company, as the lieutenant of the great king; for it is said somewhere, "Behold, I am he! I will send my messenger before thy face, who shall keep thee in the Road."{Exodus 23:20.} (52) Let therefore all the world, the greatest and most perfect flock of the living God, say "The Lord is my shepherd, and he shall cause me to lack nothing," (53) and let every separate individual say the same thing; not with the voice which proceeds from his tongue and his mouth, extending only through a scanty portion of the air, but with the wide spreading voice of the mind, which reaches to the very extremities of this universe; for it is impossible that there should be a deficiency of anything that is necessary, where God presides, who is in the habit of bestowing good things in all fullness and completeness in all living beings.

Parallels: Genesis 30:36, 46:31-47:06; Exodus 04:22, 23:20; Psalms 02:07, 23:01, 33:06; Matthew 06:28; John 01:01-14, 03:18, 10:11-14; Acts 13:33; 1Peter 05:01-04

Comparison: John 10:11-14, "I am the good shepherd. The good shepherd lays down his life for the sheep. He who is a hireling and not the shepherd, who does not own the sheep, sees the wolf coming and leaves the sheep and flees; and the wolf snatches and scatters them. This is because he is a hireling and cares nothing for the sheep. I am the good shepherd; I know my sheep, and my own know me." 1Peter 05:01-04, "So I exhort elders among you, as a fellow elder and a witness of the sufferings of Christ and a partaker in the glory that is to be revealed, shepherd the flock of God that is under your care, [serving as overseers] – not under compulsion, but voluntarily, according to the will of God; and not for sordid gain, but with eagerness; not as lording it over those in your charge, but being examples to the flock.

And when the Chief Shepherd appears, you will receive the unfading crown of glory."

On Husbandry (64-66)

(64) If therefore any envious or captious person should blame us, and say, "How then have ye, who are devoted to the employment of shepherds, and who profess to be occupied in the care and management of the flocks which belong to you, ever thought of approaching the country of the body and the passions, namely Egypt? and why have ye not turned your voyage in another direction? You must say to him in reply, with all freedom of speech, We have come hither as sojourners, not as inhabitants." (65) For in reality every soul of a wise man has heaven for its country, and looks upon earth as a strange land, and considers the house of wisdom his own home; but the house of the body, a lodging-house, on which it proposes to sojourn for a while. (66) Therefore since the mind, the ruler of the flock, having taken the flock of the soul, using the law of nature as its teacher, governs it consistently and vigorously, rendering it worthy of approbation and great praise; but when it manages it sluggishly and indulgently, with a disregard of law, then it renders it blamable. Very naturally, therefore, the one will assume the name of a king, being addressed as a shepherd, but the other will only have the title of a confectioner, or of a baker, being called a keeper of sheep, supplying the means of feasting and gluttonous eating to cattle accustomed to gorge themselves to satiety.

Parallels: Genesis 30:36, 46:31-47:06; John 10:11-14; Hebrews 11:08-16; 1Peter 05:01-04

Comparison: Comparison: John 10:11-14, "I am the good shepherd. The good shepherd lays down his life for the sheep. He who is a hireling and not the shepherd, who does not own the sheep, sees the wolf coming and leaves the sheep and flees; and the wolf snatches and scatters them. This is because he is a hireling and cares nothing for the sheep. I am the good shepherd; I know my sheep, and my own know me." 1Peter 05:01-04, "So I exhort elders among you, as a fellow elder and a witness of the sufferings of Christ and a partaker in the glory that is to be revealed, shepherd the flock of God that is under your care, [serving as overseers] – not under compulsion, but voluntarily, according to the will of God; and not for sordid gain, but with eagerness; not as lording it over those in your charge, but being examples to the flock. And when the Chief Shepherd appears, you will receive the unfading crown of glory." Hebrews 11:08-16, "By faith Abraham obeyed when he was called to go out to a place which he was to receive as an inheritance. And he went out, not knowing where he was going. By faith he lived in a land of promise, as in a foreign land, dwelling in tents with Isaac and Jacob, heirs with him of the same promise. For he was looking forward to the city which has foundations, whose architect and builder is God. By faith Sarah herself, when she was barren, received power to conceive, even when she was past the age, because she considered him faithful who had promised. Therefore from one man, and him as good as dead, were born descendants as many as the stars of heaven and as the innumerable grains of sand by the seashore. These all died in faith, not having taken hold of the promises, but having seen them and greeted them from a distance, and having acknowledged that they were strangers and exiles on the earth. For people who say such things make it clear that they are seeking a country of their own. And if they had been thinking of that country from which they had gone out, they would have had opportunity to return. But as it is, they desire a better country, that is, a heavenly one. Therefore God is not ashamed to be called their God, for he has prepared for them a city."

On Husbandry (101)

(101) For the indulgences of intemperance and gluttony, and whatever other vices the immoderate and insatiable pleasures, when completely filled with an abundance of all external things, produce and bring forth, do not allow the soul to proceed onwards by the plain and straight road, but compel it to fall into ravines and gulfs, until they utterly destroy it; but those practices which adhere to patience, and endurance, and moderation, and all other virtues, keep the soul in the straight road, leaving no stumbling block in the way, against which it can stumble and fall. Very naturally, therefore, has Moses declared that temperance clings to the right way, because it is plain that the contrary habit, intemperance, is always straying from the road.

Parallels: Genesis 49:17; Matthew 07:13-14

Comparison: Matthew 07:13-14, "Enter by the narrow gate. For the gate is wide, and the way is easy that leads to destruction, and many are those who enter by it. How narrow is the gate and hard the way, that leads to life, and few those who find it!"

On Husbandry (104)

(104) But the paths of prudence, and temperance, and the other virtues, even though they may not be utterly untraveled, are, at all events, not beaten much; for the number of those who proceed by those roads, and who philosophize in a genuine spirit, and who form associations with virtue alone, disregarding, once for all, all other allurements, is very small.

Parallels: Genesis 49:17; Matthew 07:13-14

Comparison: Matthew 07:13-14, "Enter by the narrow gate. For the gate is wide, and the way is easy that leads to destruction, and many are those who enter by it. How narrow is the gate and hard the way, that leads to life, and few those who find it!"

On Husbandry (111-113)

(111) Do you, therefore, my friend, never enter into a contest of evil, and never contend for the pre-eminence in such practices, but rather exert yourself with all your might to escape from them. And if ever, being under the compulsion of some power which is mightier than yourself, you are compelled to engage in such a strife, take care to be without delay defeated; (112) for then you, being defeated, will be a glorious conqueror, and those who have gained the victory will have got the worst. And do not ever entrust it to a herald to proclaim the victory of your rival or to the judge to crown; but do you go yourself and offer to him the acknowledgment of victory and the palm, and crown him, if he will, and bind him with wreaths of triumph, and proclaim him as conqueror yourself, pronouncing with a loud and piercing voice such a proclamation as this: "O ye spectators, and ye who have offered prizes at these games! In this contest which you have proposed to us of appetite, and passion, and intemperance, and folly, and injustice, I have been defeated, and this man whom ye behold has gained the victory. And he has gained it by such a superabundance of excellence, that even we, who might very naturally have envied our conquerors, do not grudge him the triumph." (113) Therefore, in all these unholy contests, surrender the prizes to others; but, as for those which are really holy, study yourself to gain the crown in them. And think not those contests holy which the different cities propose in their triennial festivals, when they build theatres and receive many myriads of people; for in those he who has overthrown any one in wrestling, or who has cast him on his back or on his face upon the ground, or he who is very skilful in wrestling or in the pancratium, carries off the first prize, though he may be a

man who has never abstained from any act of violence or of injustice.

> Parallels: Matthew 05:39; 1Corinthians 09:24-27; 2Timothy 02:05, 04:07-08; James 01:12; 1Peter 05:01-04; Revelation 02:10

> Comparison: Matthew 05:39, "But I tell you, do not resist an evil person. But if someone strikes you on [your] right cheek, turn to him the other also."

On Husbandry (131-135)

(131) Do you not see that the law pronounces the camel to be an unclean beast, because it chews the cud and does not part the Hoof. {Leviticus 11:4.} And yet, if we considered this sentence as it is expressed in its literal sense, I do not see what reason there is in it when it is interpreted; but if we look at it in its allegorical meaning, it is very clear and inevitable. (132) For as the animal which chews the cud, again masticates the food which is put before it and devoured by it, when it again rises up to its teeth, so also the soul of the man who is fond of learning, when it has received any speculative opinions by hearing them, does not abandon them to forgetfulness, but quietly by itself revolves over every one of them again in its mind in all tranquility, and so comes to the recollection of them all. (133) But it is not every memory which is good, but only that which is exerted on good subjects, since it is a most pernicious thing that what is bad should not be forgotten; on which account, with a view to perfection, it is necessary that the hoofs should be parted, in order that so the faculty of memory, being divided into two sections, the word which flows through the mouth may divide the lips, as being things which nature has made of a two-fold character, and may also separate the advantageous species of memory from that which is mischievous. (134) Again, the dividing the hoof without chewing the cud does not by itself appear to bring any advantage with it. For what advantage is

there in distinguishing the natures of things beginning at the top, and going down to the most unimportant points, and yet not to be able to do so in one's self, not to have one's own divisions clearly distinguished, which by some persons are with great felicity named atoms and indivisible portions? (135) for all these things are manifest displays of intelligence and excessive accuracy, sharpened to a degree of the most acute comprehension. But they have no influence in causing virtue, or in making men live a life free from reproach.

Parallels: Leviticus 11:01-47; Hebrews 10:01

On Husbandry (142-145)

(142) And although the intellect, when it has sharpened itself so as to render itself more acute than before (as a physician gives strength to bodies), dissects the natures of things, but yet derives no advantage with respect to the acquisition of virtue; it will divide the hoof, being able to divide, and to distinguish, and to discriminate between each separate thing; but it will not chew the cud so as to avail itself of any useful food which may be able, by means of its recollections, to soften the asperity of the soul which has been engendered by sins, and to produce a really gentle and pleasant motion. (143) Therefore a vast number of those who are called sophists, being admired in their respective cities, and having attracted almost all the world to look upon them with honor, on account of the accuracy of their definitions and their excessive cleverness in inventions, have grown old while vehemently bound by the passions, and have passed their whole life in them, in no respect differing from private individuals who are of no account and are held in no consideration. (144) For which reason the lawgiver very admirably compares those of the sophists who live in this manner to the race of swine, who live a life in no respect pure or brilliant, but confused and disorderly, and who are devoted to the basest habits. (145) For he says that the swine is an unclean animal, because it divides the hoof and does not chew the cud,

just as he has pronounced the camel unclean for the contrary reason because it chews the cud and does not divide the hoof. But as many animals as partake of both these qualities are very appropriately described as clean, because they have avoided impropriety in both the aforementioned particulars. For division without memory, and care, and a diligent examination of what is best, is but an imperfect good; but the combination and union of the two in the same animal is a most perfect good.

Parallels: Leviticus 11:01-47; Hebrews 10:01

On Husbandry (152-158)

(152) In the next place, will they not have displayed examples, not of treachery only, but of the greatest insensibility, if they allow others to fight in their cause, while they themselves are occupied about their domestic affairs? And shall others be willing to incur contests and dangers in the cause of their safety, which they are afraid to encounter for their own? And shall others cheerfully endure scarcity of provisions, and sleeping on the ground, and other hardships of body and soul, from their desire for victory, while they, covering their houses with stucco and nonsense, no much lifeless ornament, or gathering in their harvests from their fields, and celebrating the festival of the vintage, or coming into connection, now for the first time, with virgins who have long since been betrothed to them, and sleeping with them, as if it were the most opportune reason for marriage, pass their time in such vanities? (153) It is a good thing, no doubt, to take care of one's walls, to collect one's revenues, to feast, to revel in wine, to contract marriages, to go courting the old and withered dames (as the proverb calls them); but these are the employments of peace, and to do all these things in the crisis of a war raging in all its freshness and vigor, (154) while neither father, nor brother, nor any relation or connection whatever shares the fatigues of the war; when this, I say, is the case, must we not say that universal cowardice has occupied the whole house? Oh, but you will say there are at all

events myriads of relations who are fighting in their cause. Then, while they are encountering danger to their lives, must not those who are spending their time in luxury and delicate living appear to surpass even the worst of wild beasts in the excess of their inhumanity? (155) Again, they will say, but it is hard that others, without enduring any labor themselves, should reap the fruits of our labors. Which, then, is worst, that enemies should come into one's inheritance while one is still alive, or that friends and relations should do so after one is dead? It is absurdity even to compare things which are so widely different; (156) and yet it is not inconsistent with reason, not only that all the property which belongs to these men who shun military service, but that even they themselves, too, may become the property of their enemies when they have obtained the mastery. So those, indeed, who die in defense of the general safety, even if they have not enjoyed as yet any advantage from those possessions which they previously had, meet with death in its most pleasant form, considering that, by their saving the others, their property goes to those whom they desired to have for their successors. (157) Therefore the words of the law here admit, perhaps, of all these and even of still more excuses; but that no one of those who study evil cunning, through his ingenuity in devising excuses, may feel any confidence in their validity, we will proceed with the allegory, and say that, in the first place, the law does not only think it right for men to labor for the acquisition of good things, but also for the enjoyment of those which they have already acquired; and that it looks upon happiness as consisting in the exercise of perfect virtue, which makes life safe and complete. In the second place, that the question here is not about a house, or a vineyard, or a betrothed and espoused wife, in order that he may marry her as an accepted suitor, and that he who planted the vineyard may gather the fruit thereof and press it out, and then, drinking the unmixed wine, may be gladdened in his heart, and that the man who has built a house may dwell in it; but the question is rather about the faculties of the soul, to which the beginnings, and progress, and perfection of all praiseworthy actions are owing. (158) Now, the beginnings have usually especial connection with a suitor; for as he who courts a wife is about to become her husband, since he is not so already, so in the same manner whoever, endued with a good disposition, hopes to marry that well-born and pure maiden, education, courts her immediately. Progress has especial reference to the husbandman; for as it is an object of particular care to the planter to make his trees grow, so also is it to him, who is devoted to learning, that the speculations of wisdom should receive the greatest possible improvement. And perfection especially belongs to the building of a house when it is finished, but has not yet settled and become firm.

Parallels: Deuteronomy 20:05, 28:30; Luke 14:07-24

On Husbandry (165-166)

(165) We must therefore advise those who are beginning to learn not to go forth into such contests, for they have not sufficient knowledge; and we must counsel those who are making some progress to abstain from them, because they are not perfect; and those who have now for the first time just attained to perfection, we must urge to forbear, because in some degree their perfection has escaped their own notice. (166) But of those who disregard our warnings, Moses says, "One man will inhabit his house, and another will obtain his vineyard, and another will marry a wife." And the meaning of this is something of this kind: the powers which have been enumerated, of careful beginning, and improvement, and perfection, will never fail altogether, but will at different times approach and unite themselves with different persons, and will not be always forming the same souls, but will change about, resembling seals.

Parallels: Deuteronomy 20:05, 28:30; Luke 14:07-24

On Joseph (77-79)

(77) But I, who have got for my patient not one man but a whole city sick with those more grievous diseases which the kindred desires have brought upon it, what ought I to do? Shall I, abandoning all idea of what will be of general advantage to the whole state seek to please the ears of this or that man with an ungentlemanly and thoroughly slavish flattery? I would rather choose to die than to speak merely with the object of gratifying the ear, and to conceal the truth, disregarding all thought of what is really advantageous. (78) "Now then," as the tragedian says: "Now then let fire, let biting steel come on; Burn, scorch my flesh, and glut your appetite, drinking my dark, warm blood; for here I swear, Sooner shall those bright stars which deck the heaven descend beneath the earth, the earth itself soar upwards to the sky, than servile words of flattery creep from out my mouth to thee." {this is a fragment of Euripides from the Syleus. Fr. 2.} (79) But the people, when it is the master, cannot endure a statesman of so masculine a spirit, and one who keeps so completely aloof from the passions, from pleasure, from fear, from grief, from desire; but it arrests its well-wisher and friend and punishes him as an enemy, in doing which it first of all inflicts upon itself the most grievous of all punishments, namely, ignorance; in consequence of which state it does not itself learn that lesson which is the most beautiful and profitable of all, namely, obedience to its governor, from which the knowledge how to govern subsequently springs.

Parallels: Matthew 26:47-27:56; Luke 22:63-71, 23:33-45; John 06:53-56; Ephesians 04:18; fragment of Euripides from the Syleus. Fr. 2.

Comparison: John 06:53-56, "So Jesus said to them, "Truly, truly, I say to you, unless you eat the flesh of the Son of Man and drink his blood, you have no life in you. Whoever eats my flesh and drinks my blood has eternal life, and I will raise him up at the last day. For my flesh is true food, and my blood is true drink. He who eats my flesh and drinks my blood abides in me, and I in him." Matthew 27:45, 50-51, "Now from the sixth hour until the ninth hour there was darkness over all the land… And Jesus cried out again with a loud voice, and yielded up his spirit. And behold, the veil of the temple was torn in two, from top to bottom. And the earth shook. And the rocks were split."

On Mating With the Preliminary Studies (8)

(8) For he also says that the lamp, that archetypal model after which the copy is made, shines in one part, that is to say, in the part which is turned towards God.{Exodus 25:31.} For since that completes the number of seven, and stands in the middle of the six branches, which are divided into two lots of three each, acting as body-guards to it on either side, it sends its rays upwards toward that one being, namely God, thinking its light too brilliant for mortal sight to be able to stand its proximity.

Parallels: Exodus 25:31; Matthew 05:15, 17:01-21

On Mating With the Preliminary Studies (100-101)

(100) Very beautifully, therefore, and at the same time most unavoidably, does the sacred historian tell us in the fashion of an incidental narrative, when the memorial of that heavenly and divine food was consecrated in the golden urn, that "gomer was the tenth part of three Measures."{Exodus 16:36.} For in us men there appear to be three measures, the outward senses, and speech, and mind. The outward sense being the measure of the objects of outward sense, speech being the measure of nouns and verbs, and of whatever is said; and the mind being the measure of those things which can only be perceived by the intellect. (101) We must therefore offer first-fruits of each of these three measures as a sacred tenth, in order that our powers of speaking, and of feeling, and of comprehending, may be seen to be

irreproachable and sound, in reference to and in connection with God. For this is the true and just measure, and the things that relate to ourselves are false and unjust measures.

Parallels: Genesis 18:06; Exodus 16:36; Luke 13:21

On Mating With the Preliminary Studies (107-108)

(107) For this propitiation also is established in the tenth day of the month, when the soul addresses its supplications to the tenth portion, namely to God, and has learnt, by its own sagacity and acuteness, the insignificance and nothingness of the creature, and also the excessive perfection and pre-eminent excellence in all good things of the uncreated God. Therefore God becomes at once propitious, and propitious too, even without any supplications being addressed to him, to those who abase and humble themselves, and who are not puffed up with vain arrogance and self-opinion. (108) This is remission and deliverance, this is complete freedom of the soul, shaking off the wanderings in which it wandered, and fleeing for a secure anchorage to the one nature which cannot wander, and which rises up to return to the lot which it formerly received when it had brilliant aspirations, and when it vigorously toiled in labors which had virtuous ends for their object. For then admiring it for its exertions, the holy scripture honored it, giving it a most especial honor, and immortal inheritance, a place namely in the imperishable race.

Parallels: Genesis 18:01-08; Matthew 18:04; Acts 20:32

Comparison: Acts 20:32, "And now I commend you to God and to the word of his grace, which is able to build you up and to give the inheritance among all those who are sanctified."

On Mating With the Preliminary Studies (124-125)

(124) But there are times when virtue, as if making experiment of those who come to her as pupils, to see how much eagerness they have, does not come forward to meet them, but veiling her face like Tamar, sits down in the public road, giving room to those who are traveling along the road to look upon her as a harlot, in order that those who are over curious on the subject may take off her veil and disclose her features, and may behold the untouched, and unpolluted, and most exquisite, and truly virgin beauty of modesty and chastity. (125) Who then is he who is fond of investigating, and desirous of learning, and who thinks it not right to leave any of those things which are disguised or concealed unconsidered and examined? Who is he, I say, but the chief captain and king, he who abides and rejoices in the agreements which he has made with God, by name Judah? For says the scripture, "He turned aside out of his road to her, and said unto her, Suffer me to come in unto thee," (but he was not inclined to offer her any violence), and to see what is that power which is thus veiled, and for what purpose it is thus adorned.

Parallels: Genesis 38:14-16; Luke 01:26-27; 2Corinthians 03:12-18

Comparison: 2Corinthians 03:12-18, "Therefore, since we have such a hope, we are very bold. We are not like Moses, who would put a veil over his face to keep the Israelites from gazing at the end of the radiance of what was fading away. But their minds were hardened; for to this very day, when they read the old covenant, the same veil remains unlifted, because only in Christ is it removed. Even to this day whenever Moses is read, a veil lies over their hearts. But whenever a person turns to the Lord, the veil is taken away. Now the Lord is the Spirit, and where the Spirit of the Lord is, is freedom. And we all, with unveiled face, beholding the reflection of the

Lord's glory, are being transformed into his likeness from one degree of glory to another, for this comes from the Lord who is the Spirit."

On Mating With the Preliminary Studies (170)

(170) Does not, then, the prophetic word, by name Moses, very rightly speak in dignified language when he says, "Thou shall remember all the road by which the Lord God led thee in the wilderness, and how he afflicted thee, and tried thee, and proved thee, that he might know what was in thy heart, and whether thou would keep his commandments. Did he not afflict thee and oppress thee with hunger, and feed thee with manna which thy fathers know not, that he might make thee know that man shall not live by bread alone, but by every word that proceeds out of the mouth of God?"{Deuteronomy 8:2.}

Parallels: Deuteronomy 08:02-03; Matthew 04:04

Comparison: Matthew 04:04, "But he answered, "It is written, 'Man shall not live by bread alone, but by every word that proceeds from the mouth of God.'""

On Mating With the Preliminary Studies (177)

(177) And it is from this consideration, as it appears to me that one of the disciples of Moses, by name the peaceful, who in his native language is called Solomon, says, "My son, neglect not the instruction of God, and be not grieved when thou art reproved by him; for whom the Lord loves he chastens; and scourges every son whom he received."{Proverbs 3:11.} Thus, then, scourging and reproof are looked upon as good, so that by means of it agreement and relationship with God arise. For what can be more nearly related than a son is to his father, and a father to his son?

Parallels: Proverbs 03:11; Hebrews 12:06-08

> Comparison: Hebrews 12:06-08, "For those whom the Lord loves he disciplines. And he scourges every son whom he receives." It is for discipline that you endure. God is treating you as sons; for what son is there whom his father does not discipline? If you are left without discipline, in which all have become partakers, then you are illegitimate children and not sons."

On Rewards And Punishments (17-21)

(17) And by this enigmatical expression the two things are clearly intimated, the migration by the change of place, and the solitude by his not being found. And very appropriately is this stated; for if in real truth man had resolved at all times to show himself really superior to the passions, despising all pleasures and all appetites, then he would require to prepare himself diligently, fleeing without ever turning his head round, and forsaking his home, and his country, and his relations, and his friends; (18) for familiar custom is an attractive thing, so that there is reason to fear that if a man remains behind he may be taken prisoner, being caught by such powerful charms all round, the appearances of which will again rouse up the disgraceful though at present dormant appetites for evil pursuits, and will restore to vitality those recollections which it was creditable to have forgotten. (19) Accordingly, many persons have become corrected and improved by migrations from their native land, having been cured by such means of their frenzied and wicked desires, by reason of the sight no longer being able to furnish to the passion the images of pleasure. For in consequence of the separation which has taken place, this passion has only a vacuum through which to rove, since there is no longer any object present by which it can be inflamed. (20) And if it does rise up and quit its former abode, still let it avoid the assemblies of the multitude, embracing solitude; for there are snares in a foreign land resembling those, which are found in a man's own country into which those men must fall who are careless and do

not look before them, and who rejoice in the society of the multitude; for the multitude is a very concentration of everything that is irregular, disorderly, improper, and blamable, with which it is a most mischievous thing for the man who is now for the first time passing over to the ranks of virtue to proceed. (21) For as the bodies of those men who are only just beginning to recover from a long attack of sickness are very subject to a relapse; so the soul which is just recovering its health finds its intellectual vigor weak and wavering, so that there is room to apprehend that the evil passions may return which were wont to be excited in it by a habit of living in the society of inconsiderate men.

Parallels: Genesis 05:24; Matthew 19:29; Luke 04:01-13; Hebrews 11:08-16

On Rewards And Punishments (114)

(114) If, then, any one proves himself a man of such a character in the city he will appear superior to the whole city, and if a city show itself of such a character it will be the chief of all the country around; and if a nation do so it will be the lord of all the other nations, as the head is to the body occupying the pre-eminence of situation, not more for the sake of glory than for that of advancing the interests of those that see. For continual appearances of good models stamp impressions closely resembling themselves on all souls which are not utterly obdurate and intractable.

Parallels: Deuteronomy 28:06-13; Ephesians 05:23

Comparison: Ephesians 05:23, "For a husband is the head of his wife, as Christ is the head of the church. He himself is the Savior of The Body."

On Rewards And Punishments (117)

(117) As therefore God, by one single word of command, could easily collect together men living on the very confines of the earth, bringing them from the extremities of the world to any place which he may choose, so also the merciful Savior can bring back the soul after its long wandering, after it has been straying about in every direction, and been ill-treated by pleasure and desire, most imperious mistresses, and guide it easily from a trackless waste into a regular road when it has once determined to flee from evil without ever looking back, a flight not liable to reproach, but the cause of its preservation, which no one will do wrong to pronounce more desirable than any return.

Parallels: Deuteronomy 30:01-10; 1Thessalonians 04:16-17

On Rewards And Punishments (123-125)

(123) This is the mind which has drunk strong draughts of the beneficent power of God, and has feasted on his sacred words and doctrines. This is the mind in which the prophet says that God walks as in his palace; for the mind of the wise man is in truth the palace and the house of God. And he who is the God of all things is peculiarly called the God of this mind; and again this mind is by a peculiar form called his people, not the people of any particular rulers, but of the one only and true ruler, the Holy One of holies. (124) This is the mind which a little while ago was enslaved to many pleasures and many desires, and to innumerable necessities arising from weaknesses and desires; but its evils God crushed in slavery, having elected to bring it to freedom. This is the mind which has received a favor not to be suppressed in silence, but rather to be proclaimed abroad and announced in every quarter, on account of the authority and power of its champion and defender, by which it was not thrust down to the tail, but was raised upwards to the head. (125) But all these statements are uttered in a metaphorical form, and

contain an allegorical meaning. For as in an animal the head is the first and best part, and the tail the last and worst part, or rather no part at all, inasmuch as it does not complete the number of the limbs, being only a broom to sweep away what flies against it; so in the same manner what is said here is that the virtuous man shall be the head of the human race whether he be a single man or a whole people. And that all others, being as it were parts of the body, are only vivified by the powers existing in the head and superior portions of the body.

Parallels: Leviticus 26:11-12; Deuteronomy 28:06-13; John 02:19-21; Romans 06:01-23; Ephesians 05:23

Comparison: Romans 06:17-22, "But thanks be to God, that you who were once slaves of sin have become obedient from the heart to the standard of teaching to which you were committed, and, having been set free from sin, you have become slaves of righteousness. I am speaking in human terms, because of the weakness of your flesh. For just as you once yielded your members to impurity and to greater and greater iniquity, so now yield your members to righteousness for holiness. When you were slaves of sin, you were free in regard to righteousness. But then what return did you get from the things of which you are now ashamed? For the end of those things is death. But now that you have been set free from sin and have become slaves of God, the return you get is holiness and its end, eternal life."

On Rewards And Punishments (131-136)

(131) For then there will be no rain, no showers, no gentle springs, no soft drops of moisture, no dew, nor anything else which can contribute to the growth of plants; but, on the contrary, all things which are calculated to dry them up when beginning to grow, all things destructive of the fruit when beginning to ripen, and adapted to prevent it from ever coming

to perfection. For, says God, "I will make the heaven of brass for you, and the earth Iron."{Deuteronomy 28:23.} Implying by this enigmatical expression that neither of them shall accomplish the tasks which naturally belong to them and for which they were created; (132) for how could iron ever bear ears of corn, or how could brass produce rain, of which all animals stand in need, and especially that animal so liable to misfortune and in need of so many things, man? And God intimates here not only barrenness and the destruction of the seasons of the year, but also the beginnings of wars, and of all the intolerable and ineffable evils which arise in wars; for brass and iron are the materials for warlike arms. (133) And the earth, indeed, shall produce dust, and masses of dirt shall be brought down from above, from heaven, weighing down the fruit and destroying it by choking, in order that nothing may be omitted which can tend to complete destruction; for numerous families will be made desolate, and cities will suddenly become empty of their inhabitants, remaining as monuments of their former prosperity and records of subsequent disaster, for the warning of those who are capable of receiving correction. (134) And such a complete scarcity of all necessary things will seize the people that, being wholly destitute of and indifferent to them, they will turn even to devouring one another, eating not only the gentiles and those who are no relations to them, but even their nearest and dearest kinsfolk; for the father will take the flesh of his son, and the mother will eat of the life-blood of her daughter, brothers will eat their brothers, and children will devour their parents; and, in fact, the weaker will be continually the prey of the more powerful; and that wicked and accursed food, that of Thyestes, will seem to them like a joke when compared with the excessive and intolerable evils which their necessities bring upon them; (135) for, as in the case of other persons, while they are in prosperity they desire length of life to be able to enjoy all good things, so also even those men overwhelmed with misery will have a vehement desire for life established in them, though it can only lead them to a participation in immoderate and interminable evils, all of which are likewise irremediable. For it would have been better for such men to have escaped misery by cutting off their grief through death, which persons who are not utterly out of their senses are accustomed to do. But these men are arrived at such a degree of folly that they would be willing to live even to the longest possible time of life, being eager for and insatiably desirous of the greatest extremities of misery. (136) Such evils, that which appears at first to be the lightest of all misfortunes, namely, poverty, is naturally calculated to produce, when it is the result of the vengeance of God; for even though cold, and thirst, and want of food may be terrible, still they might at times be objects worth being prayed for, if they only produced instantaneous death without any delay. But when they last a long time and waste away both body and soul, then they are calculated to reproduce the very greatest of the calamities recorded by the tragic poets, which appear to me to be described in a spirit of fabulous exaggeration.

> Parallels: Leviticus 26:14-39; Deuteronomy 28:23-24; Revelation 08:01-09:21, 11:01-06, 15:07-17:01, 20:09

On Rewards And Punishments (139-151)

(139) Such men, becoming slaves, endure the services imposed on them by stern commands with their bodies, but when they are oppressed as to their souls with the anguish of still more bitter spectacles, they will sink under them; for they will see their enemies becoming the inheritors of houses which they have built, or of vineyards which they have planted, or of possessions which they have acquired, enjoying the good things and stores which have been prepared by others. And they will see their enemies feasting on the fattest of their cattle, and sacrificing them, and preparing them for the sweetest enjoyment, without being able to deprive those persons of anything who have thus robbed them. They will also see their wives, whom they married in holy wedlock for the purpose of propagating legitimate children, their modest, domestic, affectionate wives, insulted like so many courtesans. (140) And they will rush forward to defend and to avenge them, but beyond resisting they will not be able to effect anything, being deprived of all their strength and utterly

disabled; for they will be exposed as a mark for their enemies, an object for plunder, and ravage, and violence, and insult, and wounds, and injuries, and contumely, and utter destruction, so that nothing belong to them can escape, but no one dart of the enemy shall miss its blow, but every one of them shall be well aimed and successful. (141) They shall be cursed in their cities and in their villages, and cursed in their town-houses and in their dwellings in the fields. Cursed will be their plains and all the seed which is sown in them; cursed will be the fertile soil of the mountain district, and all the kinds of trees which produce eatable fruit; cursed will be their herds of cattle, for they will be rendered barren and unproductive; cursed will be all their fruits and all their crops, for at the most critical period of their ripening they will be found to be all full of wind and destroyed. (142) The storehouses full of food and money shall be made empty; no source of revenue shall be productive anymore; all the arts, all the various businesses and employments, and all the innumerable varieties of life, shall be of no use to those who adopt them; for the hopes of those who are anxious shall fail to be fulfilled; and, in short, whatever they touch, in consequence of their wicked pursuits and wicked actions, the head, and front, and end of which is the abandonment of the service of God, shall all be vain and unprofitable. (143) For these things are the rewards of impiety and lawless iniquity. And, in addition to these things, there are diseases of the body which separately afflict and devour each limb and each part, and which also rack and torture it all over with fevers, and chills, and wasting consumptions, and terrible rashes, and scrofulous diseases, and spasmodic convulsions of the eyes, and putrefying sores and abscesses, and cutaneous disorders extending over the whole of the skin, and disorders of the bowels and inward parts, and convulsions of the stomach, and obstructions in the passages of the lungs preventing the patient from breathing easily, and paralysis of the tongue, and deafness of the ears, and imperfections of the eyes, and a general dimness and confusion of all the other senses, things which, though terrible, will yet hardly appear so when compared with other things more grievous still; (144) when, for instance, all the vivifying qualities which existed in the blood contained in the veins have escaped from it, and when the breath which is contained in the lungs and windpipe is no longer capable of receiving a salutary admixture of the outward air so nearly connected with it; (145) and when the veins are all relaxed and dissolved, which state is followed by a complete prostration of the harmony and due arrangement of the limbs, which were indeed previously distressed by the violent rush of a briny and very bitter stream stealthily pervading them; which, when it was shut up in a narrow passage having no easy outlet, being then pressed close and pressing other parts, conduces to the production of bitter and almost intolerable pains, from which are engendered the diseases of gout and arthritic pains and diseases, for which no salutary remedy has ever been discovered, but which are incurable by any human means. (146) Some persons, when they behold these things, will be alarmed, marveling to see how those who a little while ago were fat and full of good flesh, and flourishing exceedingly in health and vigor, have so on a sudden wasted away and become merely withered muscles and a thin skin; and how the women, formerly luxurious, and tender, and delicate by reason of the luxury to which they have been accustomed from their earliest infancy, now, from the terrible afflictions to which they have been subjected, have become wild in their souls, and wild-looking in their bodies. (147) Then, then indeed, their enemies shall pursue them, and the sword shall exact its penalty; and they, fleeing to the cities, where they think that they have obtained a place of safety, being deluded by treacherous hopes, shall perish to a man being caught and destroyed by the ambuscades of their enemies. (148) And if, after all these calamities, they are not chastened, but still proceed by crooked paths, and turn off from the straight roads which lead to truth, then cowardice and fear shall be established in their souls, {Leviticus 26:36.} and they shall flee when no one pursues, and shall be routed and destroyed by false reports, as does often happen. The lightest sound of leaves falling through the air shall cause as great an agony of fear and apprehension as the most formidable war waged by the most powerful of enemies ought to produce, so that children shall be indifferent to the fate of their parents, and parents to that of their children, and brothers to that of their brethren, looking upon it that if they go to their assistance they may themselves incur the danger of captivity, while their best chance of safety consists in escaping by themselves. (149) But the hopes of wicked men do never obtain their accomplishment, and those who hope to escape thus will be still more, or at all events not less, taken prisoners than those who were previously laid hold of. And even if some such persons do escape notice, they will still be exposed to insidious attacks from their natural enemies; and these are those most furious wild beasts who are well armed by the endowments of nature, and which God, simultaneously with the original creation of the universe, made for the purpose of striking terror into those men who were incapable of taking warning, and for executing implacable justice on those whose wickedness was incurable; (150) and those who behold their cities razed to the very foundations will hardly believe that they were ever inhabited, and they will turn the sudden misfortunes which befall men after brilliant instances of prosperity into a proverb, recording all the instances which are mentioned or passed over in History. (151) There shall also come upon them asthmas, and consumptions affecting the internal organs, producing heaviness and despondency, with great afflictions, and making all life unstable, and hanging, as one may say, from a halter. And fears incessantly succeeding one another will toss the mind up and down, agitating it night and day, so that in the morning they shall pray for the evening, and in the evening they shall pray for the morning, on account of the visible horrors which surround them when awake, and the detestable images which present themselves to them in their dreams when sleeping.

Parallels: Leviticus 26:14-39; Deuteronomy 28:23-24; Revelation 08:01-09:21, 11:01-06, 15:07-17:01, 20:09

Comparison: Revelation 16:02, "So the first angel went and poured out his bowl to the earth. And foul and loathsome sores broke out on the people who had the mark of the beast and worshipped his image."

On Rewards And Punishments (152)

(152) And the proselyte who has come over being lifted up on high by good fortune, will be a conspicuous object, being admired and pronounced happy in two most important particulars, in the first place because he has come over to God of his own accord, and also because he has received as a most appropriate reward a firm and sure habitation in heaven, such as one cannot describe. But the man of noble descent, who has adulterated the coinage of his noble birth, will be dragged down to the lowest depths, being hurled down to Tartarus and profound darkness, in order that all men who behold this example may be corrected by it, learning that God receives gladly virtue which grows out of hostility to him, utterly disregarding its original roots, but looking favorably on the whole trunk from its lowest foundation, because it has become useful and has changed its nature so as to become fruitful.

Parallels: Luke 16:19-31

Comparison: Luke 16:19-31, ""There was a certain rich man who was clothed in purple and fine linen and feasted sumptuously every day. And a certain beggar named Lazarus was laid at his gate, full of sores, longing to be fed with what fell from the rich man's table. Moreover the dogs came and licked his sores. So the beggar died, and was carried by the angels to Abraham's bosom. The rich man also died and was buried. And in Hades, being in torment, he lifted up his eyes, and saw Abraham far off and Lazarus in his bosom. And he called out, 'Father Abraham, have mercy upon me, and send Lazarus to dip the tip of his finger in water and cool my tongue; for I am in agony in this flame.' But Abraham said, 'Son, remember that in your lifetime you received your good things, and Lazarus received evil things; but now he is comforted here and you are in agony. And in all this, between us and you a great chasm has been fixed, so that those who want to pass from here to you cannot, nor can anyone cross over from there to us.' And he said, 'Then I beg you, father, to send him to my father's house, for I have five brothers, so that he may warn them, lest they also come to this place of torment.' But Abraham said, 'They have Moses and the prophets; let them hear them.' And he said, 'No, father Abraham; but if someone goes to them from the dead, they will repent.' He said to him, 'If they do not hear Moses and the prophets, neither will they be convinced if some one should rise from the dead.'"

On Rewards And Punishments (163-170)

(163) If, however, they receive these exertions of power not as aiming at their destruction, but rather at their admonition and improvement, and if they feel shame throughout their whole soul, and change their ways, reproaching themselves for their errors, and openly avowing and confessing all the sins that they have committed against themselves with purified souls and minds, so as in the first place to exhibit a sincerity of conscience utterly alien from falsehood and concealing nothing evil beneath; and secondly, having their tongues also purified so as to produce improvement in their hearers, they will then meet with a favorable acceptance from their merciful Savior, God, who bestows on the race of mankind his especial and exceedingly great gift, namely, relationship to his own word; after which, as its archetypal model, the human mind was formed. (164) For even though they may be at the very extremities of the earth, acting as slaves to those enemies who have led them away in captivity, still they shall all be restored to freedom in one day, as at a given signal; their sudden and universal change to virtue causing a panic among their masters; for they will let them go, because they are ashamed to govern those who are better than themselves. (165) But when they have received this unexpected liberty, those who but a short time before were scattered about in Greece, and in the countries of the

barbarians, in the islands, and over the continents, rising up with one impulse, and coming from all the different quarters imaginable, all hasten to one place pointed out to them, being guided on their way by some vision, more divine than is compatible with its being of the nature of man, invisible indeed to everyone else, but apparent only to those who were saved, having their separate inducements and intercessions, (166) by whose intervention they might obtain a reconciliation with the Father. First of all, the merciful, and gentle, and compassionate nature of him who is invoked, who would always rather have mercy than punishment. In the second place, the holiness of all the founders of the nation, because they, with souls emancipated from the body, exhibiting a genuine and sincere obedience to the Ruler of all things, are not accustomed to offer up ineffectual prayers on behalf of their sons and daughters, since the Father has given to them, as a reward, that they shall be heard in their prayers. (167) And, thirdly, that quality, on account of which above all others, the good will of the beings above-mentioned is conciliated, and that is the improvement and amelioration of those persons who are brought to treaties and agreements, who have, with great difficulty, been able to come from a pathless wilderness into a beaten road, the end of which is no other than that of pleasing God as sons please a father. (168) And when they come cities will be rebuilt which but a short time ago were in complete ruins, and the desert will be filled with inhabitants, and the barren land will change and become fertile, and the good fortune of their fathers and ancestors will be looked upon as a matter of but small importance, on account of the abundance of wealth of all kinds which they will have at the present moment, flowing forth from the graces of God as from ever-running fountains, which will thus confer vast wealth separately on each individual, and also on all the citizens in common, to an amount beyond the reach even of envy. (169) And the change in everything will be immediate, for God will nourish the virtues against the enemies of those who have repented, who have delighted in the ruined fortunes of the nation, reviling them, and making a mockery of them, as if they themselves were destined to have a season of good fortune, which could never be put an end to, which they hope to leave, in regular succession, to their children and to their posterity; thinking, at the same time, that they will forever behold their adversaries in lasting and unchangeable misfortunes, laid up for even remote future generations; (170) not perceiving, in their insanity, that they enjoyed that brilliant fortune which fell to their share a little while before, not for their own merits, but for the sake of giving a warning and admonition to others, for whom, as they had forsaken their national and hereditary customs, the only salutary remedy which could be found was the grief which they felt to excess when their enemies carried off their property. Therefore, weeping for and bewailing their own defeat, they will turn back again to the ancient prosperity of their ancestors, retracing all their steps with great exactness, and without its even happening to them to stray from the proper course and to be wrecked.

> Parallels: Leviticus 26:01-45; Deuteronomy 30:01-10; Isaiah 54:01-13; Ezekiel 20:33-38; John 01:18; Acts 03:19; 1Thessalonians 04:16-17

On Rewards And Punishments (172)

(172) For as, when the trunk of a tree is cut down, if the roots are not taken away, new shoots spring up, by which the old trunk is again restored to life as it were; in the very same manner, if there be only left in the soul ever so small a seed of virtue, when everything else is destroyed, still, nevertheless, from that little seed there spring up the most honorable and beautiful qualities among men; by means of which, cities, which were formerly populous and flourishing, are again inhabited, and nations are led to become wealthy and powerful.

> Parallels: Job 14:07-09; Isaiah 11:01; Daniel 04:15-26; Matthew 13:03-43, 17:20; Mark 04:31-32; Luke 13:19, 17:06

Comparison: Matthew 13:31-32, "Another parable he put forth to them, saying: "The kingdom of heaven is like a mustard seed, which a man took and sowed in his field. It is the smallest of all seeds, but when it has grown it is the greatest of shrubs and becomes a tree, so that the birds of the air come and make nests in its branches."

On the Birth of Abel And the Sacrifices offered By Him And By His Brother Cain (33)

(33) These are the great mysteries of that very beautiful and much to be sought for pleasure, which she designedly concealed and kept out of sight, from a fear that if you knew of them you would turn away from any meeting with her. But who is there who could worthily describe either the multitude or the magnitude of the good things which are stored up in my treasure houses? They who have partaken of them already know it, and those whose nature is mild will hereafter know, when they have been invited to a participation in the banquet, not the banquet at which the pleasures of the satiated belly make the body fat, but that at which the mind is nourished and at which it revels among the virtues, and exults and revels in their company.

Parallels: Genesis 33:11; Matthew 22:02-14

On the Birth of Abel And the Sacrifices offered By Him And By His Brother Cain (60)

(60) Now it is very good that these three measures should, as it were, be kneaded together in the soul, and mixed up together, in order that so the soul, being persuaded that the supreme being is God, who has raised his head above all his powers, and who is beheld independently of them, and who makes himself visible in them, may receive the characters of his power and beneficence,

and becoming initiated into the perfect mysteries, may not be too ready to divulge the divine secrets to any one, but may treasure them up in herself, and keeping a check over her speech, may conceal them in silence; for the words of the scripture are, "To make secret cakes;" because the sacred and mystic statements about the one uncreated Being, and about his powers, ought to be kept secret; since it does not belong to every one to keep the deposit of divine mysteries properly.

Parallels: Genesis 18:06; Luke 01:35, 13:21; Acts 04:07, 08:10; 1Corinthians 01:24

Comparison: Luke 13:21, "It is like leaven, which a woman took and hid in three measures of flour till it was all leavened.""

On the Birth of Abel And the Sacrifices offered By Him And By His Brother Cain (124-130)

(124) Therefore when I see any good man dwelling in any house or city, I pronounce that house or that city happy, and I think that its enjoyment of its present good things is sure, and that its expectation of future happiness will be accomplished, inasmuch as, for the sake of those who are worthy, God will bestow his boundless and illimitable riches even on the unworthy. And I pray that they may live to as great an age as possible, since it is not possible that they should ever grow old, as I expect that good fortune will remain to men as long as these men are able to live in the practice of virtue. (125) When, therefore, I see or hear that any one of these men is dead, I am exceedingly downcast and grieved, and I lament those who are left behind alive as much as I lament them; for to the one I see, that the necessary end has arrived in consistency with the ordinances of nature, and that they have exhibited a happy life and a glorious death. But I look upon the others as now deprived of the great and mighty hand by which they were saved, and as likely, now that

they are bereft of it, soon to feel the evils which are due to them, unless, indeed, instead of the former men, who are gone, nature should be preparing to make other young men shoot up, as in the case of a tree which has already shed its ripe fruit for the nourishment and enjoyment of those who are able to make use of it. (126) As, therefore, good men are the strongest part of cities, with a view to their duration, so also in that state of each individual of us, which consists of soul and body, the reasoning powers which are attached to prudence and knowledge, are the firmest part of its foundation; which the legislator, using metaphorical language, calls the ransom and the first-born, on account of those reasons which I have already mentioned. (127) In this way he also says, "The cities of the Levites are ransomed forever, because the minister of God enjoys eternal freedom, according to the continuous revolutions of the ever-moving soul," and he admits incessant healing applications; for when he calls them ransomed, not once, but forever, as he says, he means to convey such a meaning as this, that they are always in a state of revolution, and always in a state of freedom, the state of revolution being implanted in them because of their natural mortality, but their freedom coming to them because of their ministration to God. (128) But it is worthwhile to consider, in no passing manner, why he granted the cities of the Levites to fugitives, thinking it right that even these, who appear entirely impious, should dwell with the most holy of men. Now these fugitives are they who have committed, unintentionally, homicide. First of all, therefore, we must repeat what is consistent with what has been already said, that the good man is the ransom of the worthless one, so that they who have sinned will naturally come to those who have been hallowed, for the sake of being purified; and, in the second place, we must consider that the Levites admit the fugitives because they themselves are potentially fugitives; (129) for as they are driven away from their country, so these others also have left their children, their parents, their brethren, their nearest and dearest things, in order that they may receive an immortal inheritance instead of a mortal one. But they differ, because the flight of the one is involuntary, being caused by an unintentional action, but the flight of the others is voluntary, from a love of what is most excellent; and because the one have the Levites for a refuge; but the Levites have the Lord of all for their refuge, in order that those who are imperfect may have the sacred scriptures for their law; but that the others may have God for theirs, by whom they are hallowed. (130) Moreover, those who have committed unintentional homicide, have been allotted the same cities as the Levites to dwell in, because they also were thought worthy of a privilege because of a holy slaughter. When therefore the soul being changed, came to honor the Egyptian God, the body, as fine gold, then all the sacred writings rushing forth of their own accord with defensive weapons, namely demonstrations according to knowledge, putting forward as their leader and general the chief priest, and prophet, and friend of God, Moses, proclaimed an unceasing war in the cause of piety, and would not hear of peace till they had put down all the doctrines of those who opposed them, so that they naturally came to inhabit the same dwellings, inasmuch as they had done similar actions, though not the same.

> Parallels: Numbers 08:05-22, 35:01-34; Joshua 20:02-03, 21:13-38; Matthew 19:29; Luke 14:26; Galatians 05:18-23; Hebrews 11:10-16
>
> Comparison: Matthew 19:29, "And whoever has left houses or brothers or sisters or father or mother or children or lands, for my name's sake, will receive a hundredfold, and inherit eternal life."

On the Change of Names (40)

(40) for if you honor your parents, or show mercy to the poor, or do good to your friends, or fight in defense of your country, or pay proper attention to the common principles of justice towards all men, you most certainly are pleasing to those with whom you associate, and you are also acceptable in the sight of God: for he sees all things with an eye which never slumbers, and he unites to himself with especial favor all that is good, and that he accepts and embraces.

Parallels: Deuteronomy 12:28; Matthew 05:16

On the Change of Names (87)

(87) For this reason God, who never changes, altered the name of Abraham, since he was about to remain in a similar condition, in order that that which was to be firmly established might be confirmed by him who was standing firmly, and who was remaining in the same state in the same manner. But it was an angel who altered the name of Jacob, being the Word, the minister of God; in order that it might be confessed and ascertained, that there is none of the things whose existence is subsequent to that of the living God, which is the cause of unchangeable and unvarying firmness. ... but of that harmony which, as in a musical instrument, contains the intensity and relaxation of sounds so as to produce an artistic combination of melody.

Parallels: Genesis 17:05, 32:24-30; John 01:01-14

On the Change of Names (125-129)

(125) But it happens to the arch-prophet to have many names: for when he interprets and explains the oracles which are delivered by God, he is called Moses; and when he prays for and blesses the people, he is called the man of God; {Deuteronomy 33:1.} and when Egypt is paying the penalty of its impious actions, he is then denominated the god of him who is the king of the country, namely, of Pharaoh.{Exodus 7:1.} And why is all this? (126) Because to alter a code of laws for the advantage of those who are to use them is the part of a man who is always handling divine things, and having them in his hands; and who is called a lawgiver by the all knowing God, and who has received from him a great gift--the interpretation of the sacred laws, and the spirit of prophecy in accordance with them. For the name Moses, being translated, signifies "gain," and it also means handling, for the reasons which I have already enumerated. (127) But to pray and to bless are not the duties of any ordinary man, but they belong to one who has not admitted any connection with created things, but who has devoted himself to God, the governor and the father of all men. (128) And any one must be content to whom it has been allowed to use the privilege of blessing. And to be able also to procure good for others belongs to a greater and more perfect soul, and is the profession of one who is really inspired by God, which he who has attained to may reasonably be called God. But also, this same person is God, inasmuch as he is wise, and as on this account he rules over every foolish person, even if such foolish person be established and strengthened by a haughty scepter, and be ever so proud on this account; (129) for the Ruler of the universe, even though some persons are about to be punished for intolerable acts of wickedness, nevertheless is willing to admit some intercessors to mediate on their behalf, who, in imitation of the merciful power of the father, exercise their power of punishment with more moderation and humanity; but to do good is the peculiar attribute of God.

Parallels: Exodus 04:16, 07:01, 11; Deuteronomy 12:28, 33:01; Matthew 05:16, 19:17, 26:47-27:56; Acts 03:18-26

Comparison: Matthew 19:17, "And he said to him, "Why do you ask me about what is good? There is only one who is good. If you want to enter life, keep the commandments.""

On the Change of Names (140)

(140) For if there be any good thing among existing things, that, or I should rather say the whole heaven and the whole world, if one must tell the truth, is the fruit of God; being preserved upon his eternal and ever flourishing nature as upon a tree. But it belongs to wise and understanding men to understand and to confess such things as these, and not to the ignorant.

Parallels: Genesis 02:08-09; Hosea 14:08-09; Matthew 07:16-21; Luke 23:33-45; Galatians 03:13

On the Change of Names (174)

(174) And he also says, "I will give unto you all the good things of Egypt , and you shall eat of the marrow of the Earth."{Genesis 45:18.} But we will say unto him, We who keep our eyes fixed on the good things of the soul do not desire those of the body. For that most delicious desire of the former things, when once implanted in the mind, is well calculated to engender a forgetfulness of all those things which are dear to the flesh.

Parallels: Genesis 45:18; John 06:31-58

On the Change of Names (211-212)

(211) Surely not, we must then explain what it is which he intends to signify. All the lessons and all the admonitions of instruction are built up and established on the nature which is calculated to receive instruction, as on a foundation previously laid; but if there is no natural foundation previously in existence, everything is useless; for men, by nature destitute of sense, would not appear at all to differ from a stock or a lifeless stone; for nothing could possibly be adapted to them so as to cleave to them, but everything would rebound and spring back as from some hard body. (212) But on the other hand, we may see the souls of those who are well endowed by nature, like a well-smooth waxen tablet, neither too solid nor too tender, moderately tempered, and easily receiving all admonitions and all lessons, and themselves giving an accurate representation of any impression which has been stamped upon them, being a sort of distinct image of memory.

Parallels: Luke 06:48-49

Comparison: Luke 06:48-49, "he is like a man building a house, who dug deep and laid the foundation on the rock. And when a flood arose, the stream broke against that house and could not shake it, because it was well built. But he who hears and does not do them is like a man who built a house on the ground without a foundation; against which the stream broke, and immediately it collapsed. And the ruin of that house was great.""

On the Change of Names (224)

(224) It is right also to praise those inquirers after truth, who have endeavored to tear up and carry off the whole trunk of virtue, root and branch: but since they have not been able to do it, have at least taken either a single shoot, or a single bunch of fruit, as a specimen and portion of the whole tree, being all that they were able to bear.{Numbers 13:25.}

Parallels: Numbers 13:17-27; John 15:01-06

On the Confusion of Tongues (62-63)

(62) I have also heard of one of the companions of Moses having uttered such a speech as this: "Behold, a man whose name is the East!"{Zechariah 6:12.} A very novel appellation indeed, if you consider it as spoken of a man who is compounded of body and soul; but if you look upon it as applied to that incorporeal being who in no respect differs from the divine image, you will then agree that the name of the east has been given to him with great felicity. (63) For the Father of the universe has caused him to spring up as the eldest son, whom, in another passage, he calls the firstborn; and he who is thus born, imitating the ways of his father, has formed such and such species, looking to his archetypal patterns.

Parallels: Zechariah 06:12; John 03:18

On the Confusion of Tongues (77-78)

(77) For this reason all the wise men mentioned in the books of Moses are represented as sojourners, for their souls are sent down from heaven upon earth as to a colony; and on account of their fondness for contemplation, and their love of learning, they are accustomed to migrate to the terrestrial nature. (78) Since

therefore having taken up their abode among bodies, they behold all the mortal objects of the outward senses by their means, they then subsequently return back from thence to the place from which they set out at first, looking upon the heavenly country in which they have the rights of citizens as their native land, and as the earthly abode in which they dwell for a while as in a foreign land. For to those who are sent to be the inhabitants of a colony, the country which has received them is in place of their original mother country; but still the land which has sent them forth remains to them as the house to which they desire to return.

> Parallels: Genesis 23:04, 47:09; Exodus 02:22; Hebrews 11:10-16
>
> Comparison: Hebrews 11:10-16, "For he was looking forward to the city which has foundations, whose architect and builder is God. By faith Sarah herself, when she was barren, received power to conceive, even when she was past the age, because she considered him faithful who had promised. Therefore from one man, and him as good as dead, were born descendants as many as the stars of heaven and as the innumerable grains of sand by the seashore. These all died in faith, not having taken hold of the promises, but having seen them and greeted them from a distance, and having acknowledged that they were strangers and exiles on the earth. For people who say such things make it clear that they are seeking a country of their own. And if they had been thinking of that country from which they had gone out, they would have had opportunity to return. But as it is, they desire a better country, that is, a heavenly one. Therefore God is not ashamed to be called their God, for he has prepared for them a city.

On the Confusion of Tongues (82)

(82) But Moses says, "I am a sojourner in a foreign land;" speaking with peculiar fitness, looking upon his abode in the body not only as foreign land, as sojourners do, but also as a land from which one ought to feel alienated, and never look upon it as one's home.

Parallels: Genesis 23:04, 47:09; Exodus 02:22; Hebrews 11:10-16

Comparison: Hebrews 11:10-16, "For he was looking forward to the city which has foundations, whose architect and builder is God. By faith Sarah herself, when she was barren, received power to conceive, even when she was past the age, because she considered him faithful who had promised. Therefore from one man, and him as good as dead, were born descendants as many as the stars of heaven and as the innumerable grains of sand by the seashore. These all died in faith, not having taken hold of the promises, but having seen them and greeted them from a distance, and having acknowledged that they were strangers and exiles on the earth. For people who say such things make it clear that they are seeking a country of their own. And if they had been thinking of that country from which they had gone out, they would have had opportunity to return. But as it is, they desire a better country, that is, a heavenly one. Therefore God is not ashamed to be called their God, for he has prepared for them a city.

On the Confusion of Tongues (107-109)

(107) And the expression, "Come, let us build ourselves a city and a tower, the top of which shall reach to heaven," has such a meaning as this concealed beneath it; the lawgiver does not conceive that those only are cities which are built upon the earth, the materials of which are wood and stone, but he thinks that there are other cities also which men bear about with them, being built in their souls; (108) and these are, as is natural, the archetypes and models of the others, inasmuch as they have received a more divine building, and the others are but imitations of them, as consisting of perishable substances. But there are two species of cities, the one better, the other worse. That is the better which enjoys a democratic government, a constitution which honors equality, the rulers of which are law and justice; and such a constitution as this is a hymn to God. But that is the worst kind which adulterates this constitution, just as base and clipped money is adulterated in the coinage, being, in fact, ochlocracy, which admires inequality, in which injustice and lawlessness bear sway. (109) Now good men are enrolled as citizens in the constitution of the first-mentioned kind of city; but the multitude of the wicked clings to the other and worst sort, loving disorder more than orderliness, and confusion rather than well-established steadiness.

Parallels: Genesis 11:04, 23:04, 47:09; Exodus 02:22; Hebrews 11:10-16

Comparison: Hebrews 11:10-16, “For he was looking forward to the city which has foundations, whose architect and builder is God. By faith Sarah herself, when she was barren, received power to conceive, even when she was past the age, because she considered him faithful who had promised. Therefore from one man, and him as good as dead, were born descendants as many as the stars of heaven and as the innumerable grains of sand by the seashore. These all died in faith, not having taken hold of the promises, but having seen them and greeted them from a distance, and having acknowledged that they were strangers and exiles on the earth. For people who say such things make it clear that they are seeking a country of their own. And if they had been thinking of that country from which they had gone out, they would have had opportunity to return. But as it is, they desire a better country, that is, a heavenly one. Therefore God is not ashamed to be called their God, for he has prepared for them a city.

On the Confusion of Tongues (146-147)

(146) And even if there be not as yet anyone who is worthy to be called a son of God, nevertheless let him labor earnestly to be adorned according to his first-born word, the eldest of his angels, as the great archangel of many names; for he is called, the authority, and the name of God, and the Word, and man according to God's image, and he who sees Israel. (147) For which reason I was induced a little while ago to praise the principles of those who said, "We are all one man's Sons."{Genesis 42:11.} For even if we are not yet suitable to be called the sons of God, still we may deserve to be called the children of his eternal image, of his most sacred word; for the image of God is his most ancient word.

Parallels: Genesis 01:26, 03:22, 11:07, 42:11; Psalms 02:07, 33:06; Matthew 28:19; John 01:01-14, 03:18; Acts 13:33; Colossians 01:15

Comparison: Colossians 01:15, “He [Jesus] is the image of the invisible God, the firstborn of all creation.”

On the Confusion of Tongues (168-179)

(168) And it is worthwhile to consider in no superficial manner what the meaning of that expression which is put by Moses into the mouth of God: "Come, let us go down and confuse their language there."{Genesis 11:7.} For here God is represented as if he were speaking to some beings who were his coadjutors. And the very same idea may be excited by what is said in the account of the creation of the world, (169) for there, too, Moses records that "the Lord God said, Come, let us now make man in our image; man in our Similitude.{Genesis 1:26.} The expression, "Let us make," implying a number of creators. And, in another place, we are told that God said, "Behold, the man, Adam, has become as one of us, in respect of his knowing good and Evil;"{Genesis 3:22.} for the expression, "as one of us," is not applicable to one person, but to many. (170) In the first place, then, we must say this, that there is no existing being equal in honor to God, but there is one only ruler and governor and king, to whom alone it is granted to govern and to arrange the universe. For the verse - A multitude of kings is never good, Let there one sovereign, one sole monarch be, {Iliad 2.204.} is not more justly said with respect to cities and men than with respect to the world and to God; for it is clear from the necessity of things that there must be one creator, and one father, and one master of the one universe. (171) This point then being thus granted, it is necessary to convert with it also what follows, so as to adapt it properly. Let us then consider what this is: God, being one, has about him an unspeakable number of powers, all of which are defenders and preservers of everything that is created; and among these powers those also which are conversant with punishment are involved. But even punishment is not a disadvantageous thing, inasmuch as it is both a hindrance to and a correction of doing wrong. (172) Again, it is by means of these powers that the incorporeal world, perceptible by the intellect, has been put together, which is the archetypal model of this invisible world, being compounded by invisible species, just as this world is of invisible bodies. (173) Some persons therefore, admiring

exceedingly the nature of both these worlds, have not only deified them in their wholes, but have also deified the most beautiful parts of them, such as the sun and the moon, and the entire heaven, which, having no reverence for anything, they have called gods. But Moses, perceiving their design, says, "O Lord, Lord, King of the Gods,"{Deuteronomy 10:17.} in order to show the difference between the ruler and those subject to him," (174) And there is also in the air a most sacred company of incorporeal souls as an attendant upon the heavenly souls; for the word of prophecy is accustomed to call these souls angels. It happens therefore that the whole army of each of these worlds, being marshaled in their suitable ranks, are servants and ministers of the ruler who has marshaled them, whom they follow as their leader, in obedience to the principles of law and justice; for it is impossible to suppose that the divine army can even be detected in desertion. (175) But it is suitable to the character of the king to associate with his own powers, and to avail himself of them, with a view to their ministrations in such matters as it is not fitting should be settled by God alone, for the Father of the universe has no need of anything, so as to require assistance from any other quarter if he wishes to make anything. But seeing at once what is becoming, both for himself and for his works of creation, there are some things which he has entrusted to his subordinate powers to fashion; and yet he has not at once given even to them completely independent knowledge to enable it to accomplish their objects, in order that no one of those things which come to be created may be found to be erroneously made. (176) These things, then, it was necessary to give an idea of beforehand; but for what reason this was necessary we must now say. The nature of animals was originally divided into the portion endowed with and into that devoid of reason, the two being at variance with one another. Again the rational division was subdivided into the perishable and imperishable species, the perishable species being the race of mankind, and the imperishable species being the company of incorporeal souls which revolve about the air and heaven. (177) But these have no participation in wickedness, having received from the very beginning an inheritance without stain and full of happiness;

and not being bound up in the region of interminable calamities, that is to say, in the body. The divisions also of the irrational part are free from any participation in wickedness, inasmuch as, having no endowment of intellect, they are never convicted of those deliberate acts of wickedness which proceed upon consideration. (178) But man is almost the only one of all living things which, having a thorough knowledge of good and evil, often chooses that which is worst, and rejects those things which are worthy of earnest pursuit, so that he is often most justly condemned as being guilty of deliberate and studied crime. (179) Very appropriately therefore has God attributed the creation of this being, man, to his lieutenants, saying, "Let us make man," in order that the successes of the intellect may be attributed to him alone, but the errors of the being thus created, to his subordinate power: for it did not appear to be suitable to the dignity of God, the ruler of the universe, to make the road to wickedness in a rational soul by his own agency; for which reason he has committed to those about him the creation of this portion of the universe; for it was necessary that the voluntary principle, as the counterpoise to the involuntary principle, should be established and made known, with a view to the completion and perfection of the universe.

> Parallels: Genesis 01:26, 03:22, 11:07; Deuteronomy 10:17; Psalms 02:07, 33:06; Matthew 28:19; Luke 01:35; John 01:01-14, 03:18, 17:16, 18:36; Acts 04:07, 08:10, 13:33; 1Corinthians 01:24; Colossians 01:15

On the Confusion of Tongues (185-186)

(185) Mixture then is a placing side by side of different bodies in no regular order, as if any one were to make a heap, bringing barley, and wheat, and peas, and all sorts of other seeds, all into one mass; but combination is not a placing side by side, but rather a mutual penetration of dissimilar parts entering into one another at all points, so that the distinctive qualities are still able to be distinguished by some artificial skill, as they say is the case with respect to wine and water; (186) for these substances

coming together form a combination, but that which is combined is not the less capable of being resolved again into the distinctive qualities from which it was originally formed. For with a sponge saturated with oil it is possible for the water to be taken up and for the wine to be left behind, which may perhaps be because the origin of sponge is derived from water, and therefore it is natural that water being a kindred substance is calculated by nature to be taken up by the sponge out of the combination, but that that substance which is of a different nature, namely the wine, is naturally left behind.

Parallels: Luke 23:33-45

On the Confusion of Tongues (193)

(193) But his especial object here is to dissolve the company of wickedness, to put an end to their confederacy, to destroy their community of action, to put out of sight and extirpate all their powers, to overthrow the might of their dominion, which they had strengthened by fearful lawlessness.

Parallels: Genesis 11:07; Luke 23:33-45

On the Confusion of Tongues (197)

(197) for when these are put to the rout, then those who have long ago been banished by the tyranny of folly, now, at one proclamation, find themselves able to return to their own country. God having drawn up and confirmed the proclamation, as the scriptures show, in which it is expressly stated that, "Even though thy dispersion be from one end of heaven to the other end of heaven, he will bring thee together from thence."{Deuteronomy 30:4.}

Parallels: Deuteronomy 30:01-10; 1Thessalonians 04:16-17; Revelation 20:04

On the Contemplative Life Or Suppliants (13)

(13) Then, because of their anxious desire for an immortal and blessed existence, thinking that their mortal life has already come to an end, they leave their possessions to their sons or daughters, or perhaps to other relations, giving them up their inheritance with willing cheerfulness; and those who know no relations give their property to their companions or friends, for it followed of necessity that those who have acquired the wealth which sees, as if ready prepared for them, should be willing to surrender that wealth which is blind to those who themselves also are still blind in their minds.

> Parallels: Genesis 12:01-04, 14:22-24; Matthew 19:21-29; Luke 18:22
>
> Comparison: Matthew 19:21, "Jesus said to him, "If you want to be perfect, go, sell what you possess and give to [the] poor, and you will have treasure in heaven; and come, follow me.""

On the Contemplative Life Or Suppliants (28-29)

(28) And the interval between morning and evening is by them devoted wholly to meditation on and to practice of virtue, for they take up the sacred scriptures and philosophize concerning them, investigating the allegories of their national philosophy, since they look upon their literal expressions as symbols of some secret meaning of nature, intended to be conveyed in those figurative expressions. (29) They have also writings of ancient men, who having been the founders of one sect or another have left behind them many memorials of the allegorical system of writing and explanation, whom they take as a kind of model, and imitate the general fashion of their sect; so that they do not occupy themselves solely in contemplation, but they likewise compose psalms and hymns to God in every kind of meter and

melody imaginable, which they of necessity arrange in more dignified rhythm.

Parallels: Genesis 40:08-22, 41:12-38; Ezekiel 17:02-24; Daniel 02:01-49, 04:09-27; Matthew 13:03-53; Galatians 04:21-31

On the Contemplative Life Or Suppliants (37-39)

(37) and they eat nothing of a costly character, but plain bread and a seasoning of salt, which the more luxurious of them to further season with hyssop; and their drink is water from the spring; for they oppose those feelings which nature has made mistresses of the human race, namely, hunger and thirst, giving them nothing to flatter or humor them, but only such useful things as it is not possible to exist without. On this account they eat only so far as not to be hungry, and they drink just enough to escape from thirst, avoiding all satiety, as an enemy of and a plotter against both soul and body. (38) And there are two kinds of covering, one raiment and the other a house: we have already spoken of their houses, that they are not decorated with any ornaments, but run up in a hurry, being only made to answer such purposes as are absolutely necessary; and in like manner their raiment is of the most ordinary description, just stout enough to ward off cold and heat, being a cloak of some shaggy hide for winter, and a thin mantle or linen shawl in the summer; (39) for in short they practice entire simplicity, looking upon falsehood as the foundation of pride, but truth as the origin of simplicity, and upon truth and falsehood as standing in the light of fountains, for from falsehood proceeds every variety of evil and wickedness, and from truth there flows every imaginable abundance of good things both human and divine.

Parallels: Matthew 03:01-17

Comparison: Matthew 03:04, "Now John wore a garment of camel's hair, and a leather belt around his waist; and his food was locusts and wild honey."

On the Contemplative Life Or Suppliants (59-62)

(59) But the entertainment recorded by Plato is almost entirely connected with love; not that of men madly desirous or fond of women, or of women furiously in love with men, for these desires are accomplished in accordance with a law of nature, but with that love which is felt by men for one another, differing only in respect of age; for if there is anything in the account of that banquet elegantly said in praise of genuine love and heavenly Venus, it is introduced merely for the sake of making a neat speech; (60) for the greater part of the book is occupied by common, vulgar, promiscuous love, which takes away from the soul courage, that which is the most serviceable of all virtues both in war and in peace, and which engenders in it instead the female disease, and renders men men-women, though they ought rather to be carefully trained in all the practices likely to give men valor. (61) And having corrupted the age of boys, and having metamorphosed them and removed them into the classification and character of women, it has injured their lovers also in the most important particulars, their bodies, their souls, and their properties; for it follows of necessity that the mind of a lover of boys must be kept on the stretch towards the objects of his affection, and must have no acuteness of vision for any other object, but must be blinded by its desire as to all other objects private or common, and must so be wasted away, more especially if it fails in its objects. Moreover, the man's property must be diminished on two accounts, both from the owner's neglect and from his expenses for the beloved object. (62) There is also another greater evil which affects the whole people, and which grows up alongside of the other, for men who give into such passions produce solitude in cities, and a scarcity of the best kind of men, and barrenness, and unproductiveness, inasmuch as they are imitating those farmers who are unskillful in agriculture, and who, instead of the deep-soiled champagne country, sow briny marshes, or stony and rugged districts, which are not calculated to produce crops of any kind, and which only destroy the seed which is put into them.

Parallels: Romans 01:18-32

Comparison: Romans 01:18-32, "For the wrath of God is revealed from heaven against all ungodliness and wickedness of men, who by their wickedness suppress the truth. For what may be known about God is plain to them, because God has shown it to them. For since the creation of the world his invisible nature, even his eternal power and deity, has been clearly seen, being understood by the things that have been made. So they are without excuse; for although they knew God they did not honor him as God or give thanks to him, but they became futile in their thinking, and their foolish hearts were darkened. Claiming to be wise, they became fools, and exchanged the glory of the immortal God for images made like mortal man and birds and animals and reptiles. Therefore God gave them up in the lusts of their hearts to impurity, to the dishonoring of their bodies among themselves, because they exchanged the truth of God for a lie and worshipped and served the creature rather than the Creator, who is blessed forever. Amen. For this reason God gave them up to dishonorable passions. Even their women exchanged natural relations for unnatural. And the men likewise gave up natural relations with women and were consumed with passion for one another, men committing shameless acts in men and receiving in their own persons the due penalty for their error. And since they did not see fit to retain the knowledge of God, God gave them over to a base mind, to do what should not be done. They were filled with all manner of unrighteousness, wickedness, covetousness, evil. Full of envy, murder, strife, deceit, malice; they are gossips, slanderers, haters of God, insolent, arrogant, boastful, inventors of evil, disobedient to parents, foolish, faithless, heartless, ruthless. Though they know God's righteous decree that those who do such things deserve death, they not only continue to do these very things, but also approve of those who practice them."

On the Contemplative Life Or Suppliants (75)

(75) These, then, are the first circumstances of the feast; but after the guests have sat down to the table in the order which I have been describing, and when those who minister to them are all standing around in order, ready to wait upon them, and when there is nothing to drink, someone will say ... but even more so than before, so that no one ventures to mutter, or even to breathe at all hard, and then some one looks out some passage in the sacred scriptures, or explains some difficulty which is proposed by someone else, without any thoughts of display on his own part, for he is not aiming at reputation for cleverness and eloquence, but is only desirous to see some points more accurately, and is content when he has thus seen them himself not to bear ill will to others, who, even if they did not perceive the truth with equal acuteness, have at all events an equal desire of learning.

Parallels: Matthew 09:10-17; Mark 02:15-22; Luke 07:36-50, 14:01-31; John 14:01-17:26

Comparison: Luke 14:01-14, "One Sabbath, when he went to dine at the house of a ruler who belonged to [the] Pharisees, they watched him. And behold, there was a man before him who had dropsy. And Jesus spoke to the lawyers and Pharisees, saying, "Is it lawful to heal on the Sabbath, or not?" But they kept silent. And he took him and healed him, and let him go. And he said to them, "Which of you, having a son or an ox that has fallen into a well, will not immediately pull him out on the Sabbath day?" And they could not reply to this. So he told a parable to those who were invited, when he noted how they chose the places of honor, saying to them: "When you are invited by anyone to a wedding feast, do not sit down in a place of honor, lest one more distinguished than you be invited by him; and he who invited you both will come and say to you, 'Give place to this man,' and then you will begin with shame to take the lowest place. But when you are invited, go and sit in the lowest place, so that when your host comes he will say to you, 'Friend, go up higher.' Then you will be honored in the presence of all who sit to eat with you. For everyone who exalts himself will be humbled, and he who humbles himself will be exalted." Then he also said to the one who invited him, "When you give a luncheon or a dinner, do not invite your friends or your brothers, your relatives or rich neighbors, lest they also invite you back, and you be repaid. But when you give a feast, invite the poor, the maimed, the lame, the blind, and you will be blessed, because they cannot repay you; for you will be repaid at the resurrection of the just.""

On the Contemplative Life Or Suppliants (78)

(78) And these explanations of the sacred scriptures are delivered by mystic expressions in allegories, for the whole of the law appears to these men to resemble a living animal, and its express commandments seem to be the body, and the invisible meaning concealed under and lying beneath the plain words resembles the soul, in which the rational soul begins most excellently to contemplate what belongs to itself, as in a mirror, beholding in these very words the exceeding beauty of the sentiments, and unfolding and explaining the symbols, and bringing the secret meaning naked to the light to all who are able by the light of a slight intimation to perceive what is unseen by what is visible.

Parallels: Matthew 13:03-53; 2Corinthians 03:14-18

Comparison: 2Corinthians 03:14-18, "But their minds were hardened; for to this very day, when they read the old covenant, the same veil remains unlifted, because only in Christ is it removed. Even to this day whenever

> Moses is read, a veil lies over their hearts. But whenever a person turns to the Lord, the veil is taken away. Now the Lord is the Spirit, and where the Spirit of the Lord is, is freedom. And we all, with unveiled face, beholding the reflection of the Lord's glory, are being transformed into his likeness from one degree of glory to another, for this comes from the Lord who is the Spirit."

On the Creation (16-19)

(16) for God, as apprehending beforehand, as a God must do, that there could not exist a good imitation without a good model, and that of the things perceptible to the external senses nothing could be faultless which was not fashioned with reference to some archetypal idea conceived by the intellect, when he had determined to create this visible world, previously formed that one which is perceptible only by the intellect, in order that so using an incorporeal model formed as far as possible on the image of God, he might then make this corporeal world, a younger likeness of the elder creation, which should embrace as many different genera perceptible to the external senses, as the other world contains of those which are visible only to the intellect. (17) But that world which consists of ideas, it was impious in any degree to attempt to describe or even to imagine: but how it was created, we shall know if we take for our guide a certain image of the things which exist among us. When any city is founded through the exceeding ambition of some king or leader who lays claim to absolute authority, and is at the same time a man of brilliant imagination, eager to display his good fortune, then it happens at times that some man coming up who, from his education, is skilful in architecture, and he, seeing the advantageous character and beauty of the situation, first of all sketches out in his own mind nearly all the parts of the city which is about to be completed--the temples, the gymnasia, the prytanea, and markets, the harbor, the docks, the streets, the arrangement of the walls, the situations of the dwelling houses, and of the public and other buildings. (18) Then, having received in his own mind, as on a waxen tablet, the form of each building,

he carries in his heart the image of a city, perceptible as yet only by the intellect, the images of which he stirs up in memory which is innate in him, and, still further, engraving them in his mind like a good workman, keeping his eyes fixed on his model, he begins to raise the city of stones and wood, making the corporeal substances to resemble each of the incorporeal ideas. (19) Now we must form a somewhat similar opinion of God, who, having determined to found a mighty state, first of all conceived its form in his mind, according to which form he made a world perceptible only by the intellect, and then completed one visible to the external senses, using the first one as a model.

Parallels: Genesis 01:01-02; John 17:16, 18:36; Colossians 01:15-18; Hebrews 11:10-16

Comparison: Hebrews 11:10-16, "For he was looking forward to the city which has foundations, whose architect and builder is God. By faith Sarah herself, when she was barren, received power to conceive, even when she was past the age, because she considered him faithful who had promised. Therefore from one man, and him as good as dead, were born descendants as many as the stars of heaven and as the innumerable grains of sand by the seashore. These all died in faith, not having taken hold of the promises, but having seen them and greeted them from a distance, and having acknowledged that they were strangers and exiles on the earth. For people who say such things make it clear that they are seeking a country of their own. And if they had been thinking of that country from which they had gone out, they would have had opportunity to return. But as it is, they desire a better country, that is, a heavenly one. Therefore God is not ashamed to be called their God, for he has prepared for them a city.

On the Creation (26-30)

(26) Moses says also; "In the beginning God created the heaven and the earth:" taking the beginning to be, not as some men think, that which is according to time; for before the world time had no existence, but was created either simultaneously with it, or after it; for since time is the interval of the motion of the heavens, there could not have been any such thing as motion before there was anything which could be moved; but it follows of necessity that it received existence subsequently or simultaneously. It therefore follows also of necessity, that time was created either at the same moment with the world, or later than it--and to venture to assert that it is older than the world is absolutely inconsistent with philosophy. (27) But if the beginning spoken of by Moses is not to be looked upon as spoken of according to time, then it may be natural to suppose that it is the beginning according to number that is indicated; so that, "In the beginning he created," is equivalent to "first of all he created the heaven;" for it is natural in reality that that should have been the first object created, being both the best of all created things, and being also made of the purest substance, because it was destined to be the most holy abode of the visible Gods who are perceptible by the external senses; (28) for if the Creator had made everything at the same moment, still those things which were created in beauty would no less have had a regular arrangement, for there is no such thing as beauty in disorder. But order is a due consequence and connection of things precedent and subsequent, if not in the completion of a work, at all events in the intention of the maker; for it is owing to order that they become accurately defined and stationary, and free from confusion. (29) In the first place therefore, from the model of the world, perceptible only by intellect, the Creator made an incorporeal heaven, and an invisible earth, and the form of air and of empty space: the former of which he called darkness, because the air is black by nature; and the other he called the abyss, for empty space is very deep and yawning with

immense width. Then he created the incorporeal substance of water and of air, and above all he spread light, being the seventh thing made; and this again was incorporeal, and a model of the sun, perceptible only to intellect, and of all the light giving stars, which are destined to stand together in heaven. (30) And air and light he considered worthy of the pre-eminence. For the one he called the breath of God, because it is air, which is the most life-giving of things, and of life the causer is God; and the other he called light, because it is surpassingly beautiful: for that which is perceptible only by intellect is as far more brilliant and splendid than that which is seen, as I conceive, the sun is than darkness, or day than night, or the intellect than any other of the outward senses by which men judge (inasmuch as it is the guide of the entire soul), or the eyes than any other part of the body.

Parallels: Genesis 01:01-05; John 17:16, 18:36; Colossians 01:15-18

On the Creation (31)

(31) And the invisible divine reason, perceptible only by intellect, he calls the image of God. And the image of this image is that light, perceptible only by the intellect, which is the image of the divine reason, which has explained its generation. And it is a star above the heavens, the source of those stars which are perceptible by the external senses, and if any one were to call it universal light he would not be very wrong; since it is from that the sun and the moon, and all the other planets and fixed stars derive their due light, in proportion as each has power given to it; that unmingled and pure light being obscured when it begins to change, according to the change from that which is perceptible only by the intellect, to that which is perceptible by the external senses; for none of those things which are perceptible to the external senses is pure.

Parallels: Genesis 01:26; John 01:01-14, 03:19; Colossians 01:15

On the Creation (69-70)

(69) So then after all the other things, as has been said before, Moses says that man was made in the image and likeness of God. And he says well; for nothing that is born on the earth is more resembling God than man. And let no one think that he is able to judge of this likeness from the characters of the body: for neither is God a being with the form of a man, nor is the human body like the form of God; but the resemblance is spoken of with reference to the most important part of the soul, namely, the mind: for the mind which exists in each individual has been created after the likeness of that one mind which is in the universe as its primitive model, being in some sort the God of that body which carries it about and bears its image within it. In the same rank that the great Governor occupies in the universal world, that same as it seems does the mind of man occupy in man; for it is invisible, though it sees everything itself; and it has an essence which is indiscernible, though it can discern the essences of all other things, and making for itself by art and science all sorts of roads leading in diverse directions, and all plain; it traverses land and sea, investigating everything which is contained in either element.

Parallels: Genesis 01:26; John 14:09; Colossians 01:15

Comparison: Colossians 01:15, "He is the image of the invisible God, the firstborn of all creation."

On the Giants (53-54)

(53) As, therefore, among men in general, that is to say, among those who propose to themselves many objects in life, the divine spirit does not remain, even though it may abide among them for a very short time, but it remains among one species of men alone, namely, among those who, having put off all the things of creation, and the inmost veil and covering of false opinion, come to God in their unconcealed and naked minds. (54) Thus also Moses, having fixed his tent outside of the tabernacle and outside of all the corporeal army, {Exodus 33:7.} that is to say, having established his mind so that it should not move, begins to worship God, and having entered into the darkness, that invisible country, remains there, performing the most sacred mysteries; and he becomes, not merely an initiated man, but also an hierophant of mysteries and a teacher of divine things, which he will explain to those whose ears are purified;

> Parallels: Exodus 33:07, 34:33-35; Matthew 13:03-53; 2Corinthians 03:12-04:04
>
> Comparison: 2Corinthians 03:14-18, "But their minds were hardened; for to this very day, when they read the old covenant, the same veil remains unlifted, because only in Christ is it removed. Even to this day whenever Moses is read, a veil lies over their hearts. But whenever a person turns to the Lord, the veil is taken away. Now the Lord is the Spirit, and where the Spirit of the Lord is, is freedom. And we all, with unveiled face, beholding the reflection of the Lord's glory, are being transformed into his likeness from one degree of glory to another, for this comes from the Lord who is the Spirit."

On the Giants (60-61)

(60) Therefore he utters no fable whatever respecting the giants; but he wishes to set this fact before your eyes, that some men are born of the earth, and some are born of heaven, and some are born of God: those are born of the earth, who are hunters after the pleasures of the body, devoting themselves to the enjoyment and fruition of them, and being eager to provide themselves with all things that tend to each of them. Those again are born of heaven who are men of skill and science and devoted to learning; for the heavenly portion of us is our mind, and the mind of every one of those persons who are born of heaven studies the encyclical branches of education and every other art of every description, sharpening, and exercising, and practicing itself, and rendering itself acute in all those matters which are the objects of intellect. (61) Lastly, those who are born of God are priests and prophets, who have not thought fit to mix themselves up in the constitutions of this world, and to become cosmopolites, but who having raised themselves above all the objects of the mere outward senses, have departed and fixed their views on that world which is perceptible only by the intellect, and have settled there, being inscribed in the state of incorruptible incorporeal ideas.

Parallels: Genesis 06:04; Matthew 19:12; John 01:12-13, 17:16, 18:36; Hebrews 11:10-16

Comparison: Matthew 19:12, "For there are eunuchs who were born that way from their mother's womb. And there are eunuchs who were made eunuchs by men. And there are eunuchs who have made themselves eunuchs for the sake of the kingdom of heaven. He who is able to accept it, let him accept it.""

On the Life of Moses I (123)

(123) And when they had been completely dispersed, and when the king was again obstinate respecting the allowing the nation to depart, a greater evil than the former ones was descended upon him. For while it was bright daylight, on a sudden, a thick darkness overspread the land, as if an eclipse of the sun more complete than any common one had taken place. And it continued with a long series of clouds and impenetrable density, all the course of the sun's rays being cut off by the massive thickness of the veil which was interposed, so that day did not at all differ from night. For what indeed did it resemble, but one very long night equal in length to three days and an equal number of nights?

Parallels: Exodus 10:21-23; Luke 23:33-45

Comparison: Luke 23:44-45, "And it was now about the sixth hour, and there was darkness over the whole land until the ninth hour - the sun failed; and the veil of the temple was torn in two."

On the Life of Moses I (145-146)

(145) No lice, no dog-flies, no locusts, which greatly injured the plants, and the fruits, and the animals, and the human beings, ever descended upon the Hebrews. Those unceasing storms of rain and hail, and thunder and lightning, which continued so uninterruptedly, never reached them; they never felt, no not even in their dreams, that most terrible ulceration which caused the Egyptians so much suffering; when that most dense darkness descended upon the others, they were living in bright daylight, a brilliancy as of noon-day shining all around them; when, among the Egyptians, all the first-born were slain, not one of the Hebrews died; for it was not likely, since even that destruction of such countless flocks and herds of cattle never carried off or

injured a single flock or a single beast belonging to the Hebrews. (146) And it seems to me that if anyone had been present to see all that happened at that time, he would not have conceived any other idea than that the Hebrews were there as spectators of the miseries which the other nation was enduring; and, not only that, but that they were also there for the purpose of being taught that most beautiful and beneficial of all lessons, namely, piety. For a distinction could otherwise have never been made so decidedly between the good and the bad, giving destruction to the one and salvation to the other.

> Parallels: Exodus 07:08-11:10; Matthew 07:13-14, 25:01-46; Revelation 20:01-21:08
>
> Comparison: Matthew 25:46, "And they will go away into eternal punishment, but the righteous into eternal life."

On the Life of Moses II (138-139)

(138) The maker then thought it well to accept these offerings, and to melt them down, and to make nothing except the laver of them, in order that the priests who were about to enter the temple might be supplied from it, with water of purification for the purpose of performing the sacred ministrations which were appointed for them; washing their feet most especially, and their hands, as a symbol of their irreproachable life, and of a course of conduct which makes itself pure in all kinds of praiseworthy actions, proceeding not along the rough road of wickedness which one may more properly call no road at all, but keeping straight along the level and direct path of virtue. (139) Let him remember, says he, let him who is about to be sprinkled with the water of purification from this laver, remember that the materials of which this vessel was composed were mirrors, that he himself may look into his own mind as into a mirror; and if there is perceptible in it any deformity arising from some agitation unconnected with reason or from any pleasure which

would excite us, and raise us up in hostility to reason, or from any pain which might mislead us and turn us from our purpose of proceeding by the straight road, or from any desire alluring us and even dragging us by force to the pursuit of present pleasures, he seeks to relieve and cure that, desiring only that beauty which is genuine and unadulterated.

Parallels: Exodus 30:17-21; Matthew 03:05-16, 07:13-14; John 13:05-14

Comparison: Matthew 07:13-14, "Enter by the narrow gate. For the gate is wide, and the way is easy that leads to destruction, and many are those who enter by it. How narrow is the gate and hard the way, that leads to life, and few those who find it!"

On the Life of Moses II (250)

(250) For now, by reason of the necessity which environed them, and from which they saw no means of extricating themselves, they were in great agitation, being full of expectation of a miserable death. But when the prophet saw that the whole nation was now enclosed like a shoal of fish, and in great consternation, he no longer remained master of himself, but became inspired, and prophesied...

Parallels: Exodus 14:13-27; Luke 05:03-09

On the Life of Moses II (274)

(274) So they rushed forth with a shout, and slew three thousand, especially those who were the leaders of this impiety, and not only were excused themselves from having had any participation in the wicked boldness of the others, but were also enrolled among the most noble of valiant men, and were thought worthy of an honor and reward most appropriate to their action, to wit the priesthood. For it was inevitable that those men should be ministers of holiness, who had shown themselves valiant in defense of it, and had warred bravely as its champions.

Parallels: Exodus 32:26; 1Peter 02:09

On the Migration of Abraham (35)

(35) and finally crowning him like a wrestler who has gained a glorious victory, he honors him moreover with a most noble proclamation, saying that "he pleased God," (and what can there be in nature that is more excellent than this panegyric?) which is the most visible proof of excellence; for if they who displease God are miserable, those who please him are by all means happy.

Parallels: 1Corinthians 09:24-27; 2Timothy 02:05, 04:07-08; James 01:12; 1Peter 05:01-04; Revelation 02:10

Comparison: James 01:12, “Blessed is the man who perseveres under trial. For when he has stood the test, he will receive the crown of life that he has promised to those who love him.”

On the Migration of Abraham (124)

(124) There are three different classes of human dispositions, each of which has received as its portion one of the aforesaid visions. The best of them has received that vision which is in the center, the sight of the truly living God. The one which is next best has received that which is on the right hand, the sight of the beneficent power which has the name of God. And the third has the sight of that which is on the left hand, the governing power, which is called lord.

> Parallels: Luke 01:35; Acts 04:07, 07:55-56, 08:10; 1Corinthians 01:24
>
> Comparison: Acts 07:56, "And he said, "Behold, I see the heavens have completely opened, and the Son of Man standing at the right hand of God.""

On the Migration of Abraham (132-133)

(132) For when the wise man entreats those persons who are in the guise of three travelers to come and lodge in his house, he speaks to them not as three persons, but as one, and says, "My lord, if I have found favor with thee, do not thou pass by thy Servant."{Genesis 18:3.} For the expressions, "my lord," and "with thee," and "do not pass by," and others of the same kind, are all such as are naturally addressed to a single individual, but not to many. And when those persons, having been entertained in his house, address their entertainer in an affectionate manner, it is again one of them who promises that he by himself will be present, and will bestow on him the seed of a child of his own, speaking in the following words: "I will return again and visit thee again, according to the time of life, and Sarah thy wife shall have a Son."{Genesis 18:10.} (133) And what is signified by this is indicated in a most evident and careful manner by the events which ensued. The country of the Sodomites was a district of the

land of Canaan, which the Syrians afterwards called Palestine, a country full of innumerable iniquities, and especially of gluttony and debauchery, and all the great and numerous pleasures of other kinds which have been built up by men as a fortress, on which account it had been already condemned by the Judge of the whole world.

Parallels: Genesis 18:03-23; Matthew 01:01, 28:19; Galatians 03:16

On the Migration of Abraham (144-146)

(144) And kings too appear to me to imitate the divine nature in this particular, and to act in the same way, giving their favors in person, but inflicting their chastisements by the agency of others. (145) But since, of the two powers of God, one is a beneficent power and the other a chastising one, each of them, as is natural, is manifested to the country of the people of Sodom. Because of the five finest cities in it four were about to be destroyed by fire, and one was destined to be left unhurt and safe from every evil. For it was necessary that the calamities should be inflicted by the chastising power, and that the one which was to be saved should be saved by the beneficent power. (146) But since the portion which was saved was not endowed with entire and complete virtues, but was blessed with kindness by the power of the living God, it was deliberately accounted unworthy to have a sight of his presence afforded to it.

Parallels: Genesis 19:01-25; Luke 01:35, 09:54; Acts 04:07, 08:10; 1Corinthians 01:24

On the Posterity of Cain And His Exile (30-31)

(30) But when he comes to that which is the peculiar attribute of the creature, he says, with the most perfect correctness, "I will go down with you;" for change of place is adapted to you: so that no one shall go down with me, for in me there is no changing; but whatever is consistent with me, that is to say, with rest, shall stand. And with those who go down in such a manner as to change their place (for change of place is akin to and closely connected with them), I will go down also, not indeed changing my situation as to its actual place, inasmuch as I fill every place with myself. (31) And this, too, I do through the pity which exists in rational nature, in order that it may be raised from the hell of the passions to the heavenly region of virtue; I being the guide, who also have made the road which leads to heaven, so that it may be a plain road for suppliant souls, and have shown it to them all, in order that they may not foolishly wander out of the way.

Parallels: Genesis 17:01-22, 18:01-21; Matthew 07:13-14; John 01:01-18, 06:38

On the Posterity of Cain And His Exile (85-88)

(85) And he divides the good by a threefold division, speaking most strictly in accordance with natural philosophy. "For it is," says he, "in thy mouth, and in thy heart, and in their hands;" that is to say, in thy words, and in thy intentions, and in thy actions; for these are the component parts of the good, of which it is naturally compounded. So that the want of one portion does not only make the whole incomplete, but does entirely destroy it; (86) for of what use is it to say what is excellent, but to think and to do what is most shameful? This is the way of the sophists. For those who make long speeches about prudence and perseverance, annoy the ears even of those who are very fond of

hearing good conversation; and yet, in their designs and in the actions of their lives they are found to err. (87) And what is the use of entertaining such sentiments as are proper, but acting and speaking most improperly, and injuring by your actions all who are exposed to the effect of them? Again, it is blameworthy even to do what is right, without any intention or reason; (88) for what is done without these is a portion of involuntary conduct, and is on no account, and under no circumstances to be praised; but if it were to happen that, as in the case of a lyre, so all the sounds of the good could be adapted to any man, and that we could make the conversation agree with the intention, and the intention with the action; then such a man would be considered perfect and really well constituted. So that he who removes the landmarks of the good is justly accursed, and is justly spoken of as such.

> Parallels: Deuteronomy 30:14; Matthew 06:01-16; Mark 12:28-34; James 02:01-26
>
> Comparison: James 02:14-17, “What good is it, my brothers, if a man says he has faith but has no works? Can such faith save him? If a brother or sister is without clothing and in need of daily food, and one of you says to them, “Go in peace, be warmed and filled,” and yet you do not give them what is necessary for their body, what use is that? So faith by itself, if it has no works, is dead.”

On the Posterity of Cain And His Exile (128-129)

(128) And the lawgiver shows this, when he says, "And a river went out of Eden to water the Paradise; and from thence it is divided into four Heads."{Genesis 2:10.} For there are four generic virtues: prudence, courage, temperance, and justice. And of these, every single one is a princess and a ruler; and he who has acquired them is, from the moment of the acquisition, a ruler and a king, even if he has no abundance of any kind of treasure;

(129) for the meaning of the expression, "it is divided into four heads," is [...]{here again is an hiatus, which Mangey does not attempt to supply.} nor distance; but virtue exhibits the pre-eminence and the power. And these spring from the word of God as from one root, which he compares to a river, on account of the unceasing and everlasting flow of salutary words and doctrines, by which it increases and nourishes the souls that love God.

Parallels: Genesis 02:10; John 04:04-42

On the Posterity of Cain And His Exile (133-136)

(133) Here who can help wondering at the minute accuracy of the lawgiver as to every particular? He calls Rebecca a maiden, and a very beautiful maiden, because the nature of virtue is unmixed and free from guile, and unpolluted, and the only thing in all creation which is both beautiful and good; from which arose the Stoic doctrine, that the only thing that was beautiful was the good. (134) Now of the four virtues, some are always virgins, and some from having been women become changed into virgins, as Sarah did; "For it had ceased to be with her after the manner of Women,"{Genesis 18:11.} when she began to conceive her happy offspring Isaac. But that which is always a virgin, is that of which Moses says, "And no man whatever knows her." For in truth, it is not permitted to any mortal to pollute incorruptible nature, nor even clearly to comprehend what it is. If indeed he were able by any means to become acquainted with it, he would not cease to hate and regret it; (135) on which account Moses, in strict accordance with the principles of natural philosophy, represents Leah as Hated.{Genesis 29:31.} For those whom the charms of pleasures, which are with Rachel, that is to say, with the outward sense, cannot be endured by Leah, who is situated out of the reach of the passions; on which account they repudiate and detest her. But as far as she herself is concerned, her alienation from the creature produces her a close connection with God, from whom she receives the seeds of

wisdom, and conceives, and travails, and brings forth virtuous ideas, worthy of the father who begot them. If therefore, you, O my soul, imitating Leah, reject mortal things, you will of necessity turn to the incorruptible God, who will shed over you all the fountains of his good. (136) "But Rebecca," says Moses, "went down to the fountain to fill her pitcher, and came up again." For from what source is it natural for the mind that thirsts after wisdom to be filled, except from the wisdom of God, that fountain which never fails, and to which the soul that descends comes up again like a virtuous disciple? For those who descend out of a vain pride, the reason of virtue receives, and taking them up by means of fame raises them to a height. On which account it is that Moses seems to me to use the expression, "Go, descend, and come Up,"{Exodus 32:7.} as if everyone who measures his own loveliness comes forth more gloriously in the eyes of the judges of truth. And he speaks of these matters with great caution.

> Parallels: Genesis 18:11, 24:16, 29:31; Exodus 32:07; Luke 01:26-34
>
> Comparison: Luke 01:26-34, “In the sixth month the angel Gabriel was sent from God to a city of Galilee named Nazareth, to a virgin betrothed to a man whose name was Joseph, of the house of David. The virgin’s name was Mary. He went to her and said, “Hail, O highly favored one, the Lord is with you!” But she was greatly troubled at the saying, and considered in her mind what sort of greeting this might be. And the angel said to her, “Do not be afraid, Mary, for you have found favor with God. And behold, you will conceive in your womb and bear a son, and you shall call his name Jesus. He will be great, and will be called the Son of the Most High; and the Lord God will give him the throne of his father David. And he will reign over the house of Jacob forever; and of his kingdom there will be no end.” And Mary said to the angel, “How can this be, since I do not know a man?”

On the Posterity of Cain And His Exile (138-139)

(138) Therefore, the man who is fond of learning, seeing men imbibing the sciences like water, from wisdom that divine fountain, runs up, and meeting them becomes a suppliant to them to know how he may allay his thirst for learning. And the soul which has received the best possible education, namely, the lesson not to envy, and to be liberal, immediately proffers to him the stream of wisdom, and invites him to drink abundantly, adding also this that she calls him who is only a servant her lord. This is the meaning of that most dogmatic assertion, that the wise man alone is free, and a king, even if he have ten thousand masters over his body. (139) Most correctly, therefore, after the servant has said, "Give me a little water to drink," does she make answer, not in the manner corresponding to his request: "I will give you to drink," but "Drink." For the one expression would have been suited to one who was displaying the riches of God, which are poured forth for all who are worthy of them and who are able to think of them; but the other expression is appropriate to one who professes that she will teach. But nothing which is connected with mere professions is akin to virtue.

Parallels: Genesis 24:15-21; John 04:04-42

On the Posterity of Cain And His Exile (143-145)

(143) Do you not see that even God does not utter his oracles, having a regard to their being in proportion to the magnitude of his own oracular power, but always having respect to the capacity of those who are to be benefited by them? Since who could receive the whole power of the words of God, which are too mighty for anyone to listen to? On which account those persons appear to speak with great truth, who say to Moses, "Do thou speak to us, and let not God speak to us, lest we Die."{Exodus 20:19.} For they know that they have not in themselves any organ which can be worthy of God who is giving

laws to his church; (144) nor, indeed, could even the whole world, both land and sea, contain his riches if he were inclined to display them, unless we think that the descent of the rains and of the other things that happen in the world are appointed to take place according to the pre-arranged periods of the seasons, and not all at once, because of the scarcity and rarity of the things themselves, and not from any regard to the advantage of those who are benefited by them; who would be injured rather than be benefited by a continual enjoyment of such gifts. (145) On this account it is, that God always judiciously limits and brings out with wise moderation his first benefits, stopping them before those who partake of them become wanton through satiety; and then he bestows others in their stead; and again a third class of advantages instead of the second set, and so on, continually substituting new blessings for those of older date, at one time giving such as are different from those which went before, and at another time such as are almost identical with them; for the creature is never wholly destitute of the blessings bestowed by God, since if he were he would be utterly destroyed; but he is unable to endure an unlimited and measureless abundance of them. On which account, as he is desirous that we should derive advantage from the benefits which he bestows upon us, he weighs out what he gives so as to proportion it to the strength of those who receive it.

Parallels: Exodus 20:19; Matthew 13:03-53

On the Posterity of Cain And His Exile (147)

(147) And beyond all other things, I especially admire her exceeding liberality; for though she had only been asked for a small draught, she gave a large one, until she had filled the whole soul of the learner with wholesome speculations. For Moses says, "She gave him to drink till he ceased from drinking," a most marvelous example to teach us humanity. For if anyone should not happen to be in want of many things, but should come forward, and out of shame ask only for a very little, let us

not give him only what he mentions, but also those things of which he makes no mention, but of which he is nevertheless in reality in need.

Parallels: Genesis 24:17-20; Acts 03:02-10

On the Prayers And Curses Uttered By Noah When He Became Sober (24)

And both the wives became mothers: the one bringing forth that disposition in the soul which loves pleasures, and the other that which loves virtue; but the lover of pleasure is imperfect, and in reality is always a child, even if he reaches a vast age of many years. But, on the other hand, the lover of virtue, though he is in old age as to his wisdom, while still in his swaddling clothes, as the proverb has it, will never grow old.

Parallels: Deuteronomy 21:15-17; Luke 02:11-12; John 01:01-18

On the Prayers And Curses Uttered By Noah When He Became Sober (64)

But let everyone, on whom the love of God has showered good things, pray to God that he may have as a dweller within him the Ruler of all things, who will raise this small house, the mind, to a great height above the earth, and will connect it with the bounds of heaven.

Parallels: Genesis 09:27; Romans 08:09-11

Comparison: Romans 08:09-11, "But you are not in the flesh, you are in the Spirit, if in fact the Spirit of God dwells in you. And if anyone does not have the Spirit of Christ, he does not belong to him. But if Christ is in you,

> although your body is dead because of sin, your spirit is alive because of righteousness. If the Spirit of him who raised Jesus from the dead dwells in you, he who raised Christ from the dead will give life to your mortal bodies also through his Spirit who dwells in you."

On The Unchangeableness of God (3)

(3) For as long as the pure rays of wisdom shine forth in the soul, by means of which the wise man sees God and his powers, no one of those who bring false news ever enters into the reason, but all such are kept at a distance outside of the sacred threshold. But when the light of the intellect is dimmed and overshadowed, then the companions of darkness having become victorious, associate themselves with the dissolute and effeminate passions which the prophet calls the daughters of men, and they bear children to them and not to God.

> Parallels: Genesis 06:04; Luke 01:35; Acts 04:07, 08:10; 1Corinthians 01:24

On the Unchangeableness of God (8-9)

(8) For it is foolishness to imagine, that it is unlawful to enter into temples, unless a man has first washed his body and made that look bright, but that one may attempt to sacrifice and to pray with a mind still polluted and disordered. And yet temples are made of stones and timber, mere lifeless materials, and it is not possible for the body, if it is devoid of life by its own nature, to touch things devoid of life, without using ablutions and purifying ceremonies of holiness; and shall any one endure to approach God without being purified as to his soul, shall any one while impure come near to the purest of all beings, and this too without having any intention of repenting? (9) Let him, indeed who, in addition to having committed no new crimes, has also endeavored to wash off his old misdeeds, come cheerfully before him; but let the man who is without any such

preparation, and who is impure, keep aloof. For he will never escape the notice of him who can look into the recesses of the heart, and who walks in its most secret places.

> Parallels: Exodus 30:17-21; Psalms 44:21; Matthew 03:05-16; John 02:19-21; Acts 03:19, 15:08; Romans 02:15-16; 1Corinthians 14:25; Revelation 20:11-15
>
> Comparison: Acts 15:08, "And God, who knows the heart, bore witness to them, giving the Holy Spirit, just as he also did to us." Romans 2:15-16, "They show that the requirements of the law are written on their hearts, their conscience also bearing witness, and their thoughts accusing or else excusing them. On that day when, according to my gospel, God judges the secrets of men by Christ Jesus."

On The Unchangeableness of God (23-32)

(23) And it seems good to the lawgiver that the perfect man should desire tranquility; for it was said to the wise man in the character of God, "But stand thou here with me," this expression showing the unchangeable and unalterable nature of the mind which is firmly established in the right way; (24) for it is really marvelous when any one touches the soul, like a lyre tuned in musical principles, not with sharp and flat sounds, but with an accurate knowledge of contrary tones, and employing only the best, not sounding any too loudly, nor on the other hand letting any be too weak, so as to impair the harmony of the virtues and of those things which are good by nature, and when he, preserving it in an equal condition plays and sings melodiously; (25) for this instrument nature has made to be the most perfect of all, and to be the model of all instruments made by the hand. And if this be properly tuned, it will utter the most exquisite of all symphonies, which consists not in the combination and tones of a melodious voice, but in a harmonious agreement of all the actions in life; (26) therefore, as the soul of man can allay the

excessive storm and swell of the sea, which the violent and irresistible gale of wickedness has suddenly raised, by the gentle breezes of knowledge and wisdom, and having mitigated its swelling and boisterous fury, enjoys tranquility resting in an unruffled calm. Do you doubt whether the imperishable, and everlasting, and blessed God, the Being endowed with all the virtues, and with all perfection, and with all happiness is unchangeable in his counsels, and whether he abides by the designs which he originally formed, without changing any of them. (27) Facility of change is indeed an attribute of man, which is of necessity incidental to their nature by reason of its external want of firmness; as in this way, for instance: - often when we have chosen friends, and have lived some short time with them, without having any thing to accuse them of, we then turn away from them, so as to place ourselves in the rank of enemies, or at least of strangers to them; (28) now this conduct shows the facility and levity of ourselves, who are unable steadily to adhere to the professions which we originally made; but God is not so easily sated or wearied. Again there are times when we determine to abide by the same judgment that we have formed; but those who join us do not equally abide by theirs, so that our opinions of necessity change as well as theirs; (29) for it is impossible for us, who are but men, to foresee all the contingencies of future events, or to anticipate the opinions of others; but to God, as dwelling in pure light, all things are visible; for he penetrating into the very recesses of the soul, is able to see, with the most perfect certainty, what is invisible to others, and being possessed of prescience and of providence, his own peculiar attributes, he allows nothing to abuse its liberty, and to stray out of the reach of his comprehension, since with him, there is no uncertainty even in the future, for there is nothing uncertain nor even future to God. (30) It is plain therefore that the creator of all created things, and the maker of all the things that have ever been made, and the governor of all the things which are subject to government, must of necessity be a being of universal knowledge; and he is in truth the father, and creator, and governor of all things in heaven and in the whole world; and indeed future events are overshadowed by the distance of future time, which is sometimes a short and sometimes a long interval. (31) But God is the creator of time also; for he is the father of its father, and the father of time is the world, which made its own mother the creation of time, so that time stands towards God in the relation of a grandson; for this world is a younger son of God, inasmuch as it is perceptible by the outward sense; for the only son he speaks of as older than the world, is idea, and this is not perceptible by the intellect; but having thought the other worthy of the rights of primogeniture, he has decided that it shall remain with him; (32) therefore, this younger son, perceptible by the external senses being set in motion, has caused the nature of time to shine forth, and to become conspicuous, so that there is nothing future to God, who has the very boundaries of time subject to him; for their life is not time, but the beautiful model of time, eternity; and in eternity nothing is past and nothing is future, but everything is present only.

> Parallels: Genesis 01:01: Deuteronomy 05:31; Mark 04:37-41; Acts 02:23; Hebrews 13:08; 2Peter 03:01-18
>
> Comparison: Acts 02:23, "this man, delivered over by the predetermined plan and foreknowledge of God, you nailed to a cross by the hand of lawless men and put him to death."

On The Unchangeableness of God (101-103)

(101) So also those who restore deposits of small value in the hope of having larger deposits entrusted to them, which they may be able to appropriate, you would call men of good faith; and yet even when they are restoring the deposits, they put a great constraint on their natural faithlessness, by which it is to be hoped, they will be unceasingly tormented. (102) And do not all those who offer but a spurious kind of worship to the only wise God, putting on a profession of a rigid life like a dress on a magnificent stage, merely with the object of making a display

before the assembled spectators, having imposture rather than piety in their souls, do not they, I say, stretch themselves on the rack as it were, and torment themselves, compelling even the truth itself to assume a false appearance. (103) Therefore, they being for a brief period overshadowed with the emblems of superstition, which is the great hindrance to holiness, and a great injury to those who have it and to those who associate with it; after that again stripping off their disguise, display their naked hypocrisy. And then like men, convicted of being aliens, they are looked upon as enemies, having entered themselves as citizens of that noblest of cities - virtue, while they have really no connection with it. For whatever is violent (biaion) is also of short duration, as its very name imports, since it closely resembles short (baion). And the ancients used the two words (baion) and (oligochronion) of short duration as synonymous.

> Parallels: Numbers 14:39-45; Deuteronomy 01:41-46; Matthew 06:01-16
>
> Comparison: Matthew 06:01-06, "[But] take heed that you do not do your righteousness before men, to be seen by them. If you do, you will have no reward from your Father in heaven. "Thus, when you give alms, do not sound a trumpet before you, as the hypocrites do in the synagogues and in the streets, that they may be praised by men. Truly, I say to you, they have received their reward. But when you give to the needy, do not let your left hand know what your right hand is doing, so that your charitable deed may be in secret. And your Father, who sees in secret, will reward you. "And when you pray, you shall not be like the hypocrites. For they love to pray standing in the synagogues and on the street corners, that they may be seen by men. Truly, I say to you, they have received their reward. But when you pray, go into your room, shut the door and pray to your Father, who is in secret. And your Father, who sees in secret, will reward you."

On The Unchangeableness of God (106-108)

(106) For what kind of person must he be who would be accounted before God to be worthy of his grace? I indeed think that the whole world put together could scarcely attain to such a pitch, and yet the world is the first, and greatest, and most perfect of all the works of God. (107) May it not then perhaps be better to understand this expression as meaning that the virtuous man being fond of investigating things, and eager for learning, amid all the different things that he has investigated, has found this one most certain fact, that all things that exist, the earth, the water, the air, the fire, the sun, the stars, the heaven, all animals and plants whatever, are the grace of God. (108) But God has given nothing to himself, for he has no need of anything; but he has given the world to the world, and its parts he has bestowed on themselves and on one another, and also on the universe, and without having judged anything to be worthy of grace, (for he gives all his good things without grudging to the universe and to its parts), he merely has regard to his own everlasting goodness, thinking the doing good to be a line of conduct suitable to his own happy and blessed nature; so that if any one were to ask me, what was the cause of the creation of the world, having learnt from Moses, I should answer, that the goodness of the living God, being the most important of his graces, is in itself the cause.

Parallels: Genesis 06:08; 1Peter 01:10-13

On The Unchangeableness of God (127-130)

(127) On which account Moses also establishes a most extraordinary law, in which he enjoins that "the man who is in part leprous shall be accounted impure, but that he who is wholly, from the sole of his foot to the crown of his head overwhelmed with leprosy, shall be considered pure;" for anyone else, I apprehend, reasoning from probability, would say

the exact contrary, and would think that the leprosy which was contracted, and which extended over only a small portion of the body, was less impure, but that the leprosy which was diffused, so as to spread over the whole body was more impure: (128) but Moses here, as it appears to me, uses this symbolical expression to intimate this most undeniable truth, that unintentional misdeeds, even if they be of the greatest enormity, are not deserving of blame, and are pure, inasmuch as they have not conscience, that terrible accuser, to testify against them: but that intentional offences, even if they do not extend over a wide surface, being convicted by the judge who passes sentence against the soul, are rightly accounted unholy, and polluted, and impure. (129) This leprosy, therefore, being of a twofold character, and putting forth two complexions, signifies voluntary depravity; for the soul, though it has healthy, and vivifying, and right reason in itself, does not use it for the preservation of its good things, but surrendering itself to persons unskilled in navigation, it overturns the whole bark of life, which might have been saved in calm fine weather; (130) but when it changes so as to assume one uniform white appearance, it displays an involuntary change; since the mind, entirely deprived of the power of reasoning, not having left in it one single seed to beget understanding, like a man in a mist or in deep darkness, sees nothing that ought to be done; but, like a blind man, falling without seeing his way before him into all kinds of error, endures continual falls and disasters one after another, in spite of all its efforts.

> Parallels: Leviticus 13:11; Matthew 15:14; Revelation 20:11-15

On The Unchangeableness of God (134-135)

(134) for as long as the divine word has not come to our souls as to a hearth of hospitality, all its actions are blameless; for the overseer, or the father, or the teacher, or whatever else it may be fit to entitle the priest, by whom alone it is possible for it to be

admonished and chastened, is at a distance: and those persons are to be pardoned who do wrong from inexperience, out of ignorance what they ought to do: for they do not look upon their deeds in the light of sins, but even sometimes they believe that they are doing right in cases in which they are erring greatly; (135) but when the real priest, conviction, enters our hearts, like a most pure ray of light, then we think that the designs which we have cherished within our souls are not pure, and we see that our actions are liable to blame, and deserving of reproach, though we did them through ignorance of what was right. All these things, therefore, the priest, that is to say, conviction, pollutes, and orders that they should be taken away and stripped off, in order that he may see the abode of the soul pure, and, if there are any diseases in it, that he may heal them.

Parallels: Leviticus 14:35; Romans 02:15-16

Comparison: Romans 02:15-16, "They show that the requirements of the law are written on their hearts, their conscience also bearing witness, and their thoughts accusing or else excusing them. On that day when, according to my gospel, God judges the secrets of men by Christ Jesus."

On The Unchangeableness of God (136-139)

(136) And the woman who met the prophet, in the book of Kings, resembles this fact: "And she is a widow;" not meaning by that, as we generally use the word, a woman when she is bereft of her husband, but that she is so, from being free from those passions which corrupt and destroy the soul, as Tamar is represented by Moses. (137) For she also being a widow, was commanded to sit down in the house of the father, the only Savior; on whose account, having forsaken forever the company and society of men, she is at a distance from and widowhood of all human pleasures, and receives a divine seed; and being filled with the seeds of virtue, she conceives, and is in travail of

virtuous actions. And when she has brought them forth, she carries off the prize against her adversaries, and is enrolled as victorious, bearing the palm as the emblem of her victory. For the name Tamar, being interpreted, means the palm-tree. (138) And every soul that is beginning to be widowed and devoid of evils, says to the prophet, "O, man of God! hast thou come to me to remind me of my iniquity and of my sin?" For he being inspired, and entering into the soul, and being filled with heavenly love, and being amazingly excited by the intolerable stimulus of heaven inflicted frenzy, works in the soul a recollection of its ancient iniquities and offences: not in order that it may commit such again, - but that, greatly lamenting and bitterly bewailing its former error, it may hate its own offspring, and reject them with aversion, and may follow the admonitions of the word of God, the interpreter and prophet of his will. (139) For the men of old used to call the prophets sometimes men of God, and sometimes seers, affixing appropriate and becoming names to their enthusiasm, and inspiration, and to the foreknowledge of affairs which they enjoyed.

Parallels: Genesis 38:11; Luke 01:26-27

On The Unchangeableness of God (155-165)

(155) But we, on whom God pours and showers his fountains of good things from above, we drank from that cistern, and we were seeking scanty moisture beneath the earth, while the heaven was raining upon us, from above without ceasing, the more excellent food of nectar and ambrosia, far better than that celebrated in the fables of the poets. (156) Moreover, should we while draining draughts stored up by the contrivance of men through distrust, seek a refuge and place of escape where the Savior of the universe has opened to us his heavenly treasury for our use and enjoyment? For Moses, the hierophant, prays that "the Lord may open to us his good treasure, his heavenly one, to give us his rain," and the prayers of the man who loves God are sure to obtain a hearing. (157) And what does he say who neither

thinks the heaven, or the rain, or a cistern, or in fact anything whatever in all creation sufficient to nourish him, but who goes beyond all these things, and relating what he has suffered, says, "The God who has nourished me from my youth up." Does not this man appear to you not to think all the collections of water under the earth put together worthy even of looking at? (158) Nor therefore would he drink out of a cistern to whom God gives draughts of unmixed wine; at one time, by the ministrations of some angel whom he has thought worthy to act as cupbearer, and at another time by his own means, placing no one between the giver and the receiver. (159) Let us then, without any delay, attempt to proceed by the royal road, since we think fit to pass by all earthly things; and the royal road is that of which there is not private individual in the world who is master, but he alone who is also the only true king. (160) And this is, as I said a little while ago, wisdom, by which alone suppliant souls can find a way of escaping to the uncreated God; for it is natural that one who goes without any hindrance along the royal road, will never feel weariness before he meets with the king. (161) But, then, those who have come near to him recognize his blessedness and their own deficiency; for Abraham, when he had placed himself very near to God, immediately perceived that he was but dust and ashes. (162) And let them turn away out of the royal road, neither to the right hand nor to the left, but let them advance along the middle of it; for any deviation in either direction is blamable, as that on the one side has a tendency to excess and that on the other side to deficiency; for the right hand is, in this instance, no less blamable than the left hand. (163) In the case of those who live according to impulse, the right hand is temerity and the left hand cowardice. As regards those who are illiberal in the management of money, on the right hand stands stinginess, and on the left hand extravagant prodigality; and those men, who are very subtle in calculating, judge craftiness to be desirable and simplicity to be a thing to be shunned. Again, some persons incline towards superstition as being placed on the right hand, and flee from impiety as a thing to be avoided on the left. (164) But that we may not, through deviating from the right road, be compelled to yield to one of two rival faults, let us desire and pray to be able to proceed straight along the middle of the road. Now, the middle between temerity and cowardice, is courage; the mean between profuse extravagance and illiberal stinginess, is temperance; that between crafty unscrupulousness and folly, is prudence; and the proper path between superstition and impiety, is piety. (165) These lie in the middle between the deviations on either side, and are all roads easily travelled, and level, and plain, which we must walk upon not with our bodily organs, but with the motions of a soul continually desiring what is best.

> Parallels: Genesis 18:27; Numbers 20:17; Deuteronomy 02:27, 05:32, 17:11, 20, 28:12-14; Jeremiah 02:13; Matthew 07:13-14; John 04:04-42
>
> Comparison: Matthew 07:13-14, "Enter by the narrow gate. For the gate is wide, and the way is easy that leads to destruction, and many are those who enter by it. How narrow is the gate and hard the way, that leads to life, and few those who find it!

On The Unchangeableness of God (176)

(176) For the divine Word brings round its operations in a circle, which the common multitude of men call fortune. And then, as it continually flows on among cities, and nations, and countries, it overturns existing arrangements and gives to one person what has previously belonged to another, changing the affairs of individuals only in point of time, in order that the whole world may become, as it were, one city, and enjoy the most excellent of constitutions, a democracy.

> Parallels: Matthew 05:45

On the Virtues (58)

(58) "Let the Lord God of spirits and of all flesh look out for himself a man to be over this multitude, to undertake the care and superintendence of a shepherd, who shall lead them in a blameless manner, in order that this nation may not become corrupt like a flock which is scattered abroad, as having no Shepherd."{Numbers 27:16.}

Parallels: Numbers 27:16-17; Matthew 09:36; Mark 06:34; John 10:11-14

Comparison: Matthew 09:36, "When he saw the crowds, he had compassion for them, because they were harassed and helpless, like sheep without a shepherd."

On the Virtues (117-120)

(117) Also the law proceeds to say, If you see the beast of one who is thy Enemy{Exodus 23:4.} wandering about, leave the excitements to quarrelling to more perverse dispositions, and lead the animal back and restore him to his owner; for so you will not be benefiting him more than yourself; since he will by this means save only an irrational beast which is perhaps of no value, but you will get the greatest and most valuable of all things in nature, namely, excellence. (118) And there will follow of necessity, as sure as shadow follows a body, the dissolution of your enmity; for the man who has received a benefit is willingly induced to make peace for the future as being enslaved by the kindness shown to him; and he who has conferred the benefit, having his own good action for a counselor, is already almost prepared in his mind for a complete reconciliation. (119) And this is an object which the most holy prophet is endeavoring to bring to pass throughout the whole of his code of laws, studying to create unanimity, and fellowship, and agreement, and that due admixture of different dispositions by which houses, and

cities, and altars, and nations, and countries, and the whole human race may be conducted to the very highest happiness. (120) But up to the present time these are only wishes; but they will be hereafter, as I at least persuade myself, most real facts, since God will give a plentiful harvest of virtue, as he does give the harvest of the fruits of the seasons; which we shall never fail to attain to if we cherish a desire for them from our earliest infancy.

Parallels: Exodus 23:04; Matthew 05:39

On the Virtues (156-160)

(156) for he commands the young plants to be nursed carefully for the space of three years, while the husbandman prunes away the superfluous off-shoots, in order that the trees may not be weighed down and exhausted by them, in which case the fruit borne by them would become small and weak through insufficiency of nourishment, and he must also dig round it and clear the ground, in order that no injurious plant may grow near it, so as to hinder its growth. And he does not allow the fruit to be gathered out of season at any one's pleasure, not only because, if that were done, it would be imperfect and produced from imperfect trees (for so also animals which are not perfect themselves cannot produce a perfect offspring), but also because the young plants themselves would be injured, and would in a manner be bowed down and kept as creepers on the earth, by being prevented from shooting up into straight and stout trunks. (157) Accordingly, many husbandmen at the commencement of the spring watch their young trees, in order at once to destroy whatever fruit they show before it gets to any growth or comes to any size, from fear lest, if it be suffered to remain on, it may bring weakness to the parent tree. For it might happen, if someone did not take care beforehand, when the tree ought to bring fruit to perfection, that it will either bear none at all, or not be able to ripen any, being completely weakened by having been allowed to satiate itself with bearing before its proper time, just as old vine stems when weighed down, are exhausted both in

root and trunk. (158) But after three years, when the roots have got some depth and have taken a firmer hold of the soil, and when the trunk, being supported as it were on a firm unbending foundation, brows up with vigor, it is then in the fourth year able to bear fruit in perfection and in proper quantity: (159) and in the fourth year he permits the fruit to be gathered, not for the enjoyment and use of man, but that the whole crop may be dedicated to God as the first-fruits, partly as a thank-offering for mercies already received, and partly from hope of good crops for the future, and of a revenue to be derived from the tree hereafter. (160) You see, therefore, what great humanity and compassion our lawgiver displays, and how he diffuses his kindness over every species of man, even if they are foreigners, or even enemies; and secondly, how he extends it also to brute beasts, even though they be not clean, and in fact to everything, to sown crops, and to trees. For the man who has learnt the principles of humanity with respect to those natures which are devoid of sense, is never likely to err with respect to those which are endowed with life; and he who never attempts to act with severity towards creatures which have only life, is taught a long way off to take great care of those which are also blessed with reason.

Parallels: Leviticus 19:23-25; Luke 13:06-09

On the Virtues (179-184)

(179) And what can this best of all things be except God? Whose honors those men have attributed to beings which are not gods, honoring them beyond all reason and moderation, and, like empty minded people that they are, wholly forgetting him. All those men therefore who, although they did not originally choose to honor the Creator and Father of the universe, have yet changed and done so afterwards, having learnt to prefer to honor a single monarch rather than a number of rulers, we must look upon as our friends and kinsmen, since they display that greatest of all bonds with which to cement friendship and kindred, namely, a pious and God-loving disposition, and we

ought to sympathize in joy with and to congratulate them, since even if they were blind previously they have now received their sight, beholding the most brilliant of all lights instead of the most profound darkness. (180) We have now then described the first and most important of the considerations which belong to repentance. And let a man repent, not only of the errors by which he was for a long time deceived, when he honored the creature in preference to that uncreated being who was himself the Creator of all things, but also in respect of the other necessary and ordinary pursuits and affairs of life, forsaking as it were that very worst of all evil constitutions, the sovereignty of the mob, and adopting that best of all constitutions, a well ordered democracy; that is to say, crossing over from ignorance to a knowledge of those things to be ignorant of which is shameful; from folly to wisdom, from intemperance to temperance, from injustice to righteousness, from cowardice to confident courage. (181) For it is a very excellent and expedient thing to go over to virtue without every looking back again, forsaking that treacherous mistress, vice. And at the same time it is necessary that, as in the sun shadow follows the body, so also a participation in all other virtues must inevitably follow the giving due honor to the living God; (182) for those who come over to this worship become at once prudent, and temperate, and modest, and gentle, and merciful, and humane, and venerable, and just, and magnanimous, and lovers of truth, and superior to all considerations of money or pleasure; just as, on the contrary, one may see that those who forsake the holy laws of God are intemperate, shameless, unjust, disreputable, weak-minded, quarrelsome, companions of falsehood and perjury, willing to sell their liberty for luxurious eating, for strong wine, for sweetmeats, and for beauty, for pleasures of the belly and of the parts below the belly; the miserable end of all which enjoyment is ruin to both body and soul. (183) Moreover, Moses delivers to us very beautiful exhortations to repentance, by which he teaches us to alter our way of life, changing from an irregular and disorderly course into a better line of conduct; for he says that this task is not one of any excessive difficulty, nor one removed far out of our reach, being neither above us in the air nor on the extreme borders of the sea, so that we are unable to take hold of it; but it is near us, abiding, in fact, in three portions of us, namely, in our mouths, and our hearts, and our hands; {Deuteronomy 30:11.} by symbols, that is to say, in our words, and counsels, and actions; for the mouth is the symbol of speech, and the heart of counsels, and the hands of actions, and in these happiness consists. (184) For when such as the words are, such also is the mind; and when such as the counsels are, such likewise are the actions; then life is praiseworthy and perfect. But when these things are all at variance with one another life is imperfect and blamable, unless someone who is at the same time a lover of God and beloved by God takes it in hand and produces this harmony. For which reason this oracular declaration was given with great propriety, and in perfect accordance with what has been said above, {Leviticus 26:12.} "Thou hast this day chosen the Lord to be thy God, and the Lord has this day chosen thee to be his people."

> Parallels: Leviticus 26:01-12; Deuteronomy 30:11-14; Matthew 22:37; Mark 12:28-34; Acts 03:19; Galatians 05:16-26; Ephesians 04:18
>
> Comparison: Mark 12:29-34, "Jesus answered, "The first is: 'Hear, O Israel, the Lord our God is one Lord. And you shall love the Lord your God with all your heart, and with all your soul, and with all your mind, and with all your strength.' The second is this: 'You shall love your neighbor as yourself.' There is no other commandment greater than these." And the scribe said to him, "You are right, Teacher. You have well said that 'He is one, and there is no other but he'; and to 'love him with all the heart, and with all the understanding, and with all the strength', and to 'love one's neighbor as oneself', is much more than all whole burnt offerings and sacrifices." And when Jesus saw [him,] that he answered wisely, he said to him, "You are not far from the kingdom of God." And after that no one dared to ask him any question."

Questions And Answers On Genesis I (4)

(4) What is the man who was created? And how is that man distinguished who was made after the image of God? (Genesis 2:7). This man was created as perceptible to the senses, and in the similitude of a Being appreciable only by the intellect; but he who in respect of his form is intellectual and incorporeal, is the similitude of the archetypal model as to appearance, and he is the form of the principal character; but this is the word of God, the first beginning of all things, the original species or the archetypal idea, the first measure of the universe. Moreover, that man who was to be created as a vessel is formed by a potter, was formed out of dust and clay as far as his body was concerned; but he received his soul by God breathing the breath of life into his face, so that the temperament of his nature was combined of what was corruptible and of what was incorruptible. But the other man, he who is only so in form, is found to be unalloyed without any mixture proceeding from an invisible, simple, and transparent nature.

> Parallels: Genesis 01:26, 02:07, 15; Matthew 22:15-22; Mark 12:13-17; John 01:01-14; Colossians 01:15-18
>
> Comparison: John 01:01-02, "In the beginning was the Word, and the Word was with God, and the Word was God. He was with God in the beginning." Colossians 01:15-16, "He is the image of the invisible God, the firstborn of all creation. For by him all things were created, in heaven and on earth, visible and invisible, whether thrones or dominions or rulers or authorities – all things were created through him and for him."

Questions And Answers On Genesis I (8)

(8) Why did God place man whom he had created in the Paradise, but not that man who is after his own image? (Genesis 2:15). Some persons have said, when they fancied that the Paradise was a garden, that because the man who was created was endowed with senses, therefore he naturally and properly proceeded into a sensible place; but the other man, who is made after God's own image, being appreciable only by the intellect, and invisible, had all the incorporeal species for his share; but I should rather say that the paradise was a symbol of wisdom, for that created man is a kind of mixture, as having been compounded of soul and body, having work to do by learning and discipline; desiring according to the law of philosophy that he may become happy; but he who is according to God's own image is in need of nothing, being by himself a hearer, and being taught by himself, and being found to be his own master by reason of his natural endowments.

> Parallels: Genesis 01:26, 02:07, 15; Matthew 22:15-22; Mark 12:13-17; John 01:01-14

Questions And Answers On Genesis I (27)

(27) Why, as other animals and as man also was made, the woman was not also made out of the earth, but out of the rib of the man? (Genesis 2:21). This was so ordained in the first place, in order that the woman might not be of equal dignity with the man. In the second place, that she might not be of equal age with him, but younger; since those who marry wives more advanced in years than themselves deserve blame, as having overturned the law of nature. Thirdly, the design of God was, that the husband should take care of his wife, as of a necessary part of himself; but that the woman should requite him in turn with service, as a portion of the universe. In the fourth place, he admonishes man by this enigmatical intimation, that he should

take care of his wife as of his daughter; and he admonishes the woman that she should honor her husband as her father. And very rightly, since the woman changes her habitation, passing from her own offspring to her husband. On which account, it is altogether right and proper that he who has received should take upon himself the liability in respect of what has been given; and that she who has been removed should worthily give the same honor to her husband which she has previously given to her parents; for the husband receives his wife from her parents, as a deposit which is entrusted to him; and the woman receives her husband from the law.

Parallels: Genesis 02:21; Ephesians 05:21-33

Questions And Answers On Genesis II (20)

(20) What is the meaning of the expression, "And the water was greatly increased, and bore up the ark which floated upon the water?" {Genesis 7:17}. The literal meaning is plain enough, but it contains an allegorical reference to our bodies, which ought to be borne up as if on the water, and by fluctuating with our necessities to subdue hunger and thirst, cold and heat, by which it is agitated, disturbed, and kept in motion.

Parallels: Genesis 07:17-18, 08:11; Matthew 03:05-16, 04:01-04

Questions And Answers On Genesis II (42)

(42) What is the meaning of the expression, "The dove returned a second time to him about evening, having in her mouth a leaf and a thin branch of olive?" {Genesis 8:11}. All these separate points are selected and approved signs - the returning, the returning about evening, the having an olive-leaf and a thin branch of that tree, and oil, and the having it in her mouth; but yet every one of these signs can be examined with a certainty beyond certainty, for the return is distinct from its previous

return, for that one bore with it an announcement of nature being wholly corrupted and rebellious, and being wholly destroyed by the deluge, that is to say, by great ignorance and insolence; but this second return brings the news of the world beginning to repent, but to find repentance is not an easy task, but is a difficult and laborious business. And it is on this account that the dove arrived in the evening, having passed the whole day from morning to evening in its visitations; in word, indeed, examining places, but in fact investigating the different parts of nature itself by continual visitation, and seeing them all clearly from beginning to end, for the evening is the indication of the end. The third sign, again, is its bringing a leaf; but a leaf is a small part of a tree, still it does not exist without a tree. And the beginning of displaying repentance is somewhat corresponding to this, since the beginning of correction has some slight indications about it, which we may call a leaf, by which it appears to receive guardianship, but can easily be shaken off; so that the hope shall in that case not be great of attaining the desired improvement, which is typified by the leaf of no other tree but of the olive alone, and oil is the material of light. For wickedness, as I have said before, is profound darkness, but virtue is luminous brilliancy, and repentance is the beginning of light. But you must not yet suppose that the beginning of repentance is only visible in branches just germinating and beginning to look green, but that it exists too while they are still dry, and while the seminal principle is dry and quiescent. And it is on this account that the fifth sign is shown, that, namely, of the dove when it comes bearing a slender branch. And the sixth sign is that this slender branch was in its mouth, for the number six is the first perfect number, since virtue bears in its mouth, that is to say in its conversation, the seeds of wisdom and justice, or, in one word, of honesty of the soul; and not only bears this, but gives some portion of participation in it even to the foolish, by drawing up water for their souls, and irrigating them with the desire of repentance for their sins.

Parallels: Genesis 07:17-18, 08:11; Matthew 03:01-17; Luke 03:01-18; Acts 03:19

Questions And Answers On Genesis II (62)

(62) Why is it that he speaks as if of some other god, saying that he made man after the image of God, and not that he made him after his own image? (Genesis 9:6). Very appropriately and without any falsehood was this oracular sentence uttered by God, for no mortal thing could have been formed on the similitude of the supreme Father of the universe, but only after the pattern of the second deity, who is the Word of the supreme Being; since it is fitting that the rational soul of man should bear it the type of the divine Word; since in his first Word God is superior to the most rational possible nature. But he who is superior to the Word holds his rank in a better and most singular pre-eminence, and how could the creature possibly exhibit a likeness of him in himself? Nevertheless he also wished to intimate this fact, that God does rightly and correctly require vengeance, in order to the defense of virtuous and consistent men, because such bear in themselves a familiar acquaintance with his Word, of which the human mind is the similitude and form.

> Parallels: Genesis 01:26, 09:06; Luke 01:26-38; John 01:01-18; Colossians 01:15-18; Philippians 02:06-11
>
> Comparison: John 01:01-02, "In the beginning was the Word, and the Word was with God, and the Word was God. He was with God in the beginning." Colossians 01:15-16, "He is the image of the invisible God, the firstborn of all creation. For by him all things were created, in heaven and on earth, visible and invisible, whether thrones or dominions or rulers or authorities – all things were created through him and for him."

Questions And Answers On Genesis III (10)

(10) Why was it said to him, "Thou shall know to a certainty that thy seed shall be a stranger in a land that is not theirs, and shall be reduced to slavery, and shall be grievously afflicted for four hundred years?" {Genesis 15:13}. That expression is admirably used, "It was said to him," since a prophet is supposed to utter something, but yet he is not pronouncing any command of his own, but is only the interpreter of another who sends something into his mind; and moreover whatever he does utter and deliver in words is all true and divine. And in the first place, he declares that a family of the human race is to dwell in a land belonging to another; for all things which are beneath the heaven are the possession of God, and those living creatures which exist on the earth may more properly and truly be said to be sojourners in a foreign land than to be dwelling in a country of their own which by nature they have not got. In the second place, he thus declares to us that every mortal is a slave after his kind. But no man is found to be free, but everyone has many masters who vex and afflict him both within and without; for instance, without there are the winter which affects him with the cold, the summer which scorches him with heat, and hunger, and thirst, and many other calamities; and within there are pleasures and concupiscences, and sorrows, and fears. But his servitude is limited to a period of four hundred years, during which the aforesaid pleasures shall rise up against him. On which account it has been said above, that Abraham passed over and sat upon them, hindering and repelling them; as far as the literal words go, repelling those carnivorous birds which were hovering over the divided animals, but in fact repelling the afflictions which come upon men. Since a man who is in his own proper nature a lover of, and also by diligent practice a studier of virtue, is a most humane physician of our race, and a true protector of it, and guardian of it from evil. For all these things have an allegorical reference to the soul. For while the soul of the wise man, descending from above from the sky, comes down upon and enters a mortal and is sown in the field of the body, it is

truly sojourning in a land which is not his own. Since the earthly nature of the body is wholly alien from pure intellect, and tends to subdue it and to drag it downwards into slavery, bringing every kind of affliction upon it, until the sorrow, bringing the attractive multitude of vices to judgment, condemns them; and thus at last the soul is restored to freedom. And it is on this account that he subsequently adds the sentence, "Nevertheless the nation which they shall send I will judge: and afterwards they shall go forth with great substance;" namely, with the same measure, and still better. Because then the mind is released from its mischievous colleague, departing out of the body and being transferred not only with freedom but also with much substance; so as to leave nothing good or useful behind to its enemies. Since every rational soul is productive, but he who thinks himself loaded and endued with virtue in his own counsel, is unable to preserve his fruit unto the end. For it becomes a virtuous man to attain to the objects which he has intended of his own accord, as also the counsels of wisdom correspond to those objects. Since, as some trees, although they appear productive at the first season of the budding of their fruits, are yet unable to bring them to maturity, so that the whole fruit before it becomes ripe is shaken off by every trifling cause; in the same manner the souls of inconstant men feel many influences which contribute to their productiveness, but nevertheless are unable to keep them sound till they arrive at perfection, as a man studious of virtue ought to do in order eventually to gather them as his own possessions.

Parallels: Genesis 15:13; Matthew 13:03-43; Luke 08:05-15

Questions And Answers On Genesis III (15)

(15) What is the meaning of the expression, "Behold there was a smoking furnace and torches of fires, which passed through the middle of those divisions?" (Genesis 15:18). The literal meaning of the statement is plain, for the fountain or root of the divine word will have the victims consumed, not by that fire which is given for our use, but by that which descends from above, out of

heaven, in order that the purity of the essence of heaven may bear witness to the sanctity of the victims. But if we regard the inward meaning of the words, all things which are done beneath the moon are here compared to a smoking furnace, on account of the vapor which rises up out of the earth and water. As also the divisions of nature are, as has been already shown, every portion of the world being divided into two parts; and by these there are kindled, as it were, torches of fire, being powers which are more rapid in motion and more efficacious, being burning, in truth, like divine fiery discourses, at one time keeping the whole universe in a state of integrity reciprocally with themselves, and at another cleansing away the superfluous darkness. But the following interpretation may also be given with propriety in a more familiar manner. Human life is like unto a smoking furnace, because it has not a pure fire and an unalloyed brilliancy, but a great deal of smoke, smoking darkly through the flame, which causes mist and darkness, and an obscuration, not of the body but of the soul, so that this last cannot discern things clearly, until God the redeemer commands the heavenly lamps to arise, I mean those more pure and more holy radiations which unite those parts previously divided in two, on the right hand and on the left, and, at the same time, illuminate them, being the causes of harmony and of lucid clearness.

Parallels: Genesis 15:09-20; Matthew 03:11-12; 1Corinthians 03:10-15; 1Peter 01:07

Special Laws I (6)

(6) Thirdly, there is the resemblance of the part that is circumcised to the heart; for both parts are prepared for the sake of generation; for the breath contained within the heart is generative of thoughts, and the generative organ itself is productive of living beings. Therefore, the men of old thought it right to make the evident and visible organ, by which the objects of the outward senses are generated, resemble that invisible and superior part, by means of which ideas are formed.

Parallels: Acts 07:51

Special Laws I (31)

(31) And it is said in the scriptures that, "Those that are attached to the living God do all Live."{Deuteronomy 4:4.} Is not this, then, a thrice happy life, a thrice blessed existence, to be contented with performing due service to the most venerable Cause of all things, and not to think fit to serve his subordinate ministers and door-keepers in preference to the King himself? And this life is an immortal one, and is recorded as one of great duration in the pillars of nature. And it is inevitably necessary that these writings should last to all eternity with the world itself.

Parallels: Deuteronomy 04:04; Mark 12:27

Special Laws I (43-44)

(43) But God replied, "I receive, indeed, your eagerness, inasmuch as it is praiseworthy; but the request which you make is not fitting to be granted to any created being. And I only bestow such gifts as are appropriate to him who receives them; for it is not possible for a man to receive all that it is easy for me to give. On which account I give to him who is deserving of my

favor all the gifts which he is able to receive. (44) But not only is the nature of mankind, but even the whole heaven and the whole world is unable to attain to an adequate comprehension of me. So know yourself, and be not carried away with impulses and desires beyond your power; and let not a desire of unattainable objects carry you away and keep you in suspense. For you shall not lack anything which may be possessed by you."

Parallels: Matthew 06:28-33

Special Laws I (52)

(52) Accordingly, having given equal rank and honor to all those who come over, and having granted to them the same favors that were bestowed on the native Jews, he recommends those who are ennobled by truth not only to treat them with respect, but even with especial friendship and excessive benevolence. And is not this a reasonable recommendation? What he says is this. "Those men, who have left their country, and their friends, and their relations for the sake of virtue and holiness, ought not to be left destitute of some other cities, and houses, and friends, but there ought to be places of refuge always ready for those who come over to religion; for the most effectual allurement and the most indissoluble bond of affectionate good will is the mutual honoring of the one God."

Parallels: Leviticus 19:34; Matthew 19:29; Luke 14:26

Special Laws I (63-64)

(63) For he thinks it right, that the man who is legally enrolled as a citizen of his constitution must be perfect, not indeed in those things in which the multitude is educated, such as divination, and augury, and plausible conjectures, but in the observances due to God, which have nothing doubtful or uncertain about them, but only indubitable and naked truth. (64) And since there is implanted in all men a desire of the knowledge of future

events, and as, on account of this desire, they have recourse to sacrifices and to other species of divination, as if by these means they would be able to search out and discover the truth (but these things are, in reality, full of indistinctness and uncertainty, and are continually being convicted by themselves). He, with great energy, forbids his disciples to apply themselves to such sources of knowledge; and he says, that if they are truly pious they shall not be deprived of a proper knowledge of the future.

Parallels: Deuteronomy 18:18; Matthew 13:11

Special Laws I (65)

(65) but that some other Prophet will appear to them on a sudden, inspired like himself, who will preach and prophesy among them, saying nothing of his own (for he who is truly possessed and inspired, even when he speaks, is unable to comprehend what he is himself saying), but that all the words that he should utter would proceed from him as if another was prompting him; for the prophets are interpreters of God, who is only using their voices as instruments, in order to explain what he chooses. Having now then said this, and other things like this, concerning the proper idea to be entertained of the one real, and true, and living God; he proceeds to express in what manner one ought to pay him the honors that are his due.

Parallels: Deuteronomy 18:18; John 05:19-30, 14:10-17

Special Laws I (81)

(81) For if it was necessary to examine the mortal body of the priest that it ought not be imperfect through any misfortune, much more was it necessary to look into his immortal soul, which they say is fashioned in the form of the living God. Now the image of God is the Word, by which all the world was made.

Parallels: Exodus 28:04-42; Leviticus 09:07-14; Psalms 33:06; John 01:01-14; Hebrews 07:26-28

Special Laws I (97)

(97) There is also a third symbol contained in this sacred dress, which it is important not to pass over in silence. For the priests of other deities are accustomed to offer up prayers and sacrifices solely for their own relations, and friends, and fellow citizens. But the high priest of the Jews offers them up not only on behalf of the whole race of mankind, but also on behalf of the different parts of nature, of the earth, of water, of air, and of fire; and pours forth his prayers and thanksgivings for them all, looking upon the world (as indeed it really is) as his country, for which, therefore, he is accustomed to implore and propitiate its governor by supplications and prayers, beseeching him to give a portion of his own merciful and humane nature to the things which he has created.

Parallels: Exodus 28:04-42; Leviticus 09:07-14; Psalms 33:06; Matthew 05:44; Hebrews 07:26-28

Special Laws I (102)

(102) For God does not allow him even to look upon a harlot, or a profane body or soul, or upon any one who, having put away her pursuit of gain, now wears an elegant and modest appearance, because such a one is unholy in respect of her former profession and way of life; though in other respects she may be looked upon as honorable, by reason of her having purified herself of her former evil courses. For repentance for past sins is a thing to be praised; and no one else need be forbidden to marry her, only let her not come near a priest. For the especial property of the priesthood is justice and purity, which from the first beginning of its creation to the end, seeks a concord utterly irreproachable.

Parallels: Deuteronomy 23:17-18; Luke 07:36-48

Special Laws I (110)

(110) And besides these commands, he also defined precisely the family of the women who might be married by the high priest, commanding him to marry not merely a woman who was a virgin, but also one who was a priestess, the daughter of a priest, that so both bridegroom and bride might be of one house, and in a manner of one blood, so as to display a most lasting harmony and union of disposition during the whole of their lives.

Parallels: Leviticus 21:13-14; Luke 01:26-27; John 03:29

Special Laws I (141-142)

(141) After this he also appointed another source of revenue of no insignificant importance for the priests, bidding them to take the first fruits of every one of the revenues of the nation namely, the first fruits of the corn, and wine, and oil, and even of the produce of all the cattle, of the flocks of sheep, and herds of oxen, and flocks of goats, and of all other animals of all kinds; and how great an abundance of these animals there must be, any one may conjecture from the vast populousness of the nation; (142) from all which circumstances it is plain that the law invests the priests with the dignity and honor that belongs to kings; since he commands contributions from every description of possession to be given to them as to rulers.

Parallels: Leviticus 27:30-33; Numbers 35:02-08; 1Peter 02:09

Special Laws I (156)

(156) Having given all these supplies and revenues to the priests, he did not neglect those either who were in the second rank of the priesthood; and these are the keepers of the temple, of whom

some are placed at the doors, at the very entrance of the temple, as door-keepers; and others are within, in the vestibule of the temple, in order that no one who ought not to do so might enter it, either deliberately or by accident. Others, again, stand all around, having had the times of their watches assigned to them by lot, so as to watch by turns night and day, some being day watchmen and others night watchmen. Others, again, had charge of the porticoes and of the courts in the open air, and carried out all the rubbish, taking care of the cleanliness of the temple, and the tenths were assigned as the wages of all these men; for these tenths are the share of the keepers of the temple.

Parallels: 1Chronicles 15:24-25; 2Chronicles 23:04, 34:09; Psalms 84:10, 141:03; Matthew 24:42-51

Special Laws I (162)

(162) Or the creatures which are fit to be offered as sacrifices, some are land animals, and some are such as fly through the air. Passing over, therefore, the infinite varieties of birds, God chose only two classes out of them all, the turtledove and the pigeon; because the pigeon is by nature the most gentle of all those birds which are domesticated and gregarious, and the turtle-dove the most gentle of those which love solitude.

Parallels: Leviticus 01:14; Luke 02:22-24

Special Laws I (166-167)

(166) And the victims must be whole and entire, without any blemish on any part of their bodies, unmutilated, perfect in every part, and without spot or defect of any kind. At all events, so great is the caution used with respect not only to those who offer the sacrifices, but also to the victims which are offered, that the most eminent of the priests are carefully selected to examine whether they have any blemishes or not, and scrutinize them from head to foot, inspecting not only those parts which are

easily visible, but all those which are more out of sight, such as the belly and the thighs, lest any slight imperfection should escape notice. (167) And the accuracy and minuteness of the investigation is directed not so much on account of the victims themselves, as in order that those who offer them should be irreproachable; for God designed to teach the Jews by these figures, whenever they went up to the altars, when there to pray or to give thanks, never to bring with them any weakness or evil passion in their soul, but to endeavor to make it wholly and entirely bright and clean, without any blemish, so that God might not turn away with aversion from the sight of it.

> Parallels: Exodus 12:05, 29:01; Leviticus 01:03-10, 03:01-06, 04:03-32, 05:15-18, 06:06, 09:02-03, 14:10, 22:19, 23:12-18; Numbers 06:16, 28:19, 29:02, 08, 13-36; Romans 12:01; Hebrews 10:01

Special Laws I (201-204)

(201) And since the elements of which our soul consists are two in number, the rational and the irrational part, the rational part belongs to the male sex, being the inheritance of intellect and reason; but the irrational part belongs to the sex of woman, which is the lot also of the outward senses. And the mind is in every respect superior to the outward sense, as the man is to the woman; who, when he is without blemish and purified with the proper purifications, namely, the perfect virtues, is himself the most holy sacrifice, being wholly and in all respects pleasing to God. (202) Again, the hands which are laid upon the head of the victim are a most manifest symbol of irreproachable actions, and of a life which does nothing which is open to accusation, but which in all respects is passed in a manner consistent with the laws and ordinances of nature; (203) for the law, in the first place, desires that the mind of the man who is offering the sacrifice shall be made holy by being exercised in good and advantageous doctrines; and, in the second place, that his life shall consist of most virtuous actions, so that, in conjunction

with the imposition of hands, the man may speak freely out of his cleanly conscience, and may say, (204) "These hands have never received any gift as a bribe to commit an unjust action, nor any division of what has been obtained by rapine or by covetousness, nor have they shed innocent blood. nor have they wrought mutilation, nor works of insolence, nor acts of violence, nor have they inflicted any wounds; nor, in fact, have they performed any action whatever which is liable to accusation or to reproach, but have been ministers in everything which is honorable and advantageous, and which is honored by wisdom, or by the laws, or by honorable and virtuous men."

Parallels: Leviticus 01:04; Acts 08:18

Special Laws I (207)

(207) And by the command that the feet of the victim should be washed, it is figuratively shown that we must no longer walk upon the earth, but soar aloft and traverse the air. For the soul of the man who is devoted to God, being eager for truth, springs upward and mounts from earth to heaven; and, being borne on wings, traverses the expanse of the air, being eager to be classed with and to move in concert with the sun, and moon, and all the rest of the most sacred and most harmonious company of the stars, under the immediate command and government of God, who has a kingly authority without any rival, and of which he can never be deprived, in accordance with which he justly governs the universe.

Parallels: Exodus 29:17; John 13:05-14; 1Thessalonians 04:16-17

Special Laws I (210-211)

(210) and we must speak in the same way of other matters. When you wish to give thanks to God with your mind, and to assert your gratitude for the creation of the world, give him thanks for the creation of it as a whole, and of all its separate

parts in their integrity, as if for the limbs of a most perfect animal; and by the parts I mean, for instance, the heaven, and the sun, and the moon, and the fixed stars; and secondly the earth, and the animals, and plants which spring from it; and next the seas and rivers, whether naturally springing from the ground or swollen by rain as winter torrents, and all the things in them: and lastly, the air and all the changes that take place in it; for winter, and summer, and spring, and autumn, being the seasons of the year, and being all of great service to mankind, are what we may call affections of the air for the preservation of all these things that are beneath the moon. (211) And if ever you give thanks for men and their fortunes, do not do so only for the race taken generally, but you shall give thanks also for the species and most important parts of the race, such as men and women, Greeks and barbarians, men on the continent, and those who have their habitation in the islands; and if you are giving thanks for one individual, do not divide your thankfulness in expression into gratitude for minute trifles and inconsiderable matters, but take in your view the most comprehensive circumstances, first of all, his body and his soul, of which he consists, and then his speech, and his mind, and his outward senses; for such gratitude cannot of itself be unworthy of being listened to by God, when uttered, for each of these particulars.

Parallels: Leviticus 09:07; Matthew 05:44

Special Laws I (235-237)

(235) And after having put forth these and similar enactments with reference to sins committed unintentionally, he proceeds to lay down rules respecting intentional offences. "If anyone," says the law, "shall speak falsely concerning a partnership, or about a deposit, or about a theft, or about the finding of something which another has lost, and being suspected and having had an oath proposed to him, shall swear, and when he appears to have escaped all conviction at the hands of this accusers, shall himself become his own accuser, being convicted by his own conscience

residing within, and shall reproach himself for the things which he has denied, and as to which he has sworn falsely, and shall come and openly confess the sin which he has committed, and implore pardon; (236) then pardon shall be given to such a man, who shows the truth of his repentance, not by promises but by works, by restoring the deposit which he has received, and by giving up the things which he has stolen or found, or of which in short he has in any way deprived his neighbor, paying also in addition one fifth of the value, as an atonement for the evil which he had done." (237) And then, after he has appeased the man who had been injured, the law proceeds to say, "After this let him go also into the temple, to implore remission of the sins which he has committed, taking with him an irreproachable mediator, namely, that conviction of the soul which has delivered him from his incurable calamity, curing him of the disease which would cause death, and wholly changing and bringing him to good health." And it orders that he should sacrifice a ram, and this victim is expressly mentioned, as it is in the case of the man who has offended in respect of the holy things;

Parallels: Leviticus 06:01-07; Acts 03:19

Special Laws I (244)

(244) But the sacrifices offered up for the sins of the high priest, or for those of the whole nation, are not prepared to be eaten at all, but are burnt to ashes, and the ashes are sacred as has been said; for there is no one who is superior to the high priest or to the whole nation, or who can as such be an intercessor for them, as to the sins which they have committed.

Parallels: Leviticus 09:07-22; Hebrews 07:26-28

Special Laws I (245-246)

(245) Very naturally, therefore, is the meat of this sacrifice ordered to be consumed by fire, in imitation of the whole burnt offerings, and this to the honor of those who offer it; not because the sacred judgments of God are given with reference to the rank of those who come before his tribunal, but because the offences committed by men of pre-eminent virtue and real holiness are accounted of a character nearly akin to the good actions of others; (246) for as a deep and fertile soil, even if it at times yields a bad crop, still bears more and better fruit than one which is naturally unproductive, so in the same manner it happens that the barrenness of virtuous and God-fearing men is more full of excellence than the best actions which ordinary people perform by chance; for these men cannot intentionally endure to do anything blamable.

Parallels: Leviticus 06:09-11, 09:07-24; Matthew 07:16-21

Special Laws I (247-272)

(247) Having given these commandments about every description of sacrifice in its turn, namely, about the burnt offering, and the sacrifice for preservation, and the sin-offering, he adds another kind of offering common to all the three, in order to show that they are friendly and connected with one another; and this combination of them all is called the great vow; (248) and why it received this appellation we must now proceed to say. When any persons offer first fruits from any portion of their possessions, wheat, or barley, or oil, or wine, or the best of their fruits, or the firstborn males of their flocks and herds, they do so actually dedicating those first fruits which proceed from what is clean, but paying a price as the value of what is unclean; and when they have no longer any materials left in which they can display their piety, they then consecrate and offer up themselves, displaying an unspeakable holiness, and a most superabundant excess of a God-loving disposition, on which account such a dedication is fitly called the great vow; for every

man is his own greatest and most valuable possession, and this even he now gives up and abandons. (249) And when a man has vowed this vow the law gives him the following command; first of all, to touch no unmixed wine, nor any wine that is made of the grape, nor to drink any other strong drink whatever, to the destruction of his reason, considering that during this period his reason also is dedicated to God; for all which could tend to drunkenness is forbidden to those of the priests who are employed in the sacred ministrations, they being commanded to quench their thirst with water; (250) in the second place they are commanded not to show their heads, giving thus a visible sign to all who see them that they are not debasing the pure coinage of their vow; thirdly, they are commanded to keep their body pure and undefiled, so as not even to approach their parents if they are dead, nor their brothers; piety overcoming the natural good will and affection towards their relations and dearest friends, and it is both honorable and expedient that piety should at all times prevail. (251) But when the appointed time for their being Released{Numbers 6:14.} from this vow has arrived, the law then commands the man who has dedicated himself to bring three animals to procure his release from his vow, a male lamb, and a female lamb, and a ram; the one for a burnt offering, the second for a sin-offering, and the ram as a sacrifice for preservation; (252) for in some sense the man who has made such a vow resembles all these things. He resembles the sacrifice of the entire burnt offering, because he is dedicating to his preserver not only a portion of the first fruits of other things, but also of his own self. And he resembles the sin-offering, inasmuch as he is a man; for there is no one born, however perfect he may be, who can wholly avoid the commission of sin. He resembles also the offering for preservation, inasmuch as he has recorded that God the Savior is the cause of his preservation, and does not ascribe it to any physician or to any power of his; for those who have been born themselves, and who are liable to infirmity, are not competent to bestow health even on themselves. Medicine does not benefit all persons, nor does it always benefit the same persons; but there are times even when it does them great injury, since its power depends on different things, both on the thing itself and also on those persons who use it. (253) And a great impression is made on me by the fact that of three animals offered up in these different sacrifices, there is no one of a different species from the others, but they are every one of the same kind, a ram, and a male lamb, and a female lamb; for God wishes, as I said a little while ago, by this commandment to point out that the three kinds of sacrifice are nearly connected with and akin to one another; because, both the man who repents is saved, and the man who is saved from the diseases of the soul repents, and because both of them hasten with eagerness to attain to an entire and perfect disposition, of which the sacrifice of the whole burnt-offering is a symbol. (254) But since the man has begun to offer himself as his first fruits, and since it is not lawful for the sacred altar to be polluted with human blood, but yet it was by all means necessary that a portion should be consecrated, he has taken care to take a portion, which, being taken, should cause neither pain nor defilement; for he has cut off {Numbers 6:18.} the hair of the head, the superfluities of the natural body, as if they were the superfluous branches of a tree, and he has committed them to the fire on which the meat of the sacrifice offered for preservation will be suitably prepared, in order that some portion of the man who has made the vow, which it is not lawful to place upon the altar, may still at all events be combined with the sacrifice, burning the fuel of the sacred flame. (255) These sacred fires are common to all the rest of the people. But it was fitting that the priests also should offer up something on the altar as first fruits, not thinking that the services and sacred ministrations to which they have been appointed have secured them an exemption from such duties. And the first fruits suitable for the priests to offer do not come from anything containing blood, but from the purest portion of human food; (256) for the fine wheaten flour is their continual offering; a tenth part of a sacred measure every day; one half of which is offered up in the morning, and one half in the evening, having been soaked in oil, so that no portion of it can be left for food; for the command of God is, that all the sacrifices of the priests shall be wholly burnt, and that no portion of them shall be allotted for food. Having now, then, to the best of our ability, discussed the matters relating to the sacrifices, we will proceed in due order to speak concerning those who offer them. (257) The law chooses that a person who brings a sacrifice shall be pure, both in body and soul; --pure in soul from all passions, and diseases, and vices, which can be displayed either in word or deed; and pure in body from all such things as a body is usually defiled by. (258) And it has appointed a burning purification for both these things; for the soul, by means of the animals which are duly fit for sacrifices; and for the body, by ablutions and sprinklings; concerning which we will speak presently; for it is fit to assign the pre-eminence in honor in every point to the superior and dominant part of the qualities existing in us, namely, to the soul. (259) What, then, is the mode of purifying the soul? "Look," says the law, "take care that the victim which thou brings to the altar is perfect, wholly without participation in any kind of blemish, selected from many on account of its excellence, by the uncorrupted judgments of the priests, and by their most acute sight, and by their continual practice derived from being exercised in the examination of faultless victims. For if you do not see this with your eyes more than with your reason, you will not wash off all the imperfections and stains which you have imprinted on your whole life, partly in consequence of unexpected events, and partly by deliberate purpose; (260) for you will find that this exceeding accuracy of investigation into the animals, figuratively signifies the amelioration of your own disposition and conduct; for the law was not established for the sake of irrational animals, but for that of those who have intellect and reason." So that the real object taken care of is not the condition of the victims sacrificed in order that they may have no blemish, but that of the sacrificers that they may not be defiled by any unlawful passion. (261) The body then, as I have already said, he purifies with ablutions and sprinklings, and does not allow a person after he has once washed and sprinkled himself, at once to enter within the sacred precincts, but bids him wait outside for seven days, and to be besprinkled twice, on the third day and on the seventh day; and after this it commands him to wash himself once more, and then it admits him to enter the sacred precincts and to share in the sacred ministrations. (262) We must consider what great prudence and philosophical wisdom is displayed in this law; for nearly all other persons are besprinkled with pure water, generally in the sea, some in rivers, and others again in vessels of water which they draw from fountains. But Moses, having previously prepared ashes which had been left from the sacred fire (and in what manner shall be explained hereafter), appointed that it should be right to take some of them and to put them in a vessel, and then to pour water upon them, and then, dipping some branches of hyssop in the mixture of ashes and water, to sprinkle it over those who were to be purified. (263) And the cause of this proceeding may very probably be said to be this:--The lawgiver's intention is that those who approach the service of the living God should first of all know themselves and their own essence. For how can the man who does not know himself ever comprehend the supreme and all-excelling power of God? (264) Therefore, our bodily essence is earth and water, of which he reminds us by this purification, conceiving that this result--namely, to know one's self, and to know also of what one is composed, of what utterly valueless substances mere ashes and water are--is of itself the most beneficial purification. (265) For when a man is aware of this he will at once reject all vain and treacherous conceit, and, discarding haughtiness and pride, he will seek to become pleasing to God, and to conciliate the merciful power of that Being who hates arrogance. For it is said somewhere with great beauty, "He that exhibits over proud words or actions offends not men alone but God also, the maker of equality and of everything else that is most excellent." (266) Therefore, to us who are amazed and excited by this sprinkling the very elements themselves, earth and water, may almost be said to utter distinct words, and to say plainly, we are the essence of your bodies; nature having mixed us together, divine art has fashioned us into the figure of a man. Being made of us when you were born, you will again be dissolved into us when you come to die; for it is not the nature of anything to be destroyed so as to become non-existent; but the end brings it back to those elements from which its beginnings come. (267) But now it is necessary to fulfill our promise and to explain the peculiar propriety involved in this use of ashes. For they are not merely the ashes of wood which has been consumed by fire, but also of an animal particularly suited for this kind of purification. (268) For the law Orders {Numbers 19:1.} that a red heifer, which has never been brought under the yoke, shall be sacrificed outside of the city, and that the high priest, taking some of the blood, shall seven times sprinkle with it all the things in front of the temple, and then shall burn the whole animal, with its hide and flesh, and with the belly full of all the entrails. And when the flame begins to pour down, then it commands that these three things shall be thrown into the middle of it, a stick of cedar, a stick of hyssop, and a bunch of saffron; and then, when the fire is wholly extinguished, it commands that some man who is clean shall collect the ashes, and shall again place them outside of the city in some open place. (269) And what figurative meanings he conceals under these orders as symbols, we have accurately explained in another treatise, in which we have discussed the allegories. It is necessary, therefore, for those who are about to go into the temple to partake of the sacrifice, to be cleansed as to their bodies and as to their souls before their bodies. For the soul is the mistress and the queen, and is superior in everything, as having received a more divine nature. And the things which cleanse the mind are wisdom and the doctrines of wisdom, which lead to the contemplation of the world and the things in it; and the sacred chorus of the rest of the virtues, and honorable and very praiseworthy actions in accordance with the virtues. (270) Let the man, therefore, who is adorned with these qualities go forth in cheerful confidence to the temple which most nearly belongs to him, the most excellent of all abodes to offer himself as a sacrifice. But let him in whom covetousness and a desire of unjust things dwell and display themselves, cover his head and be silent, checking his shameless folly and his excessive impudence, in those matters in which caution is profitable; for the temple of the truly living God may not be approached by unholy sacrifices. (271) I should say to such a man: My good man, God is not pleased even though a man bring hecatombs to his altar; for he possesses all things as his own, and stands in need of nothing. But he delights in minds which love God, and in men who practice holiness, from whom he gladly receives cakes and barley, and the very cheapest things, as if they were the most valuable in preference to such as are most costly. (272) And even if they bring nothing else, still when they bring themselves, the most perfect completeness of virtue and excellence, they are offering the most excellent of all sacrifices, honoring God, their Benefactor and Savior, with hymns and thanksgivings; the former uttered by the organs of the voice, and the latter without the agency of the tongue or mouth, the worshippers making their exclamations and invocations with their soul alone, and only appreciable by the intellect, and there is but one ear, namely, that of the Deity which hears them. For the hearing of men does not extend so far as to be sensible of them.

> Parallels: Numbers 06:13-21, 19:01-02; Matthew 08:22; Mark 12:33, 41-44; Luke 01:15, 09:60, 21:01-04

Special Laws I (275-279)

(275) from which it is plain that God looks upon even the smallest offering of frankincense by a holy man as more valuable than ten thousand beasts which may be sacrificed by one who is not thoroughly virtuous. For in proportion, I imagine, as gold is more valuable than stones, and as the things within the inner temple are more holy than those without, in the same proportion is the gratitude displayed by offerings of incense superior to that displayed by the sacrifice of victims full of blood, (276) on which account the altar of incense is honored not only in the costliness of its materials, and in the manner of its erection, and in its situation, but also in the fact that it ministers every day before anything else to the thanksgivings to be paid to God. For the law does not permit the priest to offer the sacrifice of the whole burnt offering outside before he has offered incense within at the earliest Dawn.{Exodus 30:8.} (277) And this command is a symbol of nothing else but of the fact that in the eyes of God it is not the number of things sacrificed that is accounted valuable,

but the purity of the rational spirit of the sacrificer. Unless, indeed, one can suppose that a judge who is anxious to pronounce a holy judgment will never receive gifts from any of those whose conduct comes before his tribunal, or that, if he does receive such presents, he will be liable to an accusation of corruption; and that a good man will not receive gifts from a wicked person, not even though he may be poor and the other rich, and he himself perhaps in actual want of what he would so receive; and yet that God can be corrupted by bribes, who is most all-sufficient for himself and who has no need of anything created; who, being himself the first and most perfect good thing, the everlasting fountain of wisdom, and justice, and of every virtue, rejects the gifts of the wicked. (278) And is not the man who would offer such gifts the most shameless of all men, if he offers a portion of the things which he has acquired by doing injury, or by rapine, or by false denial, or by robbery, to God as if he were a partner in his wickedness? O most miserable of all men! I should say to such a man, "You must be expecting one of two things. Either that you will be able to pass undetected, or that you will be discovered. (279) Therefore, if you expect to be able to pass undetected, you are ignorant of the power of God, by which he at the same time sees everything and hears everything. And if you think that you will be discovered, you are most audacious in (when you ought rather to endeavor to conceal the wicked actions which you have committed) bringing forward to light specimens of all your iniquitous deeds, and giving yourself airs, and dividing the fruits of them with God, bringing him unholy first fruits. And have you not considered this, that the law does not admit of lawlessness, nor does the light of the sun admit of darkness; but God is the archetypal model of all laws, and the sun, which can be appreciated only by the intellect, is the archetypal model of that which is visible to the senses, bringing forth from its invisible fountains visible light to afford to him who sees." Moreover, there are other commandments relating to the Altar.

Parallels: Exodus 30:08-09; Mark 12:41-44; Luke 21:01-04

Special Laws I (282)

(282) Very often in truth time has put an end to the occupation of a harlot, since, when women have outlived their beauty, no one any longer approaches them, their prime having withered away like that of some flowers; and what length of time can ever transform the harlotry of the soul which from its youth has been trained in early and habitual incontinence, so as to bring it over to good order? No time could do this, but God alone, to whom all things are possible, even those which among us are impossible.

Parallels: Deuteronomy 23:17-18; Matthew 19:26; Mark 10:27; Luke 07:36-48, 18:27

Comparison: Mark 10:27, "Jesus looked at them and said, "With men it is impossible, but not with God; for all things are possible with God.""

Special Laws I (293)

(293) And leaven is forbidden on account of the rising which it causes; this prohibition again having a figurative meaning, intimating that no one who comes to the altar ought at all to allow himself to be elated, being puffed up by insolence; but that such persons may keep their eyes fixed on the greatness of God, and so obtain a proper conception of the weakness of all created beings, even if they be very prosperous; and that so cherishing correct notions they may correct the arrogant loftiness of their minds, and discard all treacherous self-conceit.

Parallels: Leviticus 02:11; Matthew 16:06-12; Mark 08:15

Special Laws I (295)

(295) For, my fine fellow, you came naked into the world, and you shall leave it again naked, having received the interval between your birth and death as a loan from God; during which what ought you to do rather than take care to live in communion and harmony with your fellow creatures, studying equality, and humanity, and virtue, repudiating unequal, and unjust, and irreconcilable unsociable wickedness, which makes that animal which is by nature the most gentle of all, namely, man, a cruel and intractable monster?

Parallels: Leviticus 02:11; 1Timothy 06:07

Special Laws I (332)

(332) These are they who are symbolically called by the law the sons of a harlot. For as mothers who are harlots do not know who is the real father of their children, and cannot register him accurately, but have many, or I might almost say all men, their lovers and associates, the same is the case with those who are ignorant of the one true God. For, inventing a great number whom they falsely call gods, they are blinded as to the most important of all existing things which they ought to have thoroughly learnt, if not alone, at all events as the first and greatest of all things from their earliest childhood; for what can be a more honorable thing to learn than the knowledge of the true and living God?

Parallels: Deuteronomy 14:01; John 01:18

Special Laws II (10)

(10) For what is better than to speak with perfect truth throughout one's whole life, and to prove this by the evidence of God himself? For an oath is nothing else but the testimony of God invoked in a matter which is a subject of doubt, and to invoke God to witness a statement which is not true is the most impious of all things.

Parallels: Deuteronomy 19:18-19; Matthew 05:33-37

Special Laws II (12-15)

(12) A man, therefore, as I have said, must be sure and give effect to all oaths which are taken for honorable and desirable objects, for the due establishment of private or public objects of importance, under the guidance of wisdom, and justice, and holiness. And in this description of oaths those most lawful vows are included which are offered up in consequence of an abundance of blessings, either present or expected; but if any vows are made for contrary objects, it is not holy to ratify them, (13) for there are some men who swear, if chance so prompts them, to commit theft, or sacrilege, or adultery, or rape, or to inflict wounds or slaughter, or any similar acts of wickedness, and who perform them without any delay, making an excuse that they must keep their oaths, as if it were not better and more acceptable to God to do no iniquity, than to perform such a vow and oath as that. The national laws and ancient ordinances of every people are established for the sake of justice and of every virtue, and what else are laws and ordinances but the sacred words of nature having an authority and power in themselves, so that they differ in no respect from oaths? (14) And let every man who commits wicked actions because he is so bound by an oath, beware that he is not keeping his oath, but that he is rather violating one which is worthy of great care and attention to preserve it, which sets a seal as it were to what is honorable and just, for he is adding wickedness to wickedness, adding lawless actions to oaths taken on improper occasions, which had better

have been buried in silence. (15) Let such a man, therefore, abstain from committing iniquity, and seek to propitiate God, that he may grant to him the mercy of that humane power which is innate in him, so as to pardon him for the oaths which he took in his folly. For it is incurable madness and insanity to take upon himself twofold evils, when he might put off one half of the burden of them.

Parallels: Deuteronomy 19:18-19; Matthew 05:33-37

Special Laws II (18-19)

(18) But there are other persons, also, boastful, puffed up with pride and arrogance, who, being insatiably greedy of glory, are determined to obey none of the precepts which point to that most beneficial virtue, frugality; but even if anyone exhorts them to it, in order to induce them to shake off the obstinate impetuosity of the appetites, they look upon all their admonitions as insults, and drive their course on headlong to every kind of effeminate luxury, despising those who seek to correct them, and making a joke of and turning into ridicule all the honorable and advantageous recommendations of wisdom. (19) And if such men happen to be in such circumstances as to have any abundance and superfluity of the means of living, they declare with positive oaths that they will indulge in all imaginable expense for the use and enjoyment of costly luxury. For instance, a man who has lately come into the enjoyment of considerable riches, embraces a prodigal and extravagant course of life; and when some old man, some relation perhaps, or some friend of his father, comes and admonishes him, exhorting him to alter his ways and to come over to a more honorable and strict behavior, he is indignant beyond all measure at the advice, and being obstinate in his contentious disposition, swears that as long as he has the means and resources necessary for supplying his wants he will not practice any single way which leads to economy or moderation, neither in the city nor in the country, neither when travelling by sea nor by land, but that he will at all times and in all places show how rich and liberal he is; but as it

seems to me such conduct as this is not so much a display of riches as of insolence and intemperance.

Parallels: Luke 15:11-32

Special Laws II (44-48)

(44) for all those men, whether among the Greeks or among the barbarians, who are practitioners of wisdom, living in a blameless and irreproachable manner, determining not to do any injustice, nor even to retaliate it when done to them, shunning all association with busy-bodies, in all the cities which they inhabit, avoid all courts of justice, and council halls, and market-places, and places of assembly, and, in short, every spot where any band or company of precipitate headstrong men is collected, (45) admiring, as it were, a life of peace and tranquility, being the most devoted contemplators of nature and of all the things in it. Investigating earth and sea, and the air, and the heaven, and all the different natures in each of them; dwelling, if one may so say, in their minds, at least, with the moon, and the sun, and the whole company of the rest of the stars, both planets and fixed stars. Having their bodies, indeed, firmly planted on the earth, but having their souls furnished with wings, in order that thus hovering in the air they may closely survey all the powers above, looking upon them as in reality the most excellent of cosmopolites, who consider the whole world as their native city, and all the devotees of wisdom as their fellow citizens, virtue herself having enrolled them as such, to whom it has been entrusted to frame a constitution for their common city. (46) Being, therefore, full of all kinds of excellence, and being accustomed to disregard all those good things which affect the body and external circumstances, and being inured to look upon things indifferent as really indifferent, and being armed by study against the pleasures and appetites, and, in short, being always laboring to raise themselves above the passions, and being instructed to exert all their power to pull down the fortification which those appetites have built up, and being insensible to any impression which the attacks of fortune might make upon them,

because they have previously estimated the power of its attacks in their anticipations (for anticipation makes even those things light which would be most terrible if unexpected), their minds in this manner calculating that nothing that happens is wholly strange, but having a kind of faint perception of everything as old and in some degree blunted. These men, being very naturally rendered cheerful by their virtues, pass the whole of their lives as a festival. (47) These men, however, are therefore but a small number, kindling in their different cities a sort of spark of wisdom, in order that virtue may not become utterly extinguished, and so be entirely extirpated from our race. (48) But if men everywhere agreed with this small number, and became, as nature originally designed that they should, all blameless and irreproachable, lovers of wisdom, delighting in all that is virtuous and honorable, and thinking that and that alone good, and looking on everything else as subordinate and slaves, as if they themselves were the masters of them, then all the cities would be full of happiness, being wholly free from all the things which are the causes of pain or fear, and full of all those which produce joy and cheerfulness. So that no time would ever cease to be the time of a happy life, but that the whole circle of the year would be one festival.

Parallels: Hebrews 11:10-16

Special Laws II (74-78)

(74) But the action of lending on usury is blamable; for a man who lends on usury has not abundant means of living, but is clearly in some want; and he does so as being compelled to add the interest to his principal in order to subsist, and so he at last becomes of necessity very poor; and while he thinks that he is deriving advantage he is in reality injured, just as foolish animals are when they are deceived by a present bait. (75) But I should say to such persons, "O you who lend on usury, why do you seek to disguise your unsociable disposition by an apparent pretence of good fellowship? And why do you in words, indeed, pretend to be a humane and considerate person, while in your

actions you exhibit a want of humanity and a terrible hardness of heart, exacting more than you gave, and sometimes even doubling your original loan, so as to make the poor man an absolute beggar? (76) Therefore no one sympathizes with you in your distress, when, having endeavored to obtain more, you fail to do so, and besides lose even what you had before. But, on the contrary, all men are glad of your misfortunes, calling you a usurer, and a skinflint, and all kinds of names like those, looking on you as one who lies in wait for human misfortunes, and who esteems the misfortunes of others his own prosperity." (77) But, as some have said, wickedness is a most laborious thing; and he who lends on usury is blind, not seeing the time of repayment, in which he will scarcely, or perhaps not at all, receive the things which in his covetousness he had hoped to gain. (78) Let such a man pay the penalty of his avaricious disposition, not recovering back what he has expended, so as to make a gain of the misfortunes of men, deriving a revenue from unbecoming sources. But let the debtors be thought worthy of a humanity enjoined by the law, not paying back their loans and usurious interest upon them, but paying back merely the original sum lent. For again, at a proper season, they will give the same assistance to those who have aided them, requiting those who set the example of kindness with equal services.

Parallels: Exodus 22:25; Luke 06:34-35

Special Laws II (92-95)

(92) Moreover let the governors of cities cease to oppress them with continual and excessive taxes and tributes, filling their own stores with money, and in preserving as a treasure the illiberal vices which defile their whole lives; (93) for they do, on purpose, select as collectors of their revenues the most pitiless of men, persons full of all kinds of inhumanity, giving them abundant opportunity for the exercise of their covetousness; and they, in addition to their own innate severity of temper, receiving free license from the commands of their masters, and having determined to do everything so as to please them, practice all

the harshest measures which they can imagine, having no notion of gentleness or humanity, not even in their dreams; (94) therefore they throw everything into disorder and confusion, levying their exactions, not only on the possessions of the citizens, but also on their persons, with insults and violence, and the invention of new and unprecedented torture. And before now I have heard of some persons who, in their ferocity and unequalled fury, have not spared even the dead; but have been so brutal as even to venture to beat the dead corpses with goads; (95) and when someone blamed their brutality, in that not even death, that relief and real end of all miseries, could prevent their victims from being insulted by them, but that, instead of a grave and the customary funeral rites, they were exposed to continued insult, they made a defense worse even than the accusation brought against them, saying that they were insulting the dead, not for the sake of abusing the dumb and senseless dust, for there was no advantage in that, but for the sake of making those who through ties of blood or of friendship were nearly connected with them feel compassion for them, and so inducing them to pay a ransom for their bodies, thus doing them the last service in their power.

Parallels: Matthew 09:09-13

Special Laws II (122)

(122) But the laws established with respect to those who owed money to usurers, and to those who had become servants to masters, resemble those already mentioned; that the usurers shall not exact usurers' interest from their fellow countrymen, but shall be contented to receive back only what they lent; and that the masters shall behave to those whom they have bought with their money not as if they were by nature slaves, but only hirelings, giving them immunity and liberty, at once, indeed, to those who can pay down a ransom for themselves, and at a subsequent period to the indigent, either when the seventh year from the beginning of their slavery arrives, or when the fiftieth year comes, even if a man happen to have fallen into slavery

only the day before. For this year both is and is looked upon as a year of remission; every one retracing his steps and turning back again to his previous state of prosperity.

Parallels: Exodus 22:25; Luke 06:34-35

Special Laws II (145)

(145) And after the feast of the new moon comes the fourth festival, that of the passover, which the Hebrews call pascha, on which the whole people offer sacrifice, beginning at noonday and continuing till evening.

Parallels: Exodus 12:01-28; Matthew 27:33-56

Special Laws II (147-148)

(147) But those who are in the habit of turning plain stories into allegory, argue that the Passover figuratively represents the purification of the soul; for they say that the lover of wisdom is never practicing anything else except a passing over from the body and the passions. (148) And each house is at that time invested with the character and dignity of a temple, the victim being sacrificed so as to make a suitable feast for the man who has provided it and of those who are collected to share in the feast, being all duly purified with holy ablutions. And those who are to share in the feast come together not as they do to other entertainments, to gratify their bellies with wine and meat, but to fulfill their hereditary custom with prayer and songs of praise.

Parallels: Exodus 12:01-28; Matthew 26:30, 27:33-56; Acts 01:03

Special Laws II (155)

(155) And this feast is begun on the fifteenth day of the month, in the middle of the month, on the day on which the moon is full of light, in consequence of the providence of God taking care that there shall be no darkness on that day.

Parallels: Leviticus 23:06; Matthew 27:45; Mark 15:33; Luke 23:44

Special Laws II (161)

(161) The setting out of twelve loaves--the same number as the tribes--on the sacred table especially guarantees the things which have been said. For they are all unleavened, the clearest example of an unmixed food which has been prepared not by human skill for pleasure but by nature for the most essential use. These things are sufficient for this topic.

Parallels: Leviticus 23:06; 1Corinthians 05:08

Special Laws II (162)

(162) There is also a festival on the day of the paschal feast, which succeeds the first day, and this is named the sheaf, from what takes place on it; for the sheaf is brought to the altar as a first fruit both of the country which the nation has received for its own, and also of the whole land; so as to be an offering both for the nation separately, and also a common one for the whole race of mankind; and so that the people by it worship the living God, both for themselves and for all the rest of mankind, because they have received the fertile earth for their inheritance; for in the country there is no barren soil but even all those parts which appear to be stony and rugged are surrounded with soft veins of great depth, which, by reason of their richness, are very well suited for the production of living things.

Parallels: Leviticus 23:04-14; 1Corinthians 15:20; Hebrews 09:26

Special Laws II (164)

(164) Apart from the fact that the legislation is in a certain way teaching about the priesthood and that the one who lives by the laws is at once considered a priest, or rather a high priest, in the judgment of truth…

Parallels: 1Peter 02:09

Special Laws II (165)

(165) But if he is, whom all Greeks together with all barbarians acknowledge with one judgment, the highest Father of both gods and humans and the Maker of the entire cosmos, whose nature--although it is invisible and unfathomable not only to sight but also to perception--all who spend their time with mathematics and other philosophy long to discover, leaving aside none of the things which contribute to the discovery and service of him, then it was necessary for all people to cling to him and not as if through some mechanical device to introduce other gods into participation of equal honors.

Parallels: John 01:18

Special Laws II (176-180)

(176) The solemn assembly on the occasion of the festival of the sheaf having such great privileges, is the prelude to another festival of still greater importance; for from this day the fiftieth day is reckoned, making up the sacred number of seven sevens, with the addition of a unit as a seal to the whole; and this festival, being that of the first fruits of the corn, has derived its name of Pentecost from the number of fifty, (penteμkostos). And on it it is the custom to offer up two leavened loaves made of wheat, as a first fruit of the best kind of food made of corn; either because, before the fruit of the year is converted to the use of man, the first produce of the new crop, the first gathered corn that appears is offered as a first fruit, in order that by an insignificant emblem the people may display their grateful disposition; (177) We must disclose another reason. Its nature is wondrous and highly prized for numerous reasons including the fact that it consists of the most elemental and oldest of the things which are encased in substances, as the mathematicians tell us, the right angled triangle. For its sides, which exist in lengths of three and four and five, combine to make up the sum twelve, the pattern of the zodiac cycle, the doubling of the most fecund number six which is the beginning of perfection since it is the sum of the same numbers of which it is also the Product.{literally, "being the sum of its own parts to which it is equal." In mathematical notation: 1 + 2 + 3 = 6 = 1 x 2 x 3.} To the second power, it seems, they produce fifty, through the addition of 3 x 3 and 4 x 4 and 5 x 5. The result is that it is necessary to say that to the same degree that fifty is better than twelve, the second power is better than the first power. (178) If the image of the lesser is the most beautiful sphere of those which are in heaven, the zodiac, then of what would the better, the number fifty, be a pattern than a completely better nature? This is not the occasion to speak about this. It is sufficient for the present that the difference has been noted so that a principal point is not considered to be subordinate. (179) the feast which takes place on the basis of the number fifty has received the name "the feast

of the first produce" since during the feast it is customary to offer two leavened loaves made from wheat as the first fruit of grain, the best food. It is named "the feast of the first produce" Either because before the annual crop has proceeded to human use, the first produce of the new grain and the first fruit which has appeared are offered as first fruit. (180) For it is just and religiously correct that those who have received the greatest gift from God, the abundance of the most necessary as well as most beneficial and even the sweetest food, should not enjoy it or have any use of it at all before they offer the first fruits to the Supplier. They are giving him nothing since all things and possessions and gifts are his, but through a small symbol demonstrate a thankful and God-loving character to the one who needs no favors but showers continuous and ever-flowing favors.

Parallels: Leviticus 23:15-17; Acts 02:01-21

Special Laws II (224)

(224) Having already spoken of four commandments which, both as to the order in which they are placed and as to their importance, are truly the first; namely, the commandment about the lenity of that sovereign authority by which the world is governed, and that which commands that man should not look upon any representation or figure of anything as God, and that which forbids the swearing falsely, or indeed the swearing carelessly and vainly at all, and that concerning the sacred seventh day--all which commandments tend to piety and holiness. I now proceed to the fifth commandment, relating to the honor due to parents; which is, as I showed in the mention I made of it separately before, on the borders between those which relate to the affairs of men and those which relate to God.

Parallels: Deuteronomy 19:18-19; Matthew 05:33-37

Special Laws II (252-253)

(252) Against those who call God as a witness in favor of assertions which are not true, the punishment of death is ordained in the law; {Deuteronomy 19:19.} and very properly, for even a man of moderate respectability will never endure to be cited as a witness, and to have his name registered in support of a lie. But it seems to me that he would look upon any one who proposed such a thing to him as a thoroughly faithless enemy; (253) on which account we must say this, that him, who swears rashly and falsely, calling God to witness an unjust oath, God, although he is merciful by nature, will yet never release, inasmuch as he is thoroughly defiled and infamous from guilt, even though he may escape punishment at the hands of men. And such a man will never entirely escape, for there are innumerable beings looking on, zealots for and keepers of the national laws, of rigid justice, prompt to stone such a criminal, and visiting without pity all such as work wickedness, unless, indeed, we are prepared to say that a man who acts in such a way as to dishonor his father or his mother is worthy of death, but that he who behaves with impiety towards a name more glorious than even the respect due to one's parents, is to be borne with as but a moderate offender.

Parallels: Deuteronomy 19:18-19; Matthew 05:33-37

Special Laws III (6)

(6) But even in these circumstances I ought to give thanks to God, that though I am so overwhelmed by this flood, I am not wholly sunk and swallowed up in the depths. But I open the eyes of my soul, which from an utter despair of any good hope had been believed to have been before now wholly darkened, and I am irradiated with the light of wisdom, since I am not given up for the whole of my life to darkness. Behold, therefore, I venture not only to study the sacred commands of Moses, but

also with an ardent love of knowledge to investigate each separate one of them, and to endeavor to reveal and to explain to those who wish to understand them, things concerning them which are not known to the multitude.

> Parallels: Exodus 34:33-35; 1 Samuel 14:27-45; Matthew 05:15, 06:22-23; Luke 24:27, 44-47; Acts 17:02-03, 26:18
>
> Comparison: Luke 24:44-45, "The he said to them, "These are my words which I spoke to you, while I was still with you, that everything written about me in the law of Moses and the prophets and the psalms must be fulfilled." Then he opened their minds, so they could understand the Scriptures." Acts 26:18, "to open their eyes, to turn them from darkness to light and from the power of Satan to God, that they may receive forgiveness of sins and a place among those who are sanctified by faith in me."

Special Laws III (52-54)

(52) The law has pronounced all acts of adultery, if detected in the fact, or if proved by undeniable evidence, liable to the punishment of death; but cases in which guilt is only suspected, it does not choose should be investigated by men, but it brings them before the tribunal of nature; since men are able to judge of what is visible, but God can judge also of what is unseen, since he alone is able to behold the soul distinctly, (53) therefore he says to the man who suspects such a thing, "Write an accusation, and go up to the holy city with thy wife, and standing before the judges, lay bare the passion of suspicion which affects you, not like a false accuser or treacherous enemy, seeking to gain the victory by any means whatever, but as a man may do who wishes accurately to ascertain the truth without any sophistry. (54) And the woman, having incurred two dangers, one of her life, and the other of her reputation, the loss of which last is more grievous than any kind of death, shall judge the matter with

herself; and if she be pure, let her make her defense with confidence; but if she be convicted by her own conscience, let her cover her face, making her modesty the veil for her iniquities, for to persist in her impudence is the very extravagance of wickedness.

Parallels: Numbers 05:14-31; John 08:03-11

Special Laws III (58-63)

(58) Then the law proceeds to say, the priest, having taken an earthen vessel, shall pour forth pure water, having drawn it from a fountain, and shall also bring a lump of clay from the ground of the temple, which also I think has in it a symbolical reference to the search after truth; for the earthenware vessel is appropriate to the commission of adultery because it is easily broken, and death is the punishment appointed for adulterers; but the earth and the water are appropriate to the purging of the accusation, since the origin, and increase, and perfection of all things, take place by them: (59) on which account it was very proper for the law-giver to set them both off by epithets, saying, that the water which the priest was to take must be pure and living water, since blameless woman is pure as to her life, and deserves to live; and the earth too is to be taken, not from any chance spot, but from the soil of the ground of the temple, which must, of necessity, be most excellent, just as a modest woman is. (60) And when all these things are previously prepared, the woman with her head uncovered, bearing the barley flour in her hand, as has been already specified, shall come forward; and the priest standing opposite to her and holding the earthenware vessel in which are the water and the earth, shall speak thus: (61) "If you have not transgressed the laws of your marriage, and if no other man has been associated with you, so that you have not violated the rights of him who is joined to you by the law, you are blameless and innocent; but if you have neglected your husband and have followed empty appetites, either loving some one yourself or yielding to some lover, betraying your nearest

and dearest connections, and adulterating them by a spurious mixture, then learn that you are deservedly liable to every kind of curse, the proofs of which you will exhibit on your body. Come then and drink the draught of conviction, which shall uncover and lay bare all thy hidden and secret actions." (62) Then the priest shall write these words on a paper and dip it in the water which is in the earthenware vessel, and give it to the woman. And she shall drink it and depart, awaiting the reward of her modesty or the extreme penalty of her incontinence; for if she has been falsely accused she may hope for seed and children, disregarding all apprehensions and anxieties on the subject of barrenness and childlessness. But if she is guilty then a great weight and bulk, form her belly swelling and becoming full, will come upon her, and a terribly evil condition of her womb will afflict her, since she did not choose to keep it pure for her husband, who had married her according to the laws of her nation. (63) And the law takes such exceeding pains to prevent any irregularity taking place with respect to marriages, that even in the case of husbands and wives who have come together for legitimate embraces, in strict accordance with the laws of marriage, after they have arisen from their beds it does not allow them to touch anything before they have had recourse to washings and ablutions; keeping them very far from adultery and from all accusations referring to adultery.

Parallels: Numbers 05:14-31; John 08:03-11

Special Laws III (103)

(103) Therefore, as if we only see snakes, and serpents, and any other venomous animals, we at once, without a moment's delay, kill them before they can bite, or wound, or attack us at all, taking care not to expose ourselves to any injury from them by reason of our knowledge of the mischief which is inherent in them; in the same manner it is right promptly to punish those men who, though they have had a gentle nature assigned to them by means of that fountain of reason which is the cause and

source of all society, do nevertheless of deliberate purpose change it themselves to the ferocity of untamable beasts, looking upon the doing injury to as many people as they can to be their greatest pleasure and advantage.

Parallels: Matthew 03:07, 23:33-35

Special Laws III (116)

(116) And even suppose that someone passing by on his road is moved by a feeling of gentle compassion to take pity on and show mercy to the exposed infants, so as to take them up and give them food, and to show them other portions of the attention that is requisite, what do we think of such a humane action? Do we not look upon it as an express condemnation of the real parents, when those who are in nowise related to them show the tender foresight of parents, but the parents do not display even the kindness of strangers?

Parallels: Exodus 22:22; Luke 10:30-37

Special Laws III (151-152)

(151) Since men of wicked dispositions are never wearied of offending, but are always committing atrocious actions in the excess of their wickedness, and increasing their iniquities, and extending them beyond all bounds or limits. For the lawgiver would, if it had been in his power, have condemned those men to ten thousand deaths. But since this was not possible, he prescribed another punishment for them, commanding those who had slain a man to be hanged upon a tree. (152) And after having established this ordinance he returned again to his natural humanity, treating with mercy even those who had behaved unmercifully towards others, and he pronounced, "Let not the sun set upon persons hanging on a Tree;"{Deuteronomy 21:23.} but let them be buried under the earth and be concealed from sight before sunset. For it was necessary to raise up on high

all those who were enemies to every part of the world, so as to show most evidently to the sun, and to the heaven, and to the air, and to the water, and to the earth, that they had been chastised; and after that it was proper to remove them into the region of the dead, and to bury them, in order to prevent their polluting the things upon the earth.

Parallels: Deuteronomy 21:23; Luke 23:33-45

Special Laws III (208)

(208) And the law says, "Let everything which a man that is unclean has touched be also unclean as being polluted by a participation in that which is unclean." And this sacred injunction appears to have a wide operation, not being limited to the body alone, but proceeding as it would seem also to investigate the dispositions of the soul.

Parallels: Leviticus 22:05; Matthew 23:25-33

Special Laws IV (69-71)

(69) And what in life is there equally beautiful with truth, which the all-wise legislator erected in the most sacred place, in that part of the dress of the chief priest, where the dominant part of the soul lies, wishing to adorn it with the most beautiful and glorious of all ornaments? And next to truth he has placed power as akin to it, which he has in this case called manifestation, being the two images of the two kinds of speech which exist in us, the secret speech and the lettered speech, for the lettered speech requires manifestation, by which the secret thoughts in all our hearts are made known to our neighbor, but the secret speech has need of truth for the perfection of life and actions, by means of which the road to happiness is found out. (70) The third commandment given to a judge is to investigate the transactions themselves, in preference to showing any regard to the parties to the suit; and to attempt, in every imaginable

manner, to separate himself from all respect of persons; constraining himself to an ignorance and forgetfulness of all those things of which he has any knowledge or recollection; such as relations, friends, countrymen or foreigners, enemies or hereditary connections, so that neither affection nor hatred may overshadow his knowledge of justice; for he must stumble like a blind man, who is advancing without a staff, and who has no one to guide him in whom he can rely firmly. (71) For which reason it is fitting that a righteous judge should have it even concealed from him who the parties to the suit are, and that he should look at the undisguised, simple nature of the transactions themselves; so as not to be liable to judge in accordance with random opinion, but according to real truth, and to be guided by such an opinion as this, that judgment is of God; {Deuteronomy 1:17.} and that the judge is the minister and steward of his judgment; and a steward is not allowed to give away the things of his master, as he has received as a pledge the most excellent of all the things which exist in human life, from the most excellent of all beings.

Parallels: Deuteronomy 01:16-17; Matthew 27:02-24; Mark 15:01-15; Luke 23:01-24; John 18:29-19:22

Special Laws IV (84)

(84) So great and so excessive an evil is covetous desire; or rather, if I am to speak the plain truth concerning it, it is the source of all evils. For from what other source do all the thefts, and acts of rapine, and repudiation of debt, and all false accusations, and acts of insolence, and, moreover, all ravishments, and adulteries, and murders, and, in short, all mischief, whether private or public, or sacred or profane, take their rise?

Parallels: Exodus 20:17; Matthew 26:14-16, 24; Mark 14:21

Special Laws IV (89-91)

(89) Again, if the desire takes the direction of wishing for authority and power, it renders men's natures seditious, unequal, and tyrannical, it makes them cruel and inhuman enemies of their native countries, implacable masters unable to restrain themselves, irreconcilable forces to all who are equal to themselves in might, flatterers of those who are more powerful than themselves, in order to be able to attack them treacherously. If what is desired is beauty of person, it makes men seducers, ravishers, adulterers, pederasts, practitioners of licentiousness and incontinence, it teaches them to regard the greatest evils as the most fortunate of blessings. This passion, also, when it extends to the tongue, often causes innumerable evils; (90) for some persons desire either to be silent about what ought to be mentioned, or to mention what ought to be buried in silence, and avenging justice pursues them if they reveal things improperly, or, on the contrary, if they are unseasonably silent. (91) When it affects the parts about the belly it makes men gluttonous, insatiable, intemperate, debauched, admirers of a profligate life, delighting in drunkenness, and epicurism, slaves to strong wine, and fish, and meat, pursuers of feasts and tables, wallowing like greedy dogs; owing to all which things their lives are rendered miserable and accursed, and they are reduced to an existence more grievous than any death.

Parallels: Exodus 20:17; Matthew 26:14-16, 24; Mark 14:21

Special Laws IV (106-113)

(106) And he gives two tests and criteria of the ten animals thus Enumerated {Leviticus 11:3.} by two signs, first, that they must part the hoof, secondly, that they must chew the cud; for those which do neither, or only one of these things, are unclean. And these signs are both of them symbols of instruction and of the most scientific learning, by which the better is separated from

the worse, so that all confusion between them is prevented; (107) for as the animal which chews the cud, while it is masticating its food draws it down its throat, and then by slow degrees kneads and softens it, and then after this process again sends it down into the belly, in the same manner the man who is being instructed, having received the doctrines and speculations of wisdom in at his ears from his instructor, derives a considerable amount of learning from him, but still is not able to hold it firmly and to embrace it all at once, until he has resolved over in his mind everything which he has heard by the continued exercise of his memory (and this exercise of memory is the cement which connects ideas), and then he impresses the image of it all firmly on his soul. (108) But as it seems the firm conception of such ideas is of no advantage to him unless he is able to discriminate between and to distinguish which of contrary things it is right to choose and which to avoid, of which the parting of the hoof is the symbol; since the course of life is twofold, the one road leading to wickedness and the other to virtue, and since we ought to renounce the one and never to forsake the other. (109) For this reason all animals with solid hoofs, and all with many toes are spoken of by implication as unclean; the one because, being so, they imply that the nature of good and evil is one and the same; which is just as if one were to say that the nature of a concave and a convex surface, or of a road up hill and downhill, was the same. And the other, because it shows that there are many roads, though, indeed, they have no right to be called roads at all, which lead the life of man to deceit; for it is not easy among a variety of paths to choose that which is the most desirable and the most excellent. (110) Having laid down these definitions with respect to land animals, he proceeds to describe what aquatic creatures are clean and lawful to be used for food; distinguishing them also by two characteristics as having fins or Scales.{Leviticus 11:9.} For those which have neither one nor the other, and those which have only one of the two, he rejects and Prohibits.{Deuteronomy 14:10.} And he must state the cause, which is not destitute of sense and propriety; (111) for all those creatures which are destitute of both, or even of one of the two, are sucked down by the current, not being able to resist the force of the stream; but those which have both these characteristics can stem the water, and oppose it in front, and strive against it as against an adversary, and struggle with invincible good will and courage, so that if they are pushed they push in their turn; and if they are pursued they turn upon their foe and pursue it in their turn, making themselves broad roads in a pathless district, so as to have an easy passage to and fro. (112) Now both these things are symbols; the former of a soul devoted to pleasure, and the latter of one which loves perseverance and temperance. For the road which leads to pleasure is a down-hill one and very easy, being rather an absorbing gulf than a path. But the path which leads to temperance is up hill and laborious, but above all other roads advantageous. And the one leads men downwards, and prevents those who travel by it from retracing their steps until they have arrived at the very lowest bottom, but the other leads to heaven; making those who do not weary before they reach it immortal, if they are only able to endure its rugged and difficult ascent. (113) And adhering to the same general idea the lawgiver asserts that those reptiles which have no feet, and which crawl onwards, dragging themselves along the ground on their bellies, or those which have four legs, or many feet, are all unclean as far as regards their being eaten. And here, again, when he mentions reptiles he intimates under a figurative form of expression those who are devoted to their bellies, gorging themselves like cormorants, and who are continually offering up tribute to their miserable belly, tribute, that is, of strong wine, and confections, and fish, and, in short, all the superfluous delicacies which the skill and labor of bakers and confectioners are able to devise, inventing all sorts of rare viands, to stimulate and set on fire the insatiable and unappeasable appetites of man. And when he speaks of animals with four legs and many feet, he intends to designate the miserable slaves not of one single passion, appetite, but of all the passions; the genera of which were four in number; but in their subordinate species they are innumerable. Therefore, the despotism of one is very grievous, but that of many is most terrible, and as it seems intolerable.

Parallels: Leviticus 11:01-47; Deuteronomy 14:03-20; Matthew 07:13-14; Hebrews 10:01

Comparison: Matthew 07:13-14, "Enter by the narrow gate. For the gate is wide, and the way is easy that leads to destruction, and many are those who enter by it. How narrow is the gate and hard the way, that leads to life, and few those who find it!"

Special Laws IV (140-141)

(140) But the man to whom it happens to represent to the eyes of his mind things which are not quiet but which are in motion, and exerting energies in accordance with nature, is entitled to be set down as a perfect man, and no longer to be reckoned among learners and pupils, but among teachers and instructors; and he ought to allow all the young men who are desirous to do so, to drink of his wisdom as of an abundant stream flowing from a living fountain of lessons and Doctrines.{Deuteronomy 6:7.} And if there is anyone who, out of modesty, is wanting of courage, and therefore delays, and is slow to approach him for the purpose of learning, let him go to him of his own accord, and pour into his ears a collection of admonitions, until the channels of his soul are filled with them. (141) And let him instruct in the principles of justice all his relatives and friends, and all young men, at home and on the road, and when they are going to bed, and when they rise up; that in all their positions, and in all their motions, and in all places whether private or public, not only waking, but also while asleep, they may be delighted with the image and conception of justice. For there is no delight more exquisite than that which proceeds from the whole soul being entirely filled with justice, while devoted to the study of its everlasting doctrines and meditations, so that it has no vacant place at which injustice can effect an entrance.

Parallels: Deuteronomy 06:07; John 04:10-14

Comparison: John 04:10-14, "Jesus answered her, "If you knew the gift of God, and who it is that is saying to you, 'Give me a drink,' you would have asked him, and he would have given you living water." [The woman] said to him, "Sir, you have nothing to draw with, and the well is deep. So where do you get that living water? Are you greater than our father Jacob, who gave us the well, and drank from it himself, as well as his sons and his cattle?" Jesus answered her, "Everyone who drinks of this water will thirst again, but whoever drinks of the water that I shall give him will never thirst. The water that I shall give him will become in him a spring of water welling up to eternal life.""

Special Laws IV (187)

(187) for this is to act in imitation of God, since he also has the power to do either good or evil, but his inclination causes him only to do good. And the creation and arrangement of the world shows this, for he has summoned what had previously no being into existence, creating order out of disorder, and distinctive qualities out of things which had no such qualities, and similarities out of things dissimilar, and identity out of things which were different, and intercommunion and harmony out of things which had previously no communication nor agreement, and equality out of inequality, and light out of darkness; for he is always anxious to exert his beneficent powers in order to change whatever is disorderly from its present evil condition, and to transform it so as to bring it into a better state.

Parallels: Genesis 01:01-31; Matthew 19:17

Special Laws IV (193-194)

(193) Again, merchants and peddlers, and people in the market, and all those who deal in things necessary for life, {Leviticus 19:36.} and who in consequence are conversant with measures, and weights, and balances, since they sell things both dry and wet, are put in subjection to the superintendants of the market, and these superintendants are bound to govern them if they act with moderation, doing what is right, not out of fear, but voluntarily, for spontaneous good conduct is in every case more honorable than that which proceeds from compulsion. (194) On which account the law orders these merchants and dealers, and all other persons who have adopted this way of life, to take care to provide themselves with just balances, and measures, and weights, not practicing any wicked maneuvers to the injury of those who purchase of them, but to do and say everything with a free and guileless soul, considering this, that unjust gains are injurious, but that that wealth which is acquired in accordance with justice a man cannot be deprived of.

Parallels: Leviticus 19:36; Matthew 21:13

Special Laws IV (200-202)

(200) "O foolish minded men, do you expect to escape detection while turning the misfortunes of those men into ridicule, and committing offences against those very parts in respect of which they are unfortunate, attacking their ears by false accusations, and their eyes by putting stumbling blocks in their path? But you will never escape the notice of God, who sees everything and governs everything, while you insult in this manner the calamities of miserable men, so as to avoid meeting with similar distresses yourselves, inasmuch as your bodies are also liable to all kinds of diseases, and your outward senses are susceptible of injury and mutilation, being such as, by a very slight and ordinary cause, they are often not only impaired, but crippled by

incurable mutilations. (201) Why then should those who forget themselves, and who in their arrogance fancy that they themselves are superior to the ordinary natural weakness of mankind, and that they are out of the reach of the invisible and unexpected attacks of fortune, which often aims sudden blows at all people, and which has often wrecked men, who up to that moment had enjoyed a prosperous voyage through life, when they had almost arrived in the very harbor of ultimate happiness, why, I say, should such men triumph in and insult the misfortunes of others, having no respect for justice, the ruler of human life, who sits by the side of the great Ruler of the universe, who surveys all things with sleepless and most piercing eyes, and sees what is in recesses as clearly as if it was in the pure sunlight? (202) It seems to me that these men would not spare even the dead, in the extravagance of their cruelty, but, according to the proverb so commonly quoted, would even slay the slain over again, since they in a manner think fit to insult and ill treat those members of them which are already dead; for eyes which do not see are dead, and ears which are devoid of the power of hearing are devoid of life; so that if the man himself to whom these members belong, were to be extinct, they would then show their merciless and implacable nature, doing no humane or compassionate action, such as is shown to the dead, even by their enemies in irreconcilable wars. And this may be enough to say on this subject.

Parallels: Leviticus 19:14; Matthew 18:23-35, 26:64; Mark 14:62; Luke 22:69; Acts 02:33-34, 07:55-56; Romans 08:34; Colossians 03:01; Hebrews 01:03, 08:01, 12:02; 1Peter 03:22

Comparison: Hebrews 08:01, "Now the point in what we are saying is this: we have such a high priest, one who is seated at the right hand of the throne of the Majesty in heaven"

Special Laws IV (203-207)

(203) After this the lawgiver proceeds to connect with these commandments a somewhat similar harmony or series of injunctions; commanding breeders not to breed from animals of different species; not to sow a vineyard so as to make it bear two crops at once; and not to wear garments woven of two different substances, which are a mixed and base work. Now the first of these injunctions we have already mentioned in our treatise on adulterers, in order to make it more evident, that our people ought not to be anxious for marriages with foreigners, corrupting the dispositions of the women, and destroying also the good hopes which might be conceived of the propagation of legitimate children. For the lawgiver, who has forbidden all copulation between irrational animals of different species, appears to have utterly driven away all adulterers to a great distance. (204) And we must now speak again of this rule in this our treatise on justice. For we must take care not to pass over the opportunity of adapting it to as many particulars as possible. It is just then to bring together those things which are capable of union; now animals of the same species are by nature capable of union, as, on the other hand, all animals of different species are incapable of any admixture or union, and the man who brings unlawful connections to pass between such animals is an unjust man, transgressing the ordinances of nature; (205) but that which is the really sacred law takes such exceeding care to provide for the maintenance of justice, that it will not permit even the plowing of the land to be carried on by animals of unequal strength, and forbids a husbandman to plough with an ass and a heifer yoked to the same plough, lest the weaker animals, being compelled to exert itself to keep up with the superior power of the stronger animal, should become exhausted, and sink under the effort; (206) and the bull is looked upon as the stronger animal, and is enrolled in the class of clean beasts and animals, while the ass is a weaker animal and of the class of unclean beasts; but nevertheless he has not grudged those animals which appear to be weaker, the assistance which they can derive from

justice, in order, as I imagine, to teach the judges most forcibly, that they are never in their decisions to give the worse fate to the humbly born, in matters the investigation of which depends not on birth but on virtue and vice. (207) And resembling these injunctions is the last commandment concerning things yoked in pairs, namely, that it is unlawful to wear together substances of a different character, such as wool and linen; for in the case of these substances, not only does the difference prevent any union, but also the superior strength of the one substance is calculated rather to tear the other than to unite with it, when it is wanted to be used.

Parallels: Leviticus 19:19; Mark 02:21; 2Corinthians 05:14

That the Worse Is Wont To Attack the Better (19-21)

(19) If, therefore, you see any one desiring meat or drink at an unseasonable time, or repudiating baths or ointments at the proper season, or neglecting the proper clothing for his body, or lying on the ground and sleeping in the open air, and by such conduct as this, pretending to a character for temperance and self-denial, you, pitying his self-deception, should show him the true path of temperance, for all the practices in which he has been indulging are useless and profitless labors, oppressing both his soul and body with hunger and all sorts of other hardships. (20) Nor if anyone, using washings and purifications soils his mind, but makes his bodily appearance brilliant; nor if again out of his abundant wealth he builds a temple with brilliant ornaments of all kinds, at a vast expense; nor if he offers up catombs and never ceases sacrificing oxen; nor if he adorns temples with costly offerings, bringing timber in abundance, and skilful ornaments, more valuable than nay of gold or silver, (21) still let him not be classed among pious men, for he also has wandered out of the way to piety, looking upon ceremonious worship as equivalent to sanctity, and giving gifts to the

incorruptible being who will never receive such offerings, and flattering him who can never listen to flattery, who loves genuine worship (and genuine worship is that of the soul which offers the only sacrifice, plain truth), and rejects all spurious ministrations, and those are spurious which are only displays of external riches and extravagance.

Parallels: Isaiah 01:02-17; Matthew 06:02-18

That the Worse Is Wont To Attack the Better (128)

(128) And this voice is itself the most manifest of all the conceptions. For, as what is laid up is hidden in darkness until light shines upon it and exhibits it, in the same manner the conceptions are stored away in an invisible place, namely, the mind, until the voice, like light, sheds its beams upon them and reveals everything.

Parallels: Matthew 05:15

The Cherubim Part 1 (14-17)

(14) Now of the kind of opposition of place which is connected with standing in front of a judge for judgment, we have an example in the case of the woman who has been suspected of having committed adultery. For, says Moses, "the priest shall cause the woman to stand in front of her lord, and she shall uncover her Head."{Numbers 5:18.} Let us now examine what he intends to show by this direction. It often happens that what ought to be done is not done, in the manner in which it ought to be done, and sometimes too that which is not proper is nevertheless done in a proper manner. For instance, when the return of a deposit is not made in an honest spirit, but is intended either to work the injury of him who receives it back again, or by way of a snare to bear out a denial in the case of another deposit of greater value, in that case a proper action is done in an improper manner. (15) On the other hand, for a

physician not to tell the exact truth to a sick patient, when he has decided on purging him, or performing some operation with the knife or with the cautery for the benefit of the patient, lest if the sick man were to be moved too strongly by the anticipation of the suffering, he might refuse to submit to the cure, or through weakness of mind might despair of its succeeding; or in the case of a wise man giving false information to the enemy to secure the safety of his country, fearing lest through his speaking the truth the affairs of the adversaries should succeed, in this case an action which is not intrinsically right is done in a proper manner. In reference to which distinction Moses says, "to pursue what is just Justly,"{Deuteronomy 16:20.} as if it were possible also to pursue it unjustly, if at any time the judge who gives sentence does not decide in an honest spirit. (16) Since therefore what is said or done is openly notorious to all men, but since the intention, the consequence of which what is said is said, and what is done is done, is not notorious, but it is uncertain whether it be a sound and healthy motive, or an unhealthy design, stained with numerous pollutions; and since no created being is capable of discerning the secret intention of an invisible mind, but God alone; in reference to this Moses says that "all secret things are known to the Lord God, but only such as are manifest are known to the creature." (17) And therefore it is enjoined to the priest and prophet, that is to say to reason, "to place the soul in front of God, with the head Uncovered," {Numbers 5:14.} that is to say the soul must be laid bare as to its principal design, and the sentiments which it nourished must be revealed, in order that being brought before the judgment seat of the most accurate vision of the incorruptible God, it may be thoroughly examined as to all its concealed disguises, like a base coin, or, on the other hand, if it be found to be free from all participation in any kind of wickedness, it may wash away all the calumnies that have been uttered against its bringing him for a testimony to its purity, who is alone able to behold the soul naked.

Parallels: Numbers 05:14-18; Deuteronomy 16:20; Matthew 22:21; John 08:03-11; Acts 03:19; Revelation 20:11-15

The Cherubim Part 1 (36-38)

(36) Why, then, do you reproach us now, when you formerly had no fault to find with us, while your affairs were proceeding prosperously? For we are the same as we were before, having changed nothing of our nature, not the slightest jot. But you are now applying tests which have no soundness in them, and in consequence are unreasonably violent against us; for if you had understood from the beginning that it is not the pursuits which you follow that are the causes of your participation in good or in evil, but rather the divine reason, which is the helmsman and governor of the universe, then you would more easily have borne the events which have befallen you, ceasing to bring false accusations against us, and to attribute to us effects which we are unable to produce. (37) "If therefore this reason now again, putting an end to that strife, and dispersing the sad and desponding ideas which arise from it, should promise you tranquility of life, you will then again, with cheerfulness and joy, give us your right hand though we shall be like what we are now. But we are neither puffed up by your friendly favor, nor do we think it of great importance if you are angry with us; for we know that we are not the causes of either good or evil fortune, not even if you believe that we are, unless indeed you attribute to the sea the cause of sailors making favorable voyages, or of the shipwrecks which at times befall them, and not rather to the variations of the winds, which blow at one time gently, and at another with the most violent impetuosity; for as all water is by its own nature tranquil, (38) accordingly, when a favorable gale blows upon the stern of a ship, every rope is bent, and the ship is in full sail, conveying the mariners to the harbor; but when on a sudden the wind changes to the opposite direction, and blows against the head of the vessel, it then raises a heavy swell and great disturbance in the water, and upsets the ship and the sea, which was in no respect the cause of what has happened is blamed for it, though it notoriously is either calm or stormy according to the gentleness or violence of the winds."

Parallels: Matthew 05:45; Mark 04:37-41

The Cherubim: Of Cain And His Birth Part 2 (51-52)

(51) But it is, perhaps, possible that in some cases a virgin soul may be polluted by intemperate passions, and so become impure. On which account the sacred oracle has been cautious, calling God the husband, not of a virgin, for a virgin is subject to change and to mortality, but of virginity; of an idea, that is to say, which is always existing in the same principles and in the same manner. For as all things endowed with distinctive qualities are by nature liable to origination and to destruction, so those archetypal powers, which are the makers of those particular things, have received an imperishable inheritance in their turn. (52) Therefore is it seemly that the uncreated and unchangeable God should ever sow the ideas of immortal and virgin virtues in a woman who is transformed into the appearance of virginity? Why, then, O soul, since it is right for you to dwell as a virgin in the house of God, and to cleave to wisdom, do you stand aloof from these things, and rather embrace the outward sense, which makes you effeminate and pollutes you? Therefore, you shall bring forth an offspring altogether polluted and altogether destructive, the fratricidal and accursed Cain, a possession not to be sought after; for the name Cain being interpreted means possession.

Parallels: Luke 01:26-27, 35

The Cherubim: Of Cain And His Birth Part 2 (101-104)

(101) If therefore we call the invisible soul the terrestrial habitation of the invisible God, we shall be speaking justly and according to reason; but that the house may be firm and beautiful, let a good disposition and knowledge be laid as its foundations, and on these foundations let the virtues be built up in union with good actions, and let the ornaments of the front be the due comprehension of the encyclical branches of elementary instruction; (102) for from goodness of disposition arise skill, perseverance, memory; and from knowledge arise learning and attention, as the roots of a tree which is about to bring forth eatable fruit, and without which it is impossible to bring the intellect to perfection. (103) But by the virtues, and by actions in accordance with them, a firm and strong foundation for a lasting building is secured, in order that anything which may endeavor to separate and alienate the soul from honesty and make it such another haunt, may be powerless against so strong a defense, (104) and by means of the study of the encyclical branches of elementary education, the things requisite for the ornament of the soul are provided; for as whitewashing, and paintings, and tablets, and the arrangement of costly stones, by which men decorate not merely the walls, but even the lower parts of their houses, and all other such things as these do not contribute to strength, but only give pleasure to those who live in the house.

Parallels: Matthew 07:16-21, 24-27; Luke 06:48-49

Comparison: Matthew 07:16-20, "You will know them by their fruits. Do men gather grapes from thorn bushes, or figs from thistles? Even so, every good tree bears good fruit, but a bad tree bears bad fruit. A good tree cannot bear bad fruit, nor can a bad tree bear good fruit. Every tree that does not bear good fruit is cut down and thrown into the fire. Thus you will know them by their fruits."

> Matthew 07:24-27, "Therefore everyone who hears these words of mine and does them will be like a wise man who built his house on the rock. And the rain fell, and the floods came, and the winds blew and beat upon that house, but it did not fall, because it had been founded on the rock. And every one who hears these words of mine and does not do them will be like a foolish man who built his house upon the sand. And the rain descended, the floods came, and the winds blew and beat against that house, and it fell. And great was its fall." Luke 06:48-49, "he is like a man building a house, who dug deep and laid the foundation on the rock. And when a flood arose, the stream broke against that house and could not shake it, because it was well built. But he who hears and does not do them is like a man who built a house on the ground without a foundation; against which the stream broke, and immediately it collapsed. And the ruin of that house was great.""

The Cherubim: Of Cain And His Birth Part 2 (122-123)

(122) Therefore, if you consider the matter, you will find that all men, and especially those who have been alluded to as giving gratuitously, sell rather than give; and that they, who we fancy are receiving favors, are, in reality, purchasing the benefits which they derive; for they who give, hoping to receive a requital, such as praise or honor, and seeking for a return of the favor which they are conferring, under the specious name of a gift, are, in reality, making a bargain. Since it is usual, for those who sell, to receive a price in return for what they part with; but they who, receiving presents, feel anxiety to make a return for them, and make such a return in due season, they in reality perform the part of purchasers; for as they know how to receive, so also do they know how to requite. (123) But God distributes his good things, not like a seller vending his wares at a high

price, but he is inclined to make presents of everything, pouring forth the inexhaustible fountains of his graces, and never desiring any return; for he has no need of anything, nor is there any created being competent to give him a suitable gift in return.

Parallels: Matthew 06:03

The Decalogue (41)

(41) For if the uncreated, and immortal, and everlasting God, who is in need of nothing and who is the maker of the universe, and the benefactor and King of kings, and God of gods, cannot endure to overlook even the meanest of human beings, but has thought even such worthy of being banqueted in sacred oracles and laws, as if he were about to give him a love feast, and to prepare for him alone a banquet for the refreshing and expanding of his soul instructed in the divine will and in the manner in which the great ceremonies ought to be performed, how can it be right for me, who am a mere mortal, to hold my head up high and to allow myself to be puffed up, behaving with insolence to my equals whose fortunes may, perhaps, not be equal to mine, but whose relationship to me is equal and complete, inasmuch as they are set down as the children of one mother, the common nature of all men?

Parallels: Exodus 19:14-20:18; Matthew 22:02-14; 1Timothy 06:15; Revelation 17:14, 19:16

The Decalogue (48-49)

(48) It is, therefore, with great beauty, and also with a proper sense of what is consistent with the dignity of God, that the voice is said to have come forth out of the fire; for the oracles of God are accurately understood and tested like gold by the fire. (49) And God also intimates to us something of this kind by a figure. Since the property of fire is partly to give light, and partly to burn, those who think fit to show themselves obedient to the sacred commands shall live forever and ever as in a light which is never darkened, having his laws themselves as stars giving light in their soul. But all those who are stubborn and disobedient are forever inflamed, and burnt, and consumed by their internal appetites, which, like flame, will destroy all the life of those who possess them.

> Parallels: Exodus 19:16-19; Matthew 03:11-12; 1Corinthians 03:10-15; Hebrews 12:29; 1Peter 01:07
>
> Comparison: 1Corinthians 03:12-15, "Now if any man builds on the foundation with gold, silver, precious stones, wood, hay, straw, each man's work will become evident; for the day will show it, because it is to be revealed with fire, and the fire [itself] will test the quality of each man's work. If the work that any man has built on the foundation shall survive, he will receive a reward. If any man's work is burned up, he will suffer loss; but he himself will be saved, but only as through fire." 1Peter 01:07, "so that the trial of your faith, being more precious than gold which is perishable, even though tested by fire, may be found to result in praise and glory and honor at the revelation of Jesus Christ."

Who Is the Heir of Divine Things (44)

(44) Do thou, therefore, love the virtues, and embrace them with thy soul, and then you will be not at all desirous to kiss, which is but the false money of friendship; --"For have they not yet any part or inheritance in thy house? Have they not been reckoned as aliens before thee? And has not thou sold them and devoured the Money?"{Genesis 31:14.} So that you could neither at any subsequent time recover it, after having devoured the price of their safety and their ransom. Do you pretend, therefore, to wish to kiss, or else to wage endless war against all the judges? But Aaron will not kiss Moses, though he will love him with the genuine affection of his heart. "For," says the scripture, "he loved him, and they embraced one Another."{Exodus 18:7.}

> Parallels: Genesis 31:14, 28, 33:04; Exodus 18:07; Matthew 26:48-49; Luke 22:47-48

Who Is the Heir of Divine Things (215-220)

(215) These matters then we will examine into accurately on another occasion; but there is this other point also, which does not deserve to be passed over in silence. For the divisions into two equal parts which have been mentioned become six in number, since three animals were divided, so that the Word which divided them made up the number seven, dividing the two triads and establishing itself in the midst of them. (216) And a thing very similar to this appears to me to be very clearly shown in the matter of the sacred candlestick; for that also was made having six branches, three on each side, and the main candlestick itself in the middle made the seventh, dividing and separating the two triads; for it is made of carved work, a divine work of exquisite skill and highly admired, being made of one solid piece of pure gold. For the unit, being one and single and pure, begot the number seven, which had no mother but is born of itself alone, without taking any additional material whatever

to aid him. (217) But those who praise gold say a great many other things by way of panegyric on it, but dwell on two especial points as most particularly important and excellent; one that it does not receive poison, the other that it can be beaten out or melted out into the thinnest possible plates, while still remaining unbroken. Therefore it is very naturally taken as an emblem of that greater nature, which, being extended and diffused everywhere so as to penetrate in every direction, is wholly full of everything, and also connects all other things with the most admirable arrangement. (218) Concerning the candlestick above mentioned, the artist speaks again a second time and says, that from its different branches there are three arms projecting out on each side, equals in all respects to one another, and having on the top lamps like nuts, in the shape of flowers supporting the lights; {Exodus 25:33.} the seventh flower being fashioned on the top of the candlestick of solid gold, and having seven golden places for lights above them; (219) so that in many accounts it has been believed to be fashioned in such a manner because the number six is divided into two triads by the Word, making the seventh and being placed in the midst of them; as indeed is the case now. For the entire candlestick with its six most entire and principal parts was made so as to consist of seven lamps, and seven flowers, and seven lights; and the six lights are divided by the seventh. (220) And in like manner the flowers are divided by that which comes in the middle; and in the same manner also the lamps are divided by the seventh which comes in the middle. But the six branches, and the equal number of arms which shoot out are divided by the main trunk itself which makes up the number seven.

Parallels: Exodus 25:31-40; John 01:01-14, 08:12, 09:05

Who is the Heir of Divine Things (239)

(239) On the other hand, Moses approves, in no ordinary degree, of whatever reptiles are able to take a leap in an upward direction. At all events he says, "Ye shall eat of these winged reptiles which go upon four feet, and which have legs above their feet so as to be able by them to leap up from the Ground."{Leviticus 11:21.} But these reptiles are the emblems of souls, which like reptiles being rooted in the earthly body, when they are raised up, get strength to soar on high, taking the heaven in exchange for the earth, and immortality in exchange for destruction.

Parallels: Leviticus 11:21; Matthew 24:30-31; Mark 13:26-27; Luke 21:27-28; 1Thessalonians 04:16-17; Hebrews 10:01

Fragments Extracted From the Parallels of John of Damascus Page 343. D.

Page 343. D. Some men, making improvement, have returned back to virtue before coming to the end, the ancient principle of oligarchy having destroyed the principle of aristocracy lately engendered in the soul, which having been quiet for a little while, has subsequently come up over again with greater power than before.
Page 343. D. When a man rightly establishes himself in a virtuous life, with meditation, and practice, and good government, and when having been known by all men as a pious man and one who fears God, he falls into sin, that is a great fall, for he has ascended up to the height of heaven, and fallen down into the abyss of hell.

Parallels: Genesis 28:12; Hebrews 06:04-06, 10:26-31

Fragments Extracted From the Parallels of John of Damascus Page 349. A-B.

Page 349. A. It is not possible with God that a wicked man should lose his good reward for a single good thing which he may have done among a great number of evil actions; nor, on the other hand, that a good man should escape punishment, and not suffer it, if among many good actions he has done wickedly in anything, for it is infallibly certain that God distributes everything according to a just weight and balance.
Page 349. B. The mind is the witness to each individual of the things which they have planned in secret, and conscience is an incorruptible judge, and the most unerring of all judges.

Parallels: Matthew 10:42; Romans 02:15

Fragments Extracted From the Parallels of John of Damascus Page 367. D.

Page 367. D. Every stratagem is not blamable, since guardians of the night appear to act properly when they lie in wait for robbers, and generals when they form ambuscades against the enemy, whom they cannot catch without a stratagem; and the same principle is applicable to what are called maneuvers, and to the artifices practiced in the contests of wrestlers, for in such cases deceit is accounted honorable.

Parallels: 2Kings 10:18-28; John 01:21-23

Fragments Extracted From the Parallels of John of Damascus Page 370. B.

Page 370. B. It is as impossible that the love of the world can co-exist with the love of God, as for light and darkness to co-exist at the same time with one another.

Parallels: Genesis 01:04; John 03:19, 12:25; 1John 02:15-16

Fragments Extracted From the Parallels of John of Damascus Page 533. C.

Page 533. C. It is not lawful to speak of the sacred mysteries to the uninitiated.

Parallels: Exodus 20:19; Matthew 13:03-53

Fragments Extracted From the Parallels of John of Damascus Page 613. D.

Page 613. D. To inquire and put questions is the most useful of habits with a view to acquiring instruction.
Page 613. D. He who hungers and thirsts after knowledge, and who is eager to learn what he does not know, abandoning all other objects of care, is eager to become a disciple, and day and night watches at the doors of the houses of wise men.
Page 613. D. For anyone to know that he is ignorant is a piece of wisdom, just as to know that one has done wrong is a piece of righteousness.

Parallels: Matthew 24:42-51

Fragments Extracted From the Parallels of John of Damascus Page 748. B.

Page 748. B. "And God brought all the animals to Adam, to see what he would call Them;"{Genesis 2:19.} for God does not doubt, but since he has given mind to man, the first born and most excellent of his creatures, according to which he, being endowed with knowledge, is by nature enabled to reason; he excites him, as an instructor excites his pupil, to a display of his powers, and he contemplates the most excellent offspring of his soul. And, again, he visibly by the example of this man gives an outline of all that is voluntary in us, looking with disfavor on those who affirm that everything happens through necessity, by which some men must be influenced, he on that account commanded man to take upon himself the regulation of these things. And this is an employment peculiarly fitting for man, as being endowed with a very high degree of knowledge and most surpassing prudence, the giving of names to the animals being suited to him not only as being wise, but also as being the first nobly born creature.

For it was fitting that he should be the founder of the human race, and also the king of everything that is born of the earth, and that he should have this as an especial honor of his own, that, as he was the first who had any acquaintance with the animals, he might also be the first inventor and pronouncer of their names; for it would have been absurd for them to be left without names, and subsequently to have names given to them by some younger man, to the honor and glory of the elder.

And when Adam saw the figure of his wife, as the prophet says, and that it had been produced not by any connection, nor out of a woman, as human beings in after times were produced, but that she was as it were a nature on the borders between these two kinds, like a graft from a shoot of another vine taken off and grafted into a second one, on which account he says, "For this cause a man shall leave his father and his mother, and shall cleave to his wife, and they two shall become one Flesh;"{Genesis

2:24.} in saying which he used a most gentle expression, which was at the same time most perfectly true, meaning that they would be united by sympathy in their grief and joys.

Parallels: Genesis 02:19-24; Mark 10:08; Luke 13:32; Romans 11:16-28

Fragments Extracted From the Parallels of John of Damascus Page 774. B.

Page 774. B. All those who have stumbled, being unable to proceed with upright feet, go on slowly, being fatigued a long time before they come to their journey's end; so also the soul is hindered from proceeding successfully on the path which leads to piety if it has previously fallen in with any of the byroads of wickedness, for they are great hindrances to it, and the causes of its stumbling, by means of which the mind becoming lame, proceeds too slowly on the road, according to nature; and this road, according to nature, is that which ends at the Father of the universe.
From the same book.
The contentious investigations which men enter into about the virtues of God, improve the intellect and train it in most pleasant labors, which are also most beneficial to it, and especially when men do not (as those of the present day do) disguise themselves under a false appellation, and contend for the doctrines in appearance only, but do, in an honest and true heart, seek out truth in connection with knowledge.

Parallels: Psalms 24:05; 1Timothy 01:05, 06:09; 2Timothy 02:22

Fragments Extracted From the Parallels of John of Damascus Page 782. A-B.

Page 782. A. It is not lawful to divulge the sacred mysteries to the uninitiated until they are purified by a perfect purification; for the man who is not initiated, or who is of moderate capacity, being unable either to hear or to see that nature which is incorporeal and appreciable only by the intellect, being deceived by the visible sight, will blame what ought not to be blamed. Now, to divulge sacred mysteries to uninitiated people, is the act of a person who violates the laws of the privileges belonging to the priesthood.

Page 782. B. It is absurd that there should be a law in cities that it is not lawful to divulge sacred mysteries to the uninitiated, but that one may speak of the true rites and ceremonies which lead to piety and holiness to ears full of folly. All men must not partake of all things, nor of all discourses, above all, of such as are sacred; for those that desire to be admitted to a participation in such things, ought to have many qualifications beforehand. In the first place, what is the greatest and most important, they ought to have deep feelings of piety towards the only true and living God, and correct notions of holiness, avoiding all inextricable errors which perplex so many about images and statues, and in fact about any erections whatever, and about unlawful ceremonies, or illicit mysteries.

In the second place, they must be purified with all holy purifications, both in soul and body, as far as it is allowed by their national laws and customs. In the third place, they must give credible evidence of their entering into the common joy, so that they may not, after having partaken of the sacred food, like intemperate youths, be changed by satiety and overabundance, becoming like drunken men; which is not lawful.

> Parallels: Exodus 20:19; Deuteronomy 29:04; Matthew 11:15, 13:03-53

Fragments Extracted From the Parallels of John of Damascus Page 784. C.

Page 784. C. The reasoning of some persons is very rapidly satiated, who, though they have been borne upwards on wings for a little while, yet do presently return back again; not so much flying upwards, says Philo, as being dragged down again to the lowest depths of hell. But happy are they who do not draw back. Page 784. C. Before now, some persons who have tasted happiness, being very speedily satiated, after they have given hopes of their being in health, have fallen back into the same disease as before.

Parallels: Genesis 28:12; 2Peter 02:22

Fragments Preserved By Antonius Ser. VIII.

SER. VIII. When you are entreated to pardon offences, pardon willingly those who have offended against you, because indulgence given in requital for indulgence, and reconciliation with our fellow servants, is a means of averting the divine anger.

Parallels: Matthew 18:20-34

Fragments Preserved By Antonius Ser. LVII.

SER. LVII. Behave to your servants in the same manner in which you desire that God should behave to you; for as we hear them we shall be heard by him, and as we regard them we shall be regarded by him. Let us therefore let our compassion outrun compassion, that we may receive a like requital from him for our mercy to them.

Parallels: Matthew 18:20-34, 24:45

Made in the USA
Columbia, SC
16 June 2024

37240499R00159